D0875889

Construction
Productivity

Construction Productivity

On-Site Measurement and Management

Louis Edward Alfeld

McGraw-Hill Book Company

New York St. Louis San Francisco Auckland
Bogotá Hamburg London Madrid Mexico
Milan Montreal New Delhi Panama
Paris São Paulo Singapore
Sydney Tokyo Toronto

This publication is designed to provide accurate and authoritative information regarding its subject matter. It is sold with the understanding
that the publisher is not engaged in rendering legal, accounting, or other
professional service. If legal advice or other expert assistance is required,
the services of a competent professional person should be sought.

—*From a Declaration of Principles jointly adopted by a committee of the
American Bar Association and a Committee of Publishers.*

Library of Congress Cataloging-in-Publication Data

Alfeld, Louis Edward.
  Construction productivity.

  Includes index.
  1. Construction industry—Management.
  2. Construction industry—Labor productivity.
  I. Title.
  TH438.A43   1988   624'.0685   88-2947
  ISBN 0-07-001027-7

Copyright © 1988 by McGraw-Hill, Inc. All rights reserved. Printed in the
United States of America. Except as permitted under the United States
Copyright Act of 1976, no part of this publication may be reproduced or
distributed in any form or by any means, or stored in a data base or
retrieval system, without the prior written permission of the publisher.

1234567890   DOC/DOC   8921098

ISBN 0-07-001027-7

*The editors for this book were Nadine M. Post and Virginia Blair, the
designer was Naomi Auerbach, and the production supervisor was Dianne
Walber. This book was set in Century Schoolbook. It was composed by the
McGraw-Hill Book Company Professional & Reference Division
composition unit.*

Printed and bound by R. R. Donnelley & Sons Company.

For Thomas F. Gilbert, who showed the way.

Contents

Preface

Perhaps no other industry in the world promises as large a payback for performance improvement as does construction. Hundreds of billions, even trillions, of dollars are spent each year on construction. An improvement of even a fraction of a percent in performance would produce billions in savings. Yet perhaps no other industry in the world has so steadily resisted abandoning traditional, reactive management methods for performance-based management systems. I have written this book in an attempt to close that gap by demonstrating how contractors and owners can capture much of the potential savings.

I have narrowed the scope of my effort to focus on the jobsite. It is here, where plans, people, machines, and materials come together, that we can best observe and measure construction performance. And it is here, at the jobsite, that we must begin to improve our management methods. True, many off-site factors affect jobsite performance, perhaps in some cases to an even greater extent than on-site factors do. But at the moment, most off-site factors such as design and financing remain beyond the immediate influence of on-site construction management. So I have chosen to direct my efforts toward developing better management methods for influencing the factors over which construction management exercises a reasonable degree of control—the on-site work methods and management information systems responsible for the daily progress of a construction project.

Others have described, often in great detail, specific techniques for boosting productivity. Alternative work methods abound. My goal here is not to attempt to recount these methods or to list exhaustively the hundreds of factors that can affect productivity. Rather, I seek to lay out a useful methodology for finding out what to improve in the first place. Too often construction management chases solutions to every problem that arises while failing to recognize opportunities for real improvement because the opportunities do not appear in the guise of problems. To escape the trap of "fire fighting," one must establish priorities for management action. Priorities imply a means for ranking. And ranking implies a means for measuring.

The heart of this book is measurement—for until management learns to measure what it accomplishes, it lacks the ability to judge rationally the merits of alternative construction methods. The measurement methods I describe have evolved from the pioneering work of Thomas F. Gilbert. I have adapted his techniques to construction and have extended his vision to the world of building. Any shortcomings in the application, however, remain my own.

Louis Edward Alfeld

Construction
Productivity

Introduction

Competence in the management of construction projects is a goal to which we all aspire. Bringing together the many diverse elements of construction—labor, machines, materials, and managerial talent—and successfully organizing them to bring into existence a new structure is an extremely creative and satisfying endeavor. It gives one a deep sense of satisfaction to build well. No wonder so many people find careers in construction exciting.

But management performance varies greatly. Some projects make money; others lose it. Many contractors might claim that the difference between profit and loss depends on experience and judgment. Good managers run profitable jobs. But is that all there is to it? Must every good manager be born, not made? Or is there a science of construction management to be learned, with principles that anyone can apply with an equal chance of success?

Fortunately, an emerging science of construction management holds the promise that every manager, from the weakest to the strongest, can improve jobsite performance. The principles embodied in newly emerging management methods contain little that is entirely new; for the most part, the methods merely formalize exactly what good contractors have been doing intuitively for years. Formal management methods based on intuitive experience are readily understood by contractors, owners, and craftsmen anxious to improve their performance and their profitability. Competent management performance can be engineered, just as we have learned to engineer the structures we erect. And competence leads directly to larger construction savings and a bigger bottom line.

Management Needs

Every construction project can be improved. Improvement, however, requires that management know what to improve and how to improve it. And as we will see, this knowledge may come from unexpected sources.

We will learn in this book why profits do not measure performance. We will see why contractors who use their averages as performance standards will, in the long run, lower their performance, and we will analyze why contractors who "fight fires," jumping from one problem to another, lose money. On the other hand, we will discover how reports of lost time can provide the key to a successful job. And we will find that the most effective improvement methods may actually cost the least to adopt.

This book shows how contractors, owners, and labor can jointly benefit by adopting a performance-based management viewpoint. Such a performance viewpoint will:

- Set priorities for improvement efforts;
- Provide easy-to-use, cost-effective methods;
- Foster a cooperative labor-management relationship; and
- Cut costs while boosting profits.

The central concept is quite simple—better information—*for to improve performance, contractors need only focus their attention on how they collect, interpret, and act on jobsite information.*

But good information doesn't just pop out of a construction job. It requires a systematic effort to collect it.

Measurement and Performance

Construction performance can be measured. Measurements of performance provide management with invaluable feedback to guide daily decision making. And by regularly using such feedback, management becomes more competent. Measurements help turn even average managers into exemplary performers merely by supplying them with better information.

In the best of all worlds, information would be so perfect that the right decisions and actions would follow directly. However, because information is never perfect, we depend on managers with experience, judgment, training, and natural talent to correctly interpret the confusion of jobsite information and to come up with the best possible decisions. Contractors invest large amounts of money in training managers (in terms of both classroom and on-the-job training) and in hiring and keeping people with proven managerial talent. Yet no matter how well (or how poorly) a manager performs, the quality of decision making improves if the quality of information improves. Therefore, money invested to improve the quality of managerial information may actually do far more to boost construction performance than many times that amount spent directly on the managers themselves.

But good information doesn't just pop out of a construction job. It requires a systematic process of collection.

The material in this book develops three major points:

- A method for measuring construction performance
- A means for using measurements to improve management
- A demonstration of the method in field applications

The purpose of the book is to improve both (1) productivity in construction and (2) competence in construction management. Performance measurements provide the means to reach this goal. And improved productivity and competence offer contractors larger profits while cutting the cost of construction projects.

Improving Construction Performance

This book develops a methodology for measuring and managing construction productivity and jobsite performance. The methodology is not difficult to understand. The savings and profits from improved performance far outweigh the time and effort needed to achieve the improvement. Examples of successful applications demonstrate how the measurements help increase management competence (by supplying better feedback) and help improve jobsite performance (by fostering better management actions).

Since most of the numbers presented in the book have been formatted in columns and rows on spreadsheets, a short Appendix contains an introduction to electronic spreadsheets for personal computers to help readers understand how easy spreadsheets are to use.

Looking Ahead

Many contractors have chosen to ignore or dismiss the need for performance measurement. Some believe that projects cannot be built on extra paperwork. Others resist the introduction of computers and "high tech" management methods, often because they fear changes that might undermine their authority. And many, having found little of substance in past productivity-enhancement techniques, have stopped looking further for better ideas. However, our rapidly changing world does not condone complacency. Contractors who choose to sit on the sidelines while others develop methods to improve management competence will someday find themselves unable to compete successfully for new business. Owners, as they become more sophisticated in their understanding of the construction process, will seek out the more competent contractors whose management methods promise the best job with the least risk of failure.

The increasing size and complexity of projects, together with their compressed construction schedules, throw more people onto jobsites at one time. Management must respond to a rising need for communication, coordination, and cooperation among diverse trades, each performing increasingly specialized tasks only poorly understood by others. Most current construction management methods and project accounting methods evolved in an era when labor cost less than materials and equipment. Such traditional methods largely fail to recognize the greater skills of a better-educated labor force and continue to use labor as simply another tool in the construction process.

Overview

The material that follows is divided into nine chapters. The first three lay out the principles and methods for measuring field performance and identifying and setting priorities for improvement. Chapter 1 introduces a performance viewpoint and clarifies the distinction between accomplishments and the work methods that produce them; it is here that we learn what to measure and why. Chapter 2 shows how to use performance measurements to pinpoint priority problems and to focus management actions on opportunities for the greatest improvements; by focusing our limited management resources on the most profitable opportunities first, we stop wasting time and money on the unimportant problems. Chapter 3 presents a methodology for measuring jobsite performance; this methodology is based on an obvious, yet often overlooked, distinction between work time and lost time. Measurements of lost time and work time point directly to methods that will improve construction productivity.

The fourth and fifth chapters develop cost-effective methods for capturing desired improvements. Chapter 4 presents a methodology for analyzing work methods and for engineering improvements; here we learn how to use the least expensive means to develop the most productive construction environment. Chapter 5 extends the analytical methodology to demonstrate effective troubleshooting techniques; applications to specific cases show that these techniques lead to tremendous savings.

The last four chapters apply the methods to a variety of jobs, showing how performance information, structured into a feedback network, can raise contractor profitability and create a cooperative relationship between labor and management by improving labor working conditions. Chapter 6 analyzes the relationship between performance measurements and estimates, showing how to use these measurements to improve the estimates; contractors who rely on unimproved estimates as measurements of performance may actually be lowering their own productivity. Chapter 7 discusses the application of feedback reporting to field supervisors and presents a complete performance management system; contractors who want to develop a comprehensive reporting system can see exactly how it functions in the field. Chapter 8 extends the applications in greater detail, illustrating a range of management actions to boost performance, both in the field and in off-site fabrication shops; every facet of construction performance can be measured and improved. Finally, Chapter 9 discusses how to implement a successful measurement and management system; it is here that we must face up to the many obstacles standing in the way of improvement and overcome them.

The serious reader will need to follow the text carefully and to think clearly about the underlying logic, for this is not a simple-minded presentation. It will not be absorbed in an evening's light reading. However, those who stay with it will learn how to become more competent managers, able to guarantee successful jobs and a profitable enterprise.

A Performance Viewpoint

Every contractor wants to improve jobsite performance. But how? What elements of performance require our attention? And what do we mean by performance? Suppose a large corporate owner and a general contractor agree to develop a program to ensure high performance on a showcase project. The owner develops special training films. Lectures introduce new hires to the job. The contractor schedules weekly foremen meetings to discuss job progress and sets up awards dinners to involve foremen in job-improvement efforts. Extra attention to lunch areas, toilet facilities, and employee parking all demonstrate management's sincere interest in the welfare of the craftsmen. Surveys of work delays help identify problems. Weekly subcontractor meetings seek solutions to problems and elicit suggestions for avoiding future problems.

At the end of the project, both the owner and the contractor agree that the job went well, that performance was high, and that labor worked productively. To support their conclusions, they point to the fact that the job was completed on time and within budget, that the work quality was high, and that only a few minor labor problems surfaced during the work.

But is this all we have? Doesn't one get the feeling that something more is required before making a judgment regarding the performance of the job? We would also like to have measurements of performance improvement and to know how much was spent to achieve it. In other words, was the benefit worth the expense? We want to base judgments of jobsite performance not only on what was accomplished but also on how it was done and at what cost. But how do we distinguish the accomplishments at the jobsite from the methods used to achieve them? And how do both accomplishments and methods relate to performance? Let us begin with a simple story.

Seeing and Believing

Dale Driver proudly pointed toward the busy construction site across the street. "That's my first million-dollar job," he said, "and I've got two more coming. Just you wait and see; in 10 years I'll be the biggest contractor in town."

Bob Smiley nodded. "Yes sir, I bet you will be."

"Now, Bob, if you want to work for me, you've got to understand that I don't waste time and that nobody on my jobs wastes time. The reason I'm successful is that I know how to push a job. And my foremen know how to push a job. We go flat out all the time and we make money. You understand my point?"

"Yes sir, I sure do," Bob replied, watching the line of concrete trucks inching forward in the dust. "I'd sure like to get a chance to work for you, and I know I could do it."

"Well," said Driver, "you come to me with a good recommendation. You've been a foreman before. I'm gonna give you a chance to prove yourself. You start Monday morning, taking over Red's crew, 'cause I'm moving Red over to 14th Street to let him put a little fear into those guys and get 'em movin' faster. We gotta be out of there week after next. Red'll shake 'em up and run the deadbeats out."

"Yes sir, that's fine with me. I'm ready to start."

"Red's done a good job here," said Driver. "He's staying up with a tight schedule. We got another pour set for next Friday. I don't want you to miss it."

"You understand," added Driver as he turned to climb into the cab of his pickup, "you're on probation for a while until I see what you can do. But once you prove to me you've got a big enough boot to keep the men on the job all day, you won't ever have to worry again about where your next paycheck's comin' from."

As the truck pulled out onto the street, Bob waved, but Driver didn't notice. He was already figuring how to cut a few more bucks out of a bid he was trying to get in by the end of the week.

The following Wednesday afternoon Driver sat in his truck watching the work crews on the job. There was Bob Smiley, talking to two of the laborers and laughing with them about something. Yesterday, too, Driver had seen Smiley joking with the crew, and it wasn't right. Foremen were on the job to get the job done, not to entertain the troops. He'd heard that Smiley was playing Mr. Nice Guy. It didn't look as though he was cut out for a foreman's job after all. Sure as hell, they'd miss the scheduled pour on Friday now and put the job behind. He'd better get Red back over here tomorrow.

"People these days!" thought Driver, shaking his head as he walked across the street to fire Smiley. "They just don't know how to work anymore." In less than a minute, he'd told Smiley to collect his pay and be gone.

It was Friday noon before Driver got back to the job. As he pulled up, he was surprised to see concrete trucks lined up on the road ahead of him. "Well I'll be damned," he exclaimed, "if old Red hasn't jumped back on schedule in spite of the mess Smiley left. That guy is sure one heck of a ramrod."

Driver waved Red over to the trailer door. "Hey, I got to hand it to you," grinned Driver. "You sure know how to push a job. I didn't think we could make this pour until Monday or Tuesday."

Red shook his head. "Me neither. When you took me off the job last Friday, I sure thought we'd never make it. But when I came back yesterday, I was sure surprised to see it nearly ready. We could have poured yesterday afternoon, but I didn't know we were ready so I didn't order the concrete in time."

Driver looked at Red with a puzzled frown. "What do you mean, it was ready yesterday? I thought we were behind."

"No sir," he said, "Smiley had it all ready. He did one heck of a job. Had everybody pitchin' in to beat the schedule." Red chuckled. "They were gonna beat my schedule to prove what a lazy son-of-a-gun I was."

Driver's story may be overdramatized, but it is not uncommon. How often do we judge the performance of others by what we see them do, not by what they actually do? In doing so, we confuse their *methods* with their *accomplishments*.

The confusion between methods and accomplishments raises the question of just how we should judge performance. How can we tell if one construction job is performed better or worse than another? What measurements best describe construction performance? To answer these questions, we first need to lay a groundwork that will allow us to agree on what we mean by performance and on how we ought to go about measuring it.

Work and Motivation

Before proceeding, think for a moment about two commonly misapplied measurements of performance—work and motivation. Many contractors accept the false idea that performance means the same thing as hard work. They work hard and they demand that their employees work hard. Their supervisory and managerial people put in long hours, catch up on paperwork in the evenings and over weekends, and sacrifice friends and family for the sake of "working hard." According to this work ethic, any people who do not get to work early and look busy all day long must not be interested in keeping their jobs. Promotions often depend on how much time people give to the job, not on what they are able to accomplish. And those who do not work hard enough, whether in the office or in the field, find that they must soon seek employment elsewhere.

Construction companies that foster such attitudes believe that hard work is the only way to stay alive in a competitive business. Union and nonunion construction labor generally accept the same misleading principles—that working hard and looking busy measure an individual's worth on the job. This belief is just not true, because it looks only at work *methods* while ignoring *accomplishments*.

A second mistaken belief comes from thinking that motivation underlies the work ethic. Unless people are "motivated," they will not perform well. And, in the absence of other measurements of performance, motivation is frequently taken as a measurement in itself. Some contractors substitute judgments concerning individual motivation for measurements of performance. In their view, poor motivation (as evidenced by an unwillingness to "work hard" and a "bad attitude") means poor performance, regardless of actual accomplishment. Unfortunately, many competent people lose jobs or miss promotions because they "aren't motivated."

The problem here is not the supervisor or contractor who demands hard work and motivation as proof of good performance. Rather, it is the lack of an alternative point of view that offers actual measurements of performance and a methodology for using these measurements to improve performance. As we proceed through this book, this alternative point of view should become clear.

Competent Performance

Construction methods are an essential element of jobsite performance. But methods are not the same thing as performance. Pictures of a completed job, for example, can tell us a great deal about its cost, size, and materials yet reveal little or nothing about the performance of the work force that built it. A 50-ft concrete bridge span could have been erected with staging and centering support, or it could have been precast and lifted into place; the completed bridge (accomplishment) and the construction technique (method) that put it in place represent two different aspects of the contractor's performance. We must learn to distinguish between them in order to develop useful measurements of jobsite performance.

Look at accomplishment

Imagine a specific construction task and the work methods employed to complete it—framing a wall, for example. We see a carpenter measure, mark, and cut a 2 × 4, then raise and nail it into place. The method seems straightforward. Now we attempt to measure it. A stopwatch tells us how long it takes to measure and cut the board. To measure the energy used, we weigh the board and compute how far it was lifted into place. Then we count the number of hammer swings needed to secure it. We even interview the carpenter to discover how he or she felt about the job while doing it: Were the sawhorses the right height, did the saw cut well, and was the hammer too light or too heavy? But no matter how many measurements we collect of the methods, we cannot tell whether the *accomplishment* is valuable. We do not know if the wall is in the right place or of the right size. Is it plumb? Is it solid? Is it being built too early, too late, or right on schedule? In other words, is the accomplishment something we value and are willing to pay for?

To answer questions concerning the performance of the job, we must look at the whole job—both the carpenter's methods *and* what he or she accomplished with them. The carpenter might have completed the framing by using a 14-oz or a 20-oz hammer, by using a handsaw or a power saw, and by listening to a radio or working in silence, with none of these alternative methods greatly affecting his or her performance. *Performance includes both the carpenter's methods and what the carpenter accomplished with them.*

Clearly, a contractor can change the carpenter's framing methods by insisting that a plumb bob be used instead of a level, by forbidding radios on the jobsite, or by adding a second carpenter. But common sense tells us that we should not change the work methods just because we can do so—that we should make a change only if it will result in producing *a more valuable performance.* Every contractor seeks to improve performance. Valuable performance comes from using methods that lead to *valuable accomplishments.*

Worthy performance

But not all valuable performances may be worth the cost of obtaining them. Spending endless hours measuring and remeasuring the exact location and size of rough-in framing for interior walls may produce perfectly aligned studs, but this may make little visible difference to the finished job. In such a case, although we may admire the accomplishment, we would not be willing to pay for it. Or adding additional carpenters to the job may speed the completion, but would it be worth the cost if the job then had to wait two weeks for an electrician? What we want, therefore, is not just a valuable performance, but a worthy performance. *Worthy performance occurs when the value of the accomplishment exceeds the cost of the method.*

Expressed as a ratio, we can define *worth* as value divided by cost:

$$\text{Worth} = \frac{\text{value}}{\text{cost}}$$

In managing construction work, we look to maximize the worth of a job. In framing the interior of a house, for example, we want to erect the walls according to the plans and specifications while using the least amount of the carpenter's time. Getting all the walls in right creates value. Doing it in the minimum time cuts costs. Therefore, the overall worth of the job increases as the value goes up and the costs go down. Competent construction managers and craftsmen achieve valuable results without excessive costs.

In other words, competent individuals create worth by creating valuable accomplishments while minimizing costly methods. Thus, for a construction site, we can use the worth ratio to define *performance,* in this case as a ratio of accomplishment to methods:

$$\text{Performance} = \frac{\text{accomplishment}}{\text{methods}}$$

Here the accomplishment is what we value, and it is the methods that cost us money. Performance thus describes how well we accomplished the job with the methods we used. Furthermore, competent performance is worthy performance—valuable accomplishments created with the least costly methods. In sum, we can express the combined relationship as:

$$\text{Performance (worth)} = \frac{\text{accomplishment (value)}}{\text{methods (cost)}}$$

This performance ratio tells us that we can raise our individual and company competence by increasing the value of our accomplishments while reducing the amount of time, energy, and money we expend on methods. The performance ratio shows that *our competence depends on how much we are able to accomplish, not on how much we put into the effort.*

A contractor who can consistently build the same-quality homes for less than his or her competitors is more competent because of accomplishing more, not because of spending more on the methods. However, to build a better house for less money, the contractor may have invested large sums in equipment, training, prefabricated materials, and scheduling. The effect of this investment is to increase the value of the accomplishment by producing more homes. Contractors improve their performance by investing time, energy, and money in *reducing* the cost of the methods required to accomplish a given construction task, not by spending more money on methods unrelated to accomplishment. The contractor and owner at the first of this chapter who sought to improve jobsite performance by investing in a wide variety of methods (films, lectures, awards, and surveys) did so without knowing whether or not these methods contributed to the accomplishments they desired. The performance ratio, by leading us to measurements of accomplishment, can help us pinpoint exactly those work methods which have the largest potential payback for improvement. To understand how to do this, let us first turn our attention to distinguishing between accomplishments and methods.

Accomplishments and Methods

The performance ratio clarifies the need to separate accomplishments from methods in assessing jobsite performance. Accomplishments represent finished work of value to the job; methods describe how the work was completed. The number of foundations dug is an accomplishment; the number of manhours on the backhoe represents the method. Measurements of accomplishments are not the same thing as measurements of methods. And neither type of measurement, by itself, tells us much about the worth of the performance in question. We do not know if the foundations are the correct depth, and we do not know if a bulldozer could have done the job more cheaply.

Two views of measurement

To help illustrate the distinction between measurements of accomplishments and measurements of methods, let us attempt to measure the performance of two imaginary plumbers, Mr. Tightwrench and Mr. Leaks. Both arrive at the jobsite with their tools, ready to go to work, but we need only one. So we propose to test three plumber skills—plan reading, pipe layout, and soldering—in order to determine which plumber is the more competent. Each plumber will take two sets of tests, one written and one practical. One set of tests will be administered in the trailer by the project engineer, and the other set will be administered outside on the job by the plumber foreman. Table 1.1 shows Mr. T's and Mr. L's scores on the two tests.

After both plumbers have completed the tests, the engineer and the plumber foreman compare their results. The engineer has a hard time deciding which plumber is the more competent; both scored very well

TABLE 1.1   Comparison of Two Types of Performance Measurements

		Score			Score	
Skill	Engineer's test	T	L	Foreman's test	T	L
1. Plan reading	Correctly identifies plan symbols.	100%	98%	Work items correctly located from blueprints.	100%	20%
2. Pipe layout	Follows right steps in pipe layout.	100%	98%	Percentage of pipe cut to correct length.	100%	0%
3. Soldering	Knows right solder type and torch temperature.	80%	85%	Percentage of joints that do not leak.	100%	0%

on the written test. The plumber foreman, however, has no problem at all and immediately chooses Mr. Tightwrench. But why do the different measurements give such different results? Why does the engineer's test miss discovering Mr. Leaks' incompetence?

Look more closely at the measurements chosen by the foreman; *they all measure accomplishments.* They all measure something of value to the job. Conversely, each of the engineer's tests measures how much each plumber knows about the *methods* used to accomplish plumbing tasks. The scores on the engineer's test show that both plumbers know a great deal about how to accomplish a task, but the scores on the foreman's test show that only Mr. Tightwrench applies these methods with competence to achieve valuable results.

Observing the worker's methods

But does this mean that Mr. Leaks is totally incompetent? If we were to peer over Mr. Leaks' shoulder while he was working at the tasks set out for him by the plumber foreman, we might discover something very remarkable. As we watch Mr. Leaks read the blueprints to attempt to locate various work areas in the building, we notice that because the split-level floors are identified only by elevations, he has erred in assuming that the ground floor is the lobby level when, in fact, the two are one-half flight apart.

Further, we would see that in the second task Mr. Leaks followed all the right steps in laying out the dimensions for the pipe to be cut but failed only in the last step, forgetting to add an extra ½ in at each end for the overlap joint. Had Mr. Leaks made this small correction to his measurements, all his pipe cuts would have been correct. His pipe layout methods are very nearly the same as Mr. Tightwrench's, but he lacks one critical skill—remembering to allow for the overlap.

Finally, observing Mr. Leaks' performance in soldering pipe joints, we see that he does every step right except that he repeatedly fails to buff out the inside of the elbow joints, thus leaving a tarnished surface to which the solder cannot fully adhere.

Accomplishments count

Our analysis of Mr. Leaks' shortcomings leads us to the conclusion that he knows a great deal about plumbing (the engineer's scores of plumbing methods) but can do hardly anything of value (the foreman's scores of plumbing accomplishment). Further, when we look closely at Mr. Leaks' methods as he goes about performing the foreman's tasks, we see that his methods do not differ greatly from Mr. Tightwrench's. In fact, with only small changes to Mr. Leaks' methods, his performance might have been as competent as Mr. Tightwrench's.

From this example, we come to an interesting conclusion: *People may be very much alike in their methods while, at the same time, differing greatly in what they are able to accomplish.*

Measure Accomplishments First

As we have seen, contractors value the accomplishments of the people who work for them, provided these accomplishments produce something of worth. If carpenters are able to frame an entire house in a week, we do not care if they play a radio while they work or whether they use a folding rule or a tape measure. We care only for what they accomplish, not how they do it. *Accomplishments alone have value; methods are the cost we pay to get something accomplished.*

Improving performance

Now if small changes in methods can produce significant changes in accomplishment, then we ought to be willing to invest small amounts of money to change work methods so as greatly to increase the resulting accomplishment. If we can substitute a level for a plumb bob and thereby cut an hour off the time a carpenter takes to frame each interior wall, it will be well worth the cost of the level to save the time. Through such small investments, we can significantly raise the worth of our performance. For although the accomplishment remains the same (the interior walls), the cost of building the walls goes down (the price of a level less the savings in hourly wages). The worth of our performance goes up whenever we can push the ratio of accomplishment (value) to methods (cost) higher, either by raising value or reducing cost.

$$\text{Performance (worth)} \ = \ \frac{\text{accomplishment (value)}}{\text{methods (cost)}}$$

The relationship between accomplishment and methods tells us that we should not attempt to measure methods until we have first measured accomplishment. It serves no purpose to observe and judge the steps a plumber takes in making a pipe joint unless we first know that the plumber's joints leak. We have no reason to evaluate a person's ability to read blueprints until we see that the person has difficulty in using blueprints. Or, to state it another way, we should have some reason to believe that a greater potential value exists before we look to the cost of capturing it.

We want to change work methods only if this will produce a more valuable accomplishment. But we cannot readily judge which methods to change simply by observing them, for we cannot expect to observe in detail all the work methods of everyone on a jobsite. *Therefore, we start by measuring the accomplishment we value.* Only when our measurements show a deficiency in the accomplishment do we need to examine the methods that caused the deficiency.

The need to measure

To improve the worth of their endeavors, contractors first need measurements of what it is they accomplish. Only after they can pinpoint the deficiencies in their accomplishments can they reasonably expect to discover what methods they need to change in order to overcome these deficiencies. To do this, *contractors need to learn to collect quantifiable measurements of their accomplishments.*

Quantifiable measurements of construction accomplishment can lead to improved jobsite performance, while studies of methods alone will rarely help to improve a job. For example, suppose we were to visit a job at a remote site that was experiencing difficulties keeping its equipment running. Upon looking into the problem, we might discover that replacement parts are not kept in stock, that maintenance personnel lacked training on some items of equipment, and that the absence of a heated repair shed hampered people working on the equipment outside in the cold.

From this information, we could devise a better method for ordering extra spare parts and stocking them, we could develop courses to teach mechanics additional skills, and we could erect a heated temporary repair shed. And for each proposed change, we could calculate the cost.

Keeping the equipment running is the accomplishment we value and are willing to pay for; we go through the numbers to determine the least costly way to achieve our goal. In order to measure the worth of alternative methods, we must first translate both the accomplishment and the intended changes in work methods into economic terms. If the value of keeping equipment running exceeds the cost, then the investment in changing the method is worth it.

But until we know that we have an equipment problem, we have no need to examine the parts-ordering process, the skill of the mechanics, or the air temperature. In other words, measurements of the methods, *by themselves,* offer little promise of discovering worthwhile means to improve performance. Decisions concerning how much money to spend to install a computer (and to train someone) to keep track of spare parts, how much to budget for training mechanics, and how much to pay for renting and erecting a temporary shelter cannot be made without reference to the expected increase in the value of what we want to accomplish. Knowing the magnitude of the equipment problem we face (or anticipating the size of the problem before it arises) gives us both a reason for investigating methods and a means to judge the relative worth of the changes required.

Performance, Profits, and Productivity

Most of us readily acknowledge that a difference does exist between *what* people do and *how* they do it. But we frequently overlook this difference in our everyday management actions. In construction, *accomplishment is the finished work-in-place; methods are the way the work was done.* Yet in daily practice this distinction between accomplishments and methods blurs. Contractors tend to focus most of their attention on the methods, without giving a great deal of thought to overall performance. Yet when one stops to think about it, most construction companies employ pretty much the same construction methods. However, companies differ considerably in what they accomplish. Some are highly profitable; others fail. Just like Mr. Tightwrench and Mr. Leaks, companies may be very much alike in their methods while, at the same time, differing greatly in what they are able to accomplish. It follows, therefore, that small investments made to improve methods may have a surprisingly large impact upon performance. And as construction performance rises, so, too, should construction profits. However, although performance and profits are related, they are not at all the same thing.

Profits do not measure performance

Profit is the difference between what a contractor receives for a job and what it costs to do the job. Profit measures how much money a contractor makes. Clearly, a contractor can make money on a job without performing well. Circumstances can lead a client to accept a bid and sign a contract for far more than a job is worth. With an over-priced job, even an incompetent contractor can make a profit. Some contractors make their profits by cutting corners and doing less than they should to satisfy their clients; although such contractors do not stay in business long, a seemingly endless number of incompetent contractors stand ready to enter the business to take the places of those who fail. Every contractor needs to earn a profit to stay in business, but only the competent contractors—those whose performance consistently produces worth—earn profits regularly and, in the process, build the long-term goodwill necessary to remain successful against their competitors.

Because profits measure only the difference between the price of a job and the cost of a job, profits do not provide a good measurement of performance. We often assume that because a construction firm has been in business for many years and has earned profits over that time, the firm is competent in its performance. However, while the two may be related, it is a mistake to associate profits with performance. Profits may come from many sources—such as timely materials purchases, overpriced jobs, or clever accounting methods—that have little bearing on the performance of the on-site construction process. Conversely, high performance may not lead to profitability. Many competent contractors lose money and go out of business for reasons not associated with their ability to perform well. For example, lack of financing, strikes, inattention to cash-flow problems, dishonest employees, and an inability to bid and market construction services are all reasons for profit losses. Profitability and performance measure two different aspects of the construction business.

Productivity measures only one performance dimension

And what about productivity? Doesn't productivity equate to high performance and profitability? Like performance, *productivity* is defined as a ratio that relates measurements of output to measurements of input. The ratio is often given as:

$$\text{Productivity} = \frac{\text{output}}{\text{input}}$$

In many ways the productivity ratio appears to be the same thing as the performance ratio—with *output* corresponding to accomplishment and value, and *input* to methods and cost. However, this definition of productivity, used most often by economists, can mislead us by shifting our attention away from the jobsite and toward larger issues better-suited for economic researchers. We do not wish to get bogged down in definitions of output and input at this time; in Chapter 4 we shall see that the methodology of performance engineering nicely avoids the larger economic issues altogether by defining productivity in the narrower (and far more useful) context of jobsite labor manhours divided by work-in-place (or the inverse, work-in-place divided by labor manhours).

Labor productivity, the relationship between manhours and work accomplished, offers an important and very useful measurement of jobsite performance. But, because it measures only a single output (work accomplished) relative to a single input (labor manhours), labor productivity does not equal performance. For example, a contractor may be able to construct a house with a minimum of manhours because she carefully plans the job ahead of time, uses skilled workers, and provides the right equipment and materials when they are needed. Her labor productivity is high. Yet she may pay excessive rental charges to keep all the equipment on site all of the time, and she may pay too much for higher-grade materials that exceed the specifications. Overall, her performance suffers. Good productivity can lead to high performance, but it is not the only contribution (or, necessarily, the most important contribution) to jobsite performance.

It is time now to turn our attention to measurements of performance so that we can learn how to locate those construction methods which will cost the least to improve and which will contribute the most to increasing the worth of the completed job.

Chapter

2

Measurements of Performance

The performance viewpoint distinguishes between accomplishments and the work methods employed to achieve these accomplishments. Measurements of accomplishment can point to deficiencies in work methods. By correcting such deficiencies, management improves construction performance.

We seek better measurements of construction performance in order to improve it. Useful measurements, because they provide management with valuable feedback concerning jobsite performance, lead to reducing the cost of construction relative to the value of work-in-place. Three considerations determine which measurements to collect:

- We must meet management's *need for information* in order to support actions that will improve performance.

- We must collect the most *relevant* measurements, taking care not to overlook important dimensions of performance measurements.

- Whatever measurement system we develop must prove *practical* in daily use.

This chapter lays out a methodology for measuring construction performance. We begin by examining how measurements can be used to establish relevant standards for each job to help spot performance deficiencies. We then turn our attention to developing appropriate measurements for construction accomplishments.

The Performance Ability Ratio (PAR)

Chapter 1 defined *performance* as a ratio of accomplishment to methods. The *worth* of performance was given as the value of the accomplishment divided by the cost of the methods. However, it is not enough merely to assess the value of a particular piece of work-in-place, to calculate the cost of getting it there, and thereby to evaluate the worth of the performance. Knowing that a four-person ironworker crew has placed 4 tons of rebar in four hours tells us something about the worth of the crew's performance but does not tell us *how well they are doing*. To provide us with a means for judging their *relative worth,* our measurements of performance must compare actual performance against a yardstick of desired performance. We need to know whether or not 4 tons-in-place for 16 manhours of work is reasonable, relative to some accepted standard of performance. In other words, how many manhours should it normally take to place 4 tons of rebar? (Or, conversely, how many tons should a crew of four normally be able to place in four hours?)

Setting worthy standards

Construction standards, which set forth the amount of manhours normally required for a given task, form the basis for construction estimating. Estimators carefully figure the amount of work required for a construction task and then multiply the number of units of work by the number of manhours needed to accomplish a single unit of the work in order to get a figure for the total manhours required to complete the task. The standards used in estimating vary widely and, even within a single job, may vary according to the estimator's perception of expected job conditions.

Yet estimates normally come from data that tell us only the *average* of how much time is needed to complete a single unit of work. The average is clearly not the best we can do. If we truly seek to improve jobsite performance, we must never be satisfied with average performance. Only exemplary performance provides us with a worthwhile yardstick by which to measure our relative performance. *Exemplar* performance is the historically best instance of the performance. Exemplar performance, therefore, is the most worthy instance of performing a particular construction task or job—that instance in which *the value of the accomplishment most exceeds the cost of the methods.*

Exemplar and current performance

For example, suppose current records for a construction job show that ironworker performance for a four-person crew spending four hours placing similar rebar averages 3.2 tons placed for every 16 manhours (MH) worked. (Normally we would write 3.2 tons per 16 MH as 0.2 ton/MH, an expression equivalent to 3.2/16.) Suppose, further, that on good days the crew places as much as 4.8 tons in 16 MH (0.3 ton/MH). Now the 4.8 tons (or 0.3 ton/MH) would represent the exemplar, the best the crew is able to achieve. The measurement of their relative job performance would then be given as the ratio of their exemplar to their average (or current) performance. This ratio is the *performance ability ratio* (*PAR*) and is given as:

$$\text{Performance ability ratio (PAR)} = \frac{\text{exemplar performance } (P_x)}{\text{current performance } (P_c)}$$

A PAR equal to 1.0 would mean that current work equals the best. A PAR greater than 1.0 indicates a potential for performance improvement. The larger the PAR, the greater the room for improvement. In the example above, if the average of 3.2 tons reflected current work, then the PAR for placing rebar would be given as:

$$\text{PAR} = \frac{4.8 \text{ (tons per 16 MH)}}{3.2 \text{ (tons per 16 MH)}} = 1.5$$

A note on numerical conventions

Expressing the ratio in the more conventional terms of units per single manhour provides the same answer:

$$\text{PAR} = \frac{0.3 \text{ ton/MH}}{0.2 \text{ ton/MH}} = 1.5$$

Many contractors, however, prefer to measure work rates in terms of manhours per unit-in-place, or, in this case, manhours per ton of in-place rebar. Inverting the calculations above gives us 16 MH per 3.2 tons (16/3.2), or 5.0 MH/ton for the average. The exemplar would be 16 MH per 4.8 tons (16/4.8), or 3.33 MH/ton. If we use this MH/unit convention, then we must also invert the PAR calculation, giving us:

$$\text{PAR} = \frac{\text{current performance } (P_c)}{\text{exemplar performance } (P_x)}$$

Refiguring the PAR now gives us the same number:

$$\text{PAR} = \frac{5.0 \text{ MH/ton (average)}}{3.33 \text{ MH/ton (exemplar)}} = 1.5$$

The PAR is always calculated so that the smaller number is divided into the larger number to give a result greater than 1.

Choosing the exemplar

The PAR can be used in many ways. By comparing current performance to the exemplar, it serves as a measurement of the relative worth of jobsite performance. But whose exemplar should be used? This job's, the company's best, the industry's best? And what measurement of current performance should be used? Today's, last week's, this task's, all tasks', all jobs'? The answer is simple: Any of them. Depending on our purpose in measuring performance, our choice of exemplar and current performance will vary. The PAR is a *dynamic* measurement. It will change over time because the current performance will change and because, if we are competently managing performance, the exemplar will improve. If we chose the company's best historical performance as our exemplar and measure current performance against it, then sooner or later we ought to be able to improve on the exemplar, thereby setting a new standard for future PAR measurements.

In most instances, construction companies will want to set the exemplar as their own historical best, principally because they can measure their own bests and seldom know their competitors' bests. However, different jobs may be so unlike in their characteristics and conditions that it would make no sense to compare them. An exemplar for piping from a job in Alaska may not apply to a job in Texas. And an exemplar for piping installed at ground level may not apply to piping on the same job installed 40 ft in the air. To avoid mixing apples and oranges, we may need to determine every task's own exemplar in order to make useful judgments concerning measurements of relative worth. Yet, as we shall see, as long as the measurements are consistent, a great deal of comparison among different tasks will be possible.

Besides offering a relative standard for comparing performance among tasks and jobs, the exemplar also provides a dynamic standard. It will change over time as performance improves. Every day offers the opportunity to do better than the day before.

The size of the PAR

No company can maintain a PAR of 1.0; current average performance is bound to be lower than exemplar performance. Variation is inevitable. Yet the closer to 1.0 the PAR, the more competent the company. A high PAR, on the other hand, indicates incompetence, which is to say that *large variations between the exemplar and current performance reveal unique opportunities for management improvement.*

On construction jobs, PARs can vary widely for different types of work. In general, the more repetitive and uncomplicated the task, the lower the PAR, and vice versa. Over time on a single job, as people become more skilled at the task, the PAR ought to decrease. PARs for similar tasks on jobs with several crews working under similar conditions will also vary. Table 2.1 shows the range for some representative PAR measurements.

TABLE 2.1   Representative PAR Measurements

Task	Range of measured PAR
Installing H-pile lagging	1.1 to 1.4
Rebuilding conveyor belt	1.2 to 1.4
Pulling wire and connections	1.2 to 1.6
Installing ½- to 2-in pipe	1.3 to 2.8
Installing 4-in pipe	1.3 to 3.3
Installing 5- to 8-in pipe	1.3 to 3.0
Placing soldier beams	1.8 to 2.6
Installing nuclear pipe hangers	1.7 to 10.0
Nuclear welding (all pipe)	3.2 to 19.2

As most would have guessed, the industry's worst PARs occur in nuclear construction, where it is not uncommon to find PARs greater than 5. While some of the high variation in nuclear-construction performance can be attributed to the exacting nature of the work and the difficult conditions under which much of it is performed, the greatest cause of these large PARs is directly due to inadequate measurement and feedback. Good measurement and feedback would have allowed managers to focus their attention on improving the work methods that offered the greatest payback in terms of increased productivity and higher-quality construction.

Focus on Your Best

The performance of individual workers on any jobsite varies, with some performing better than others. Field supervisors know this and are usually alert for evidence of poor performance. Yet few field supervisors go out of their way to find examples of superior performance. By failing to spot exemplars, jobsite managers miss an opportunity to boost overall performance by discovering the best methods to accomplish the work.

The performance curve

Figure 2.1 shows one way to look at overall jobsite performance. Here we see a hypothetical graph of worker performance on the job. The vertical axis plots the number of people on the job, and the horizontal axis plots their performance. If we could measure individual performance well enough to construct such a graph, it would look much like Figure 2.1. Only a few people really perform either very poorly or very well. Most perform about average. Figure 2.1 is called a *bell curve;* bell curves are often used in behavioral science to describe characteristics of large groups of people. Some people will be at one end, some at

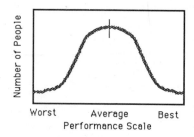

Figure 2.1 Typical distribution of jobsite performance.

the other, and most in the middle. Construction workers are no different; most are average performers, with some "sorry cases" at one extreme and a few outstanding master craftsmen capable of exemplar performance at the other end.

The difference between average performance and the best performance in Figure 2.1 can be measured by the PAR. Dividing the average into the best (or exemplar) gives a ratio. If the distance between the average and the best is very great, the ratio will be large; if the distance between the two is small, the ratio will be small.

Traditional management techniques

Many field managers on construction jobs focus on the worst end of the performance scale. Foremen and supervisors frequently come down hard on those workers and crews which they feel do not perform as well as the others. How often have hard-nosed foremen bragged about their ability to boot their workers in the tail, threatening to run them off the job if they don't work? Such foremen see force as the key to getting work done; they tolerate no "laziness" on their jobs. If they let one worker get away with lying down on the job, they believe that others will let up as well.

Figure 2.2 diagrams the usual result of such a management technique. Poorer workers are pushed into performing closer to the average (or else lose their jobs). Clearly, overall performance has improved relative to the bell curve in Figure 2.1; overlaying the two curves shows that more workers now exhibit average performance. But *more average performers do not improve the average.* Notice that for the amount of effort that goes into it and for the hard feelings that sometimes result, the gains don't look all that big.

Upgrading the average

Figure 2.3 illustrates an alternative approach to on-site management. Here the focus of management's attention is on the best instead of on

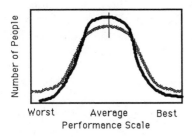

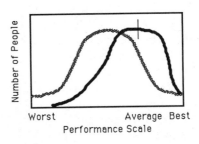

Figure 2.2 More average performers do not improve the average.

Figure 2.3 Average performance shifted toward exemplar performance.

the worst: (1) Accurate measurements of performance identify exemplar workers and crews; (2) management then studies the exemplar performers to find out what makes them the best and takes actions to make sure that the rest of the labor force follows the same superior work methods. The overall performance curve in Figure 2.3 shows considerable improvement over the normal bell curve in Figure 2.1. This improvement comes from management actions to shift average performance toward the best, thereby narrowing the gap between average and exemplar performance. Figure 2.3 indicates a job with a small PAR.

Note that the left side of the curve in Figure 2.3, representing the poorer performers, has also shifted toward improvement. Two factors account for this. First, as the average performance on the job improves, even slackards improve; they find that they must improve or else stand out so clearly as incompetent that they risk losing their jobs. The second factor is stronger, however; in most cases workers are not incompetent or lazy by nature but only slightly below average in their performance. As the average improves, they unconsciously improve, pacing their own work to try to match that of their buddies. (And all without any shouting on the foreman's part.)

To illustrate how the PAR can actually point the way to improved performance, let us turn to the story of how one contractor made it work.

Relco Roofing

Alan Marshall was dissatisfied with the falling earnings of Relco Roofing, the company his father and uncle founded just before he was born. Having just graduated from business school, Alan had given in to the joint pleadings of his father and uncle to join the firm as vice president. The starting salary was not great, but the promise that the business would be his in a few years finally convinced him to pass up other offers and join the family firm, a career decision he long thought he would never make. Now, after six months in the business, Alan had come to the realization that the ancient accounting methods used by the firm vastly overstated its real earnings. Nothing had been set aside, for example, to fund the proposed retirement of the firm's founders; much of the projected future earnings would have to be funneled into a retirement plan. Staring at the accounting sheets in front of him, Alan once again doubted the wisdom of his decision to join Relco.

Relco's problems

Relco's business consisted of two divisions—commercial and residential roofing. The commercial side seemed to be holding its own, neither growing nor sliding. The residential side, on the other hand, needed immediate attention. It was growing at a rapid rate while making less and less money every month.

If something isn't done quickly, thought Alan with bitter humor, we'll soon be turning away work, which will be good, because we'll be losing money on every job.

Relco's residential roofing business regularly employed about 30 crews that did homes and apartment buildings for local contractors. Although Relco's prices were not the lowest in the business, its large work force allowed it to get the job done quickly. Contractors preferred to pay a little more for Relco because they knew that they could rely on Relco to come in and roof the job at the earliest possible moment and in the shortest possible time.

Labor turnover in the roofing business had always been high, but lately it seemed that Relco was hiring more and more temporary people who left after a few months on the job. Even the "full-time" roofers rarely stayed in the business more than a few seasons, having figured out that there are easier ways to make a living than crawling around on hot roofs all summer long. Increasingly, Relco's new hires were young men and women with little education, no skills, and a strong disrespect for hard-driving foremen. In looking over the production figures for past years, Alan could see that the average productivity for his roofing crews was dropping fast. Clearly, the downward productivity trend needed to be halted and reversed. But how?

Foreman training

In a meeting with his father and uncle, Alan laid out the problem of falling productivity in residential roofing and pinpointed poor supervision as the cause. Relco's foremen, some of them in the business for many years, could not cope with the changing character of the labor force—fewer skills, different motivations, and "relaxed" attitudes toward supervision. Foremen needed to learn new supervisory skills, Alan argued. They needed to learn to communicate, to motivate, to lead.

Alan went on to propose a foreman training program for Relco's field supervisors. The program, conducted by a professional trainer, would cost only $8000 over a six-week period. Each of Relco's 28 foreman would attend six half-day sessions, once a week. The cost, therefore, would be $8000 divided by 28 foremen, each at four hours per week for six weeks—only about $12 per manhour, just about what Relco paid foremen in wages anyway.

"But we're still paying the wages too," pointed out Alan's uncle, "and they're not on the job. So you have to double the cost of the training."

"Even so," Alan argued, "we can't afford not to. We'll be out of business in another year unless we do something."

"Sounds reasonable to me," Alan's father said as he adjourned the meeting. "But just to be safe, we ought to get a second opinion, and I know just the person."

Alan felt discouraged.

A consultant's viewpoint

The next day Colton Turner showed up in Alan's office. "Your father asked me to take a look at your problem. Can you show me around?" During the morning, while showing "Colt" around the office and driving him to see two of the jobsites, Alan learned that Colt had never worked in construction before. His consulting work was largely confined to several industrial clients. Alan's discouragement deepened when he learned that Colt, now semiretired, was charging Relco $1000 per day for his services. After a leisurely lunch, Colt spent several hours looking over records of past jobs, writing down rows of figures, and using his pocket calculator on them. Colt surprised Alan by coming in to his office before 4:00 P.M. to announce that he was finished and would like to give him a report and get on his way. Anticipating a few obvious conclusions about the need for foreman training and a recommendation to extend his consulting services for a week or two, Alan motioned Colt into a chair.

"Your problem," Colt began, "is not your foremen. They seem to be a pretty competent lot. The problem is your crews. They're the ones who need the training."

"But," sputtered Alan in protest, "you never even talked to any of the foremen."

"Let me explain," Colt continued. And, within the hour, Alan found himself agreeing that Relco ought to spend the $16,000 for training the labor force, not the foremen. Colt left with a check for $1000, and Alan never saw him again.

Within a year Relco's residential division had completely turned around. Turnover had dropped. Productivity was up. Profits were way up. "Son," Alan's father told him, "I knew you could do it. Your idea of starting a training program was just what the company needed. I'm proud of you." But what did Colt do that changed Alan's mind about who to train, and why did it work so well?

Performance analysis

Table 2.2 shows some of the production data collected by Colt for five of Relco's crews. Because of the detailed daily production records kept by Relco, Colt was able to pull out the number of squares of shingles laid by each crew for 12 weeks over the course of several summer months.

Colt also checked through the records to get the names of the individuals working on each crew. He then tracked the attendance record for each individual, matching the person to the crew to which he or she was assigned and when. The resulting data showed that nearly every crew started off the summer with new workers and poor production records. Over the course of the summer, though, production improved as the workers learned the job. Those crews which had the

TABLE 2.2 Comparison of Relco's Weekly Production per Crew

	A	B	C	D	E	F	G	H	I
1	Week	Crew productivity (squares/MH)					Weekly	Weekly	Weekly
2							average	exemplar	PAR
3		Crew A	Crew B	Crew C	Crew D	Crew E			
4	Formula						(B:F)/5		(H/G)
5									
6	1	10.4	9.4	8.8	10.1	10.2	9.8	10.4	1.06
7	2	11.2	8.8	9.3	10.5	10.4	10.0	11.2	1.12
8	3	11.0	9.6	11.0	11.8	12.6	11.2	12.6	1.13
9	4	13.0	10.8	12.4	12.0	14.0	12.4	14.0	1.13
10	5	12.4	12.4	13.9	13.2	14.4	13.3	14.4	1.09
11	6	14.6	14.0	14.8	14.0	17.4	15.0	17.4	1.16
12	7	16.0	12.7	15.6	15.8	15.9	15.2	16.0	1.05
13	8	15.7	14.7	17.1	16.4	18.9	16.6	18.9	1.14
14	9	17.8	15.0	18.3	18.1	19.8	17.8	19.8	1.11
15	10	18.4	17.0	17.5	18.0	21.2	18.4	21.2	1.15
16	11	20.0	15.9	18.0	19.3	21.1	18.9	21.1	1.12
17	12	21.2	17.5	19.2	20.2	22.0	20.0	22.0	1.10
18									
19	Average	15.1	13.2	14.7	15.0	16.5	14.9		
20	Exemplar	21.2	17.5	19.2	20.2	22.0		22.0	
21	Crew PAR	1.40	1.33	1.31	1.35	1.33			

largest fraction of "old-timers" and the lowest turnover during the summer gained most in productivity, while those crews which suffered the highest absenteeism and turnover showed the lowest production rates.

Table 2.2 gives the calculated productivity (in squares/MH) for Crews A through E for each of the 12 weeks. Column G shows the weekly average for all crews, and column H shows the exemplar for each week. Column I then calculates the weekly PAR by dividing the average from column G into the exemplar in column H. Row 19 across the bottom gives the 12-week averages for each of the five crews. Row 20 then shows each crew's exemplar for its best week during the summer. And row 21 computes each crew's PAR (by dividing the crew's 12-week average into its exemplar).

When Colt computed the PAR for all five crews in column I, he found that for any given week it was close to 1.1, indicating very little variation in terms of crew performance or the foremen's competence. But the PAR for each crew (in row 21), computed from its best production record at the end of the summer and its average over the course of the summer, averaged more than 1.3, indicating a greater potential for improvement.

Colt concluded that the problem was not the foremen, since all seemed to average about the same production rates, but rather the length of time required for "on-the-job training" to improve the roofing skills of the crew members. The data showed that it took an average of eight weeks to develop a skilled work crew, and 12 weeks to develop a highly skilled crew. By that time most of the summer help was leaving and the process of retraining new workers had to start over again. Colt's proposal, to run an intensive two-week training program for every new hire, created skilled crews in three weeks, not eight, and these crews reached peak production in just four weeks, not 12. Besides, the greater pride the workers took in their new skills helped cut absenteeism and turnover.

Interpreting the PAR

The Relco story illustrates one use of the PAR. Colt obtained a productivity measurement of crew performance by dividing the squares of roofing shingles laid per week per crew by the number of manhours expended per crew for each week throughout the summer. Examine a portion of Colt's data in Table 2.2. The weekly performance for each of five crews over a 12-week period is shown in columns B through F. The average performance (column G) for all five crews for any single week gives a measurement of current performance, while the best production rate for any crew for the week (shown in boldface and copied to column H) provides the exemplar. Dividing the exemplar by the average for each week gives an overall PAR for the crews for each week (column I).

The PAR numbers in the right-most column show that the ratio of the exemplar for the week to the average production for the week falls between a high of 1.16 in week 6 and a low of 1.05 in week 7. Because little variation exists between the best crew and the average crew, all the PAR numbers are close to 1.0. Such small variation indicates that all foremen are performing at relatively the same level of competence each week. If, instead, the weekly PAR was 1.4 or higher, we would know that some foremen were doing a far better job than the average and that it might well pay to attempt to bring all foremen up to the best. In this case, however, since all foremen are very nearly the same, little can be gained by trying to reduce the variation among the foremen.

Now look at the numbers at the bottom of the table. Here the PAR for each crew is calculated for the entire 12-week period. Dividing a crew's exemplar production rate (row 20) by its average production rate for the summer (row 19) reveals much higher PARs (row 21), indicating a great deal of variation over time for each crew. These high PARs show a great potential for improvement within crews if only the learning that takes place slowly could be accelerated.

Colt showed Alan the following argument. Suppose each crew begins the summer spending one-half day in training for two weeks. During the remainder of the day they work at applying their new skills on the job. Such a training program ought to cut overall productivity in half for the first two weeks (since crews are really only working half of the day). The average productivity might then be only five squares/MH, not 10. Now, following the two weeks of training, the crews begin working full time and ought to be able to average 15 squares/MH in the third week, the same average they normally achieved over the course of the entire summer. By the fifth week, all crews ought to be close to the exemplar of 22 squares/MH. With these numbers the *average* production over the 12-week period for all crews would jump from 14.9 to 18.6 squares/MH, a gain of 25 percent. Although starting lower, the higher productivity in later weeks would more than offset the productivity losses during training.

Alan readily agreed that a potential improvement of 25 percent was well worth pursuing, even at the cost of a training program.

Dimensions of Performance Measurements

Knowing the importance of performance measurements does not tell us what to measure or how to measure it. A simple table of the six possible measurements, however, provides an easy-to-use guide for describing and measuring any aspect of construction accomplishment.

The need for measurements

We have seen the potential value of computing the PAR but have not yet seen how to measure the accomplishments and methods that are needed to compute it. What are the dimensions of construction performance? Most contractors can readily tell a good job from a poor one. But how? What qualities set one job apart as superior from the rest? How does an owner know whether or not a contractor performs well? The two most common measurements of construction performance ask if a job was completed on time and within budget. These measurements compare actual contractor performance with expected performance. *On-time completion* means that the job finished as it was scheduled. *Within budget* means no cost overruns. For our purposes, however, measurements of schedule and budget offer too little information for day-to-day project management. They do not tell us where the problems lie, and they do not point us toward solutions. Time and budget measurements frequently come too late to guide daily management decision making; they are better-suited as gross measurements of a completed job. On-site management needs more refined measurements for job control, measurements that provide timely feedback concerning current performance.

Six measurement dimensions

Three categories of measurements, encompassing six dimensions, are sufficient to describe every aspect of construction performance:

Quality
   1. Accuracy
   2. Workmanship
Quantity
   3. Productivity
   4. Schedule
Resources
   5. Manpower
   6. Materials, tools, and equipment

Any single construction accomplishment will require one or more of the six dimensions in order to be measured accurately. The six dimensions identify the full range of variation in accomplishments. The amount of variation depends upon the work methods chosen. For example, accuracy and productivity would be used to describe an electri-

TABLE 2.3   Questions for Measuring Performance Requirements

Quality Questions

1. *Accuracy* measures how closely the job conforms to plans, specifications, code requirements, and accepted industry standards for workmanship. Will any variation from the plans and specifications affect the worth of the finished task? Will errors result in rework? Do minor errors make a difference?

2. *Workmanship* measures significant differences in the worth of the finished job created by master-craftsmanship skills (assuming, of course, that all work meets standards for accuracy). Is it a showcase job that will be critically judged? Is it a novel design that requires special care in assembly?

Quantity Questions

3. *Productivity* measures differences in the *rate* at which the work is accomplished over time. Will any variation in productivity rates (number of units installed per manhour) significantly affect job costs? Will higher (or lower) productivity rates affect manpower and schedule?

4. *Schedule* measures how closely the job adheres to an optimum construction schedule. Will any variation from the schedule affect the job? Will an early or late completion of tasks affect other aspects of the job?

Resource Questions

5. *Manpower* measures differences in labor costs not reflected in the measurements of productivity in question 3. Will any variation in the skills of the labor force make a difference to the job? Will any variation in the type of craftsmen or craftsman classifications affect job costs? Is there a minimum or maximum number of people that should be on the job at any one time? Will crew size affect job costs? Will inattention to jobsite safety raise job costs?

6. *Materials, tools, and equipment* collects measurements of construction resources other than manpower. Can variations in job costs be attributed to differences in materials, tools, and equipment use? Will significant variations in the amount and type of equipment and tools used affect the job? Will material waste, loss, or theft create significant job costs?

cian's accomplishment of pulling wire through conduits and making connections, but the amount of materials consumed and equipment used would hardly differ among craftsmen performing the same task. To judge whether or not a dimension applies to a specific construction task, ask the questions listed in Table 2.3. If the answers to any of them are yes, then that dimension may be needed in order to measure the accomplishment accurately.

Measuring accomplishments

Table 2.4 shows how the dimensions of performance measurements apply to a sample of construction accomplishments. While all the dimensions are used in Table 2.4, remember that a dimension of performance applies only when an accomplishment can vary significantly along that dimension. For example, a masonry crew laying up a brick

TABLE 2.4   Examples of Performance Measurements

Accomplishment	Measurement	Dimension	Unit
Formwork for concrete wall	Correct placement?	Accuracy	Inches
	Complete when ready to pour?	Schedule	Hours
	Solidly braced?	Accuracy	Yes/No
	Productive work?	Productivity	Sq ft/MH
	Reasonable labor cost?	Manpower	Dollars
	Little wasted materials?	Materials	Dollars
Rough-stone stairway	Steps level and solid?	Accuracy	Yes/No
	Aesthetic appearance OK?	Workmanship	Yes/No
	Productive work?	Productivity	Steps/MH
	Reasonable labor cost?	Manpower	Dollars
	Little wasted stone?	Materials	Dollars
	Completed on time?	Schedule	Days
Lavatory fixtures	Fixtures work properly?	Accuracy	Yes/No
	Installation neat and proper?	Accuracy	Yes/No
	Productive work?	Productivity	Units/MH
	Reasonable labor cost?	Manpower	Dollars
	Completed on time?	Schedule	Days
Steel frame	All connections correct?	Accuracy	Yes/No
	Safe work practices?	Manpower	Yes/No
	Productive work?	Productivity	Tons/MH
	Reasonable labor cost?	Manpower	Dollars
	Completed on time?	Schedule	Days
	Reasonable equipment cost?	Equipment	Dollars
Hung ceiling	Ceiling level?	Accuracy	Inches
	Supports well anchored?	Accuracy	Yes/No
	Edges neat and proper?	Accuracy	Yes/No
	Productive work?	Productivity	Sq ft/MH
	Reasonable labor cost?	Manpower	Dollars
	Little wasted materials?	Materials	Dollars
	Completed on time?	Schedule	Days
Foundation excavation	Reasonable equipment cost?	Equipment	Dollars
	Reasonable labor cost?	Manpower	Dollars
	Safe work practices?	Manpower	Yes/No
	Completed on time?	Schedule	Days
	Size of hole correct?	Accuracy	Feet
Telephone system	Do all phones work?	Accuracy	Yes/No
	Productive work?	Productivity	Lines/MH
	Reasonable labor cost?	Manpower	Dollars
	Completed on time?	Schedule	Days

panel can hardly vary the materials or tools. Their crew size and skills may affect the work only marginally. Yet productivity and schedule, the two primary dimensions of most construction tasks, will certainly apply. Accuracy, too, will be a critical measurement of masonry performance. And if the masonry panel forms an extremely visible part of a main entrance area, a measurement of workmanship may also apply. Table 2.4 also includes a column for units of measurements to indicate what measurements might be collected.

Productivity and manpower

The examples in Table 2.4 repeat some of the same measurements, dimensions, and units. For example, both "Productive work?" and "Reasonable labor cost?" appear for all but one of the accomplishments. Because hourly labor performs most construction tasks, productivity (installed units per manhour or, conversely, manhours per installed unit) measures a key dimension of performance. However, because the skill of the labor force may vary considerably and because the hourly wage rate may also vary according to craft skills, measuring the labor cost of the completed work provides another dimension for comparing performance. A very productive job, performed with highly skilled (and highly paid) labor, may indeed turn out to be less costly than the same job performed by less-skilled (and lower-paid) labor who require twice as long to complete the work.

Productive and unproductive hours

In addition to differences between skill and wage rates, the amount of *labor manhours paid on the job but not actually worked* may need to be considered. A crew, for example, may complete a task in the early afternoon yet remain at the jobsite doing little or nothing until quitting time. Should all the hours for the day be charged to the task, thereby lowering the measured productivity of the crew? Or should only the hours worked be charged to the task in order to get an accurate measurement of productivity, while charging the additional "lost" hours to overhead? Contractors differ in how they account for on-site labor hours. Chapter 7 explains how a manhour accounting system should be designed to obtain accurate measurement of on-site productivity.

Schedule

The measurement question "Completed on time?" appeared for every accomplishment in Table 2.4. Normally, schedule is a critical dimension of construction performance. Depending on the task at hand, the units of measurement may range from hours to days, weeks, or even months.

Measure only variation

Although Table 2.4 includes examples of all six dimensions of performance measurements, not every job need be measured along every dimension. *We measure only when a variation along a dimension is
likely to cause a significant variation in the accomplishment.* In the
case of the foundation excavation in Table 2.4, for example, labor productivity was not included as a measurement since the excavation
equipment is likely to be a far larger factor in determining job performance. Labor cost, however, is measured. If the excavation included
installation of lagging between H-piles, then the productivity of labor
in placing the lagging (a labor-intensive task) would be measured.
And safety, while a central concern of every job, requires special attention on jobs with dangers of injury from falls (the leading cause of
injuries in construction).

Developing Measurements and Units

While most contractors readily understand most of the dimensions
and units of measurement given above, they may find it difficult to
apply the concepts to a real job. Let us spend a moment, therefore, going step by step through a typical construction job and collecting performance measurements.

Suppose we wish to measure the weekly performance of an electrical
crew installing metal conduit and boxes, running wire, and making
connections in a commercial building project. What measurements apply here? To develop the appropriate measurements for the job, it is
best to go down the list of all measurements to ensure that none is
overlooked. We begin with Table 2.5, developing a checklist of appropriate measurements.

Now, looking over the list of questions to be answered in Table 2.5,
we see that we have identified eight measurements that will be critical to the weekly performance of the job. They are:

Job measurement	Unit	Comment
Labor	MH	The number of paid manhours
Overtime	MH	Paid manhours at overtime rates
Foremen	MH	Paid manhours at foreman rates
Schedule	Days	Days ahead or behind schedule
Labor wage rate	$/MH	Labor cost per manhour
Foreman wage rate	$/MH	Foreman cost per manhour
Productivity rates	Units/MH	Amount installed per labor manhour
Materials	$	Dollar cost of waste and loss

TABLE 2.5   Checklist of Performance Requirements and Measurements

Quality Questions	Measurement and unit
1. Accuracy	
(a) Will variation from standards of accuracy significantly lower the worth of the finished job?	
Yes; if wiring does not serve needs, rework will be required.	Labor (MH) and materials ($)
Yes; if wiring is not safe, rework will be required.	Labor (MH) and materials ($)
(b) Will errors or variation result in rework?	
Yes, if work fails to meet plans, specs, or code requirements.	Labor (MH) and materials ($)
(c) Do minor errors make a difference?	
No, only in appearance.	
2. Workmanship	
(a) Is it a showcase job that will be critically judged?	
No, conduit will be covered.	
(b) Will master-craftsmanship or exemplar skill create significant differences in finished work?	
No.	
(c) Is it a novel design that requires special care in assembly?	
No.	

Quantity Questions	
3. Productivity	
(a) Will variation in productivity rates (number of units installed per manhour) affect job costs?	
Yes, higher productivity will require fewer MH.	Productivity (units/MH)
(b) Will higher (or lower) productivity rates affect manpower and schedule?	
Yes, higher productivity will require fewer people and speed the job.	Labor (MH) and schedule (days)
Yes, lower productivity will require more people or more overtime to meet the same schedule or else result in schedule delays.	Labor (MH) and overtime (MH) and schedule (days)
4. Schedule	
(a) Will variation from the schedule affect the job?	
Yes, it may create additional planning and control problems.	Foremen (MH)
(b) Will early or late completion of tasks affect other aspects of the job?	
Yes, late work will hold up other trades and cause out-of-sequence work, leading to overtime, overstaffing, or delays.	Overtime (MH) and labor (MH) and schedule (days)

TABLE 2.5   Checklist of Performance Requirements and Measurements *(Continued)*

Resource Questions	
5. Manpower	
(a) Will variation in the skills of the labor force make a difference to the job?	
Yes, higher-skilled craftsman and foremen may cost more per hour.	Foremen ($/MH) and labor ($/MH)
Skilled people may make fewer rework errors.	Labor (MH)
Skilled people may require less direct supervision.	Foremen (MH)
(b) Will variation in the type of craftsmen affect job costs?	
Yes, hourly rates for trades and trade classifications may vary.	Labor ($/MH)
(c) Will the number of people on the job at any one time affect the job cost?	
Yes, understaffing may slow the work pace and cause delays (while overstaffing may lead to productivity loss).	Schedule (days)
(d) Will crew size affect job costs?	
Yes, for the same number of craftsmen, smaller crews may require more foremen for supervision.	Foremen (MH)
(e) Does the job pose special risks of injuries from falls or equipment that demand extra safety protection?	
Yes, floor openings and scaffolds must meet Occupational Safety and Health Administration (OSHA) standards, and electricians must follow safe practices.	Labor (MH) and foremen (MH)
6. Materials, tools, and equipment	
(a) Will significant variations in the amount and type of equipment and tools used affect the job?	
No. Electricians use standard tools and equipment in good condition.	
(b) Will material waste, loss, or theft create significant job costs?	
Yes.	Materials ($)

Using Measurements of Productivity

All the measurements, except productivity, appear relatively straightforward and easy to get. Job records show wage rates and hours worked by labor and foremen, both straight time and overtime. Materials costs for the job, in excess of the cost for the estimated amounts, can be attributed to waste or theft, if any, or to an error in the quantity estimate. And we clearly know whether we finished the job on time. But what about productivity? How do we measure that?

Grouping similar accomplishments

For item 3.a in Table 2.5, one measurement of the units installed might be the ratio of the linear feet of installed conduit to the number of boxes installed. Now if we find that this ratio does not vary greatly relative to the average of past jobs, then we might safely lump the conduit and boxes together and simply count the feet of conduit installed as a representative measurement of the amount of work accomplished. Similarly, if the amount of wire pulled and the number of terminations made are also proportional to the amount of conduit installed, then we may lump them all together in a single unit of measurement—the number of feet of completed, wired conduit.

Knowing the amount of installed conduit thus gives us a measurement of the amount of work accomplished. And knowing the number of manhours it took to install the conduit, mount the boxes, pull the wire, and complete the terminations gives us a measurement of the cost of the installation method. Dividing the feet of installed conduit by the manhours worked gives us a measurement of average productivity in feet per manhour (or manhours per foot, if one prefers to invert the calculation).

Separating dissimilar accomplishments

However, we must examine the job to be sure that the number of bends, the amount of cutting and connections, and the location of the conduit are also average for work of this kind. If a portion of the work is unusual (say that the conduit must be bolted to the underside of a concrete slab 30 ft above the floor), then this amount of work ought to be counted separately from the rest. Differences in conduit sizes and locations may lead to differences in productivity during installation. In such cases, we need to measure each portion of the work separately.

Let us assume that we have successfully grouped similar accomplishments and have distinguished those which are dissimilar. Table 2.6 shows our results. The two types of conduit include the boxes, wire, and terminations necessary to complete the work. Three different installment conditions distinguish between work at floor level, on ladders, and on scaffolds. The measurements of the amounts placed and the manhours charged allow us to compute our productivity for the job in question.

Table 2.6 shows 315 labor manhours charged among the six possible classifications of work. Presumably, climbing ladders accounts for the relatively low productivity in overhead work, and setting up and climbing scaffolds accounts for the even lower productivity when working above 12 ft. Such measurements, if collected over many jobs,

TABLE 2.6   Productivity of Electrical Conduit Installation

	A	B	C	D
1		Amount	Manhours	Productivity
2	Accomplishment	placed (ft)	charged	(ft/MH)
3				
4	One-half-inch conduit			
5	(a) up to head height	600	42	14.3
6	(b) overhead	800	77	10.5
7	(c) above 12 ft	200	34	5.9
8				
9	One-inch conduit			
10	(a) up to head height	400	32	12.5
11	(b) overhead	700	75	9.3
12	(c) above 12 ft	300	55	5.5
13				
14	Total MH		315	

would give an estimator accurate numbers for estimating future work. The numbers would also give a contractor the means for calculating his or her PAR among jobs.

Measuring crew productivity

At first glance it would seem possible to collect measurements of individual performance (work accomplished and manhours charged) in order to calculate the productivity for every craftsman on the job and therefore to compute a PAR among individuals. In practice, however, individual performance measurements usually prove impractical, if not impossible.

Attempts to measure individual productivity in construction tend to fail for two reasons. First, tracking the number of tasks accomplished by each individual is difficult, particularly when the crew works as a team. It is impossible to charge individual time to specific work items when several crew members may assist in the different subtasks required for final installation. Second, most people resist individual performance measurements because they fear that these may be used to penalize them unfairly. Construction workers, in particular, pride themselves on being able to accomplish a wide variety of demanding tasks; everyone recognizes that some excel at one task, others at another task. Depending on which task is measured, even normally superior performers may not do well.

Fortunately we need not impose an impossible reporting burden on each craftsman or on ourselves. Instead, aggregate measurements of crew performance will serve us quite well. (Table 2.6, for example, records 315 hours worked by nine craftsmen in one week.) In general, therefore, we use measurements of crew performance because these are relatively easy to obtain and tell us a great deal about the adequacy of the work methods used to accomplish the work-in-place.

Measuring contractor performance

Suppose, now, that the numbers in Table 2.7 represent productivity measurements collected over five similar jobs, all running at about the same time and under more or less the same conditions. What do they tell us about the contractor's performance?

To get the PAR for each type of conduit installation, we divide the average performance for all jobs into the exemplar performance from the single best job (in this case, Job 5 represents the exemplar every time). For example, the largest PAR of 1.7, given for ½-in conduit placed at heights over 12 ft, is calculated from the average (6.2 ft per manhour) divided into the exemplar (10.3 ft per manhour). This large PAR tells us that a significant variation exists in the performance of crews installing this work on different jobs. This variation results from differences in management competence. The supervisor for Job 5 has crews installing the conduit nearly 3 times as fast as the supervisor for Job 3. What is it that makes Job 5 so superior?

Let us assume that all five jobs are really comparable—similar amounts of work installed under similar conditions. If we were able to measure the productivity of individual craftsmen on all the jobs carefully, we would certainly discover variations in individual performance as well. But given the large difference between Job 5 and the

TABLE 2.7 Comparing Productivity Measurements for Five Current Jobs

	A	B	C	D	E	F	G	H
1	Accomplishment	Job 1	Job 2	Job 3	Job 4	Job 5	Average	PAR
2								
3	*Formula*							*(F/G)*
4								
5	One-half inch conduit							
6	(a) up to head height	14.3	12.7	10.3	15.4	**19.1**	14.4	1.3
7	(b) overhead	10.5	9.8	9.8	13.6	**14.9**	11.7	1.3
8	(c) above 12 ft	5.9	4.1	3.9	7.0	**10.3**	6.2	1.7
9								
10	One-inch conduit							
11	(a) up to head height	12.5	10.6	9.5	13.0	**14.8**	12.1	1.2
12	(b) overhead	9.3	7.4	6.6	9.9	**11.2**	8.9	1.3
13	(c) above 12 ft	5.5	4.3	2.7	6.0	**8.5**	5.4	1.6

rest of the jobs, we know it is highly unlikely that the difference results from a single "super craftsman" at Job 5 and a distribution of many incompetents among the other crews. It is far more likely that the supervisor on Job 5 employs superior methods to place the crews (with their tools and materials) up in the air and to keep them working once they are up there. *Discovering the secret of Job 5 and transferring this knowledge to the supervisors at the other jobs should lead to higher productivity rates and a lower PAR.* Let us look at a case in which such measurements actually led to dramatic results.

A Foreman at the End of Her Rope

It was hot work in the summer Georgia sun, climbing rebar all day long. The electrical union working the big nuclear plant out in the red clay hills and scrub pine had the job of installing unistrut in the great concrete walls. The unistrut resembled a metal channel embedded vertically every 5 ft or so in the face of a concrete wall. Horizontal supports protruded from the channel to carry long tracks of cable tray. In this tray, high on the walls, electricians would eventually lay miles of wire to power and control the plant. At this point in time, however, the electricians were still a long way from getting to the heart of their craft skills—wires. They were toiling like ants, doing donkey work, wiring unistrut to the rebar. But at $18.72 per hour it was well-paid donkey work.

Some 20 crews were already at work on the unistrut, and more would come in the weeks to come. Even as the great masses of steel and concrete began to take shape, only a small fraction of the work had been completed. Each individual in a crew was assigned a wall of vertical rebar and a pile of unistrut. The job required a person to climb the rebar, using a safety harness, while struggling to grasp a heavy 4- to 8-ft length of unistrut. Once up, the electrician measured the location and wired the unistrut to the rebar in a temporary position. Later, when plywood forms covered the rebar, an electrician had to climb down inside the forms and bolt the unistrut pieces to the face of the form to keep them from shifting during concrete placement.

The work was hard and hot, not at all what electricians were trained to do. Electricians, so they always claimed, got paid to work with their brains, not their brawn. After each piece of unistrut was safely wired in place and the electrician was back on the ground, it was time for a well-deserved break—a trip to the can, a cigarette, a cup of water, a chat with a fellow worker—before starting to search for the next piece to go up. Needless to say, productivity was low, far lower than anyone doing estimates in an air-conditioned engineering office had ever guessed it might be. And, in spite of hassling by the foremen, none of the workers on the job felt any incentive to speed the work pace.

A new foreman

The rapidly expanding labor force demanded new foremen to run the new crews. Foreman promotion was quick. Be on the project for a few weeks, do a good job, and chances were you would get a crack at a foreman's job. (Turnover among foremen was high too. A lot of pressure for an extra buck an hour.) Bonnie Redon, a young local woman and a hard worker, got a chance one day and, without further training or ceremony, took over one of the sweltering crews.

Within two weeks, the amount of unistrut installed per manhour for Redon's crew jumped up to 2 and 3 times that of other crews. Each week, reports of manhours worked and amounts installed for each crew gave foremen and supervisors a measurement of performance. Redon's reports looked like mistakes. That is, until the superintendent went down to see Bonnie and her crew at work.

He found Bonnie and three of her crew sitting in the shade of one of the walls, looking at a set of blueprints and tying rope around lengths of unistrut. As the superintendent approached, waving the impossible reports, Bonnie rose to meet him.

After a few minutes of talk, a walk along the walls to look at the electricians up on the rebar, and another look at the rope, the superintendent returned to the trailer grinning. Bonnie hadn't figured out how to beat the reporting system; she had figured out how to beat the heat and the hassle.

Bonnie's brainstorm

As Bonnie explained it, before she became a foreman she had spent long hours in the sun climbing that rebar with the unistrut and knew first-hand how difficult the work was. There just had to be an easier way to do it, she thought. And she had resented the hassling that she and the others got whenever they took a break. No one could keep climbing that rebar all day without a rest. The tough part, thought Bonnie, was climbing up and down carrying the unistrut. Once you were up, it wasn't so bad, but as soon as you wired the unistrut in place, you had to go down for another piece. So no one had any reason to hurry.

Bonnie's brainstorm came when she picked up some rope the laborers had been using to raise scrap lumber from the lower foundation levels. Why not just tie the unistrut together and pull it up the rebar?

Bonnie laid out all the unistrut pieces that would be needed for a wall, tied them all together with 10 to 12 ft between each piece, and gave the loose end to one of her electricians, Ned. After Ned climbed up to position, he hauled up the first piece and wired it into place, then side-stepped along the rebar to the next position, pulled up the second piece of unistrut, wired it on, and continued down the wall. When Ned reached the end and climbed down, he and Bonnie agreed that the work went very fast this way and was much easier. Bonnie told him to take a 15-minute break. He'd earned it.

By the end of the day, Bonnie had rounded up every scrap of rope she could find and her whole crew was using the new method. Every time one did a wall, one got 15 minutes off. Naturally, everyone quickly figured out how to move down those walls in a hurry. And, Bonnie figured, even with the 15-minute breaks, they were still wasting a lot less time on the ground than they were before. Plus, they all liked the work better now and didn't have to put up with the hassle.

The day after the superintendent introduced Bonnie's method at the weekly general foremen's meeting, the company had to send a truck into town to buy more rope. Every electrical foreman on the jobsite, it seemed, was yelling for it.

The Bonnie Redon story shows us how measurements of crew performance, when compared among crews, can uncover surprising variations in performance due to differences in work methods. And, by following up to find the causes of the variations, exemplar performers can be identified and their methods copied. Table 2.7, which compared PARs for electrical work, pointed out a similar variation in the exemplar performance of the supervisor for Job 5.

Measurements and Performance

We have seen that we can measure jobsite performance along six different dimensions: accuracy, workmanship, productivity, schedule, manpower, and the materials, tools, and equipment that go into a job. These performance measurements provide us with a means to uncover opportunities for improvement, opportunities presented in the form of large PARs, the ratio of our exemplar performance to our average. By striving to bring average performance up to exemplar performance, we continually improve our work methods and therefore raise the worth of our performance.

But to what extent are the measurements really important? Do they really justify the effort and time required to collect them? Do measurements tell us something that we could not find out by simpler means? The answers to these questions depend on many things. They depend on the individual contractor and the nature of the work. Small jobs, few in number and consisting of unique installations (such as a specialty contractor in residential airconditioning, for example), might not benefit greatly from formal measurement methods. Yet if the work is repetitive (a guttering contractor) or requires many manhours (a boiler contractor), measurements may well help pinpoint opportunities for improved performance. Small contractors who know their jobs inside and out rely on their experience and intimate knowledge of the job to find ways to improve. But as contractors grow in size and such close contact with every job becomes impossible, *measurements become essential to performance improvement.*

In the next chapters we will see how measurement methods offer even greater management insights. For the moment, we may safely conclude that measurements and performance improvement are interrelated; while either one may be possible without the other, the two together exemplify competent management.

The Worth of Performance

While many contractors agree that efforts to improve productivity may be worthwhile, few know how to calculate the benefits and costs of such efforts. Performance measurements not only point out areas of high potential gain, they can also provide the information needed to calculate the worth of this gain. And knowing the worth of the potential gain, we can then go about systematically examining alternative methods to capture this gain, weighing the costs of each method against the worth. Let us begin, therefore, by learning how to calculate worth.

Calculating Worth

Perhaps the best way to explain the concept of worth calculations is to jump right into an example to show how it's done. In this example we will assume that we are already measuring our productivity on a weekly basis and thus have the data necessary for the calculations.

A simple example

Table 3.1 gives the data for our example. Here we see numbers representing five separate work items (A through E) being installed by a contractor. Columns B through D show the estimated amount of work to install, the estimated manhours (MH), and the expected unit rate (given in amount per manhour, column B divided by column C). Columns E through G show the actual numbers to date; column E shows the amounts (collected by field counts) of installed items, column F shows the manhours charged to each item (collected from weekly time sheets), and column G computes the average unit rate to date by dividing the actual manhours (column F) into the installed amounts (column E). Column H shows the best unit rates so far for any single

TABLE 3.1 Summary of Unit-Rate Performance (Amount per Manhours) to Date

	A	B	C	D	E	F	G	H	0I
1	Item to	Estimate			Actual to date			Best-week	
2	install	Amount	MH	Unit rate	Amount	MH	Unit rate	unit rate	PAR
3									
4	*Formula*			*(B/C)*			*(E/F)*		*(H/G*
5									
6	Item A	16000	12000	1.33	8000	8000	1.00	1.55	1.
7	Item B	18000	18000	1.00	5000	4000	1.25	1.40	1.
8	Item C	15000	30000	0.50	5000	8000	0.63	0.70	1.
9	Item D	1250	5000	0.25	400	1500	0.27	0.50	1.
10	Item E	4000	2000	2.00	500	500	1.00	1.30	1.
11									
12	Total		67000			22000			

week—the exemplars. The exemplars come from the weekly counts of work accomplished and manhours charged to each item (not shown). Dividing the weekly amounts by the weekly manhours gives a weekly unit rate for each item. The exemplars were found by going back through all the weekly unit-rate calculations and picking out the single best weekly unit rate for each item. Finally, column I computes the performance ability ratios (PARs) by dividing the exemplar from column H by the average from column G. The PARs range from a low of 1.1 for items B and C to a high of 1.9 for item D.

Given this information, is it worthwhile for the contractor to attempt to improve one or more of the unit rates? If so, which ones? If we were asked to look over the data and make a guess to test our judgment before we get into an analysis of the numbers, we might be hard put to know where to begin.

Comparing the estimated unit rates to the actual to-date unit rates in Table 3.1, we see that items B and C are doing better than the estimate, that items A and E are behind, and that item D is right about on target. The best-week unit rates in column H show that the exemplars have exceeded the estimate for all items except E. So how does the job stand at this point in time? At the present average rate of production, can the job be completed within the manhour estimate?

Projecting rates

To answer the questions concerning job status, we first extend Table 3.1 to the right to create Table 3.2. Column J repeats the row headings from column A. In column K we subtract the amount to date (column E) from the estimated amount (column B). This difference gives us the amount remaining to be installed. Dividing the amount left to install in column K by the *average rate to date* (column G in Table 3.1) gives us the manhours needed to complete each of the items (assuming that the average rate of production will be sustained for the remainder of the project). Column L provides the results of this calculation. The sum of the individual item projections in column L—41,088 MH—projects the total manhours required to complete the job if the average unit rate to date prevails for the remainder of the project.

In Table 3.2, the amounts left to install (column K) are the differences between the estimated amounts in column B and the amounts installed to date in column E. Column O, the manhours left in the estimate, represents the differences between the estimated manhours in column C and the actual manhours to date in column F (from Table 3.1). The sum for column O shows 45,000 MH remaining out of the original 67,000 MH estimated for the whole job. Our projection at average unit rates in column L gives 41,088 MH, a projected savings of 3922 MH over the estimate (subtracting column L from column O).

Working at estimated rates

What if the remainder of the work were to be installed at the original *estimated* unit rates in column D instead of the average unit rates to date in column G? By dividing the estimated unit rates (column D) into the amount remaining to install (column K), we get the manhours required to finish the job at the estimated rates. Column M shows this result. If the rest of the job goes exactly according to estimate, a total of 44,150 MH will be required to finish the job—only 850 MH less than the original estimate.

Compare this result to our earlier calculations for completing the job at the *average* unit rates. If the remainder of the work could be accomplished at the average unit rates to date (given in column G in

TABLE 3.2 Analysis of Job to Date

	J	K	L	M	N	O	P	Q
1	Item	Amount left	MH at av	MH at est	MH at best	MH left in	Potential	Potential
2	to install	to install	unit rate	unit rate	unit rate	estimate	MH savings	MH worth
3								
4	*Formula*	(B − E)	(K/G)	(K/D)	(K/H)	(C − F)	(O − N)	(L − N)
5								
6	Item A	8000	8000	6000	5161	4000	− 1161	2839
7	Item B	13000	10400	13000	9286	14000	4714	1114
8	Item C	10000	16000	20000	14286	22000	7714	1714
9	Item D	850	3188	3400	1700	3500	1800	1488
10	Item E	3500	3500	1750	2692	1500	− 1192	808
11								
12	Total		41088	44150	33125	45000	11875	7962

Table 3.1), then the job could be completed in the manhours shown in column L. Since the average unit rates total only 41,088 MH as compared to 44,150 MH at the estimated unit rates, the difference represents a potential savings of 3062 MH if the job could be completed at the average unit rates rather than at the estimated unit rates.

Working at exemplar rates

But suppose it were possible to complete the job at the *best* unit rates so far—the exemplars. How many more manhours might be saved? Dividing the amounts left to install (column K) by the *best* unit rates (column H) gives the numbers shown in column N. Working at the exemplar unit rates for the remainder of the job, we find that it would take only 33,125 MH to complete the job—a savings of 7963 MH over working at the average unit rates, and 11,025 MH better than working at the estimated unit rates. By subtracting the manhours required to complete the job at the exemplar unit rates (column N) from the manhours left in the original budget estimate (column O), we get the result in column P. Here we see the potential savings in manhours over the original estimate if the exemplar unit rates could be achieved for the remainder of the job—a total of 11,875 MH.

Now clearly it will not be possible to realize all the potential savings in column P. The best weekly unit rates may not be sustainable for each item over the remainder of the job. But if we must pick one of the items to concentrate our efforts on, which one should it be? Column P shows item C as having the largest potential savings—7714 MH. But is this really the place to concentrate our efforts? If we assume that we can actually sustain the average unit rates to date (in column G) for the remainder of the job, then some of the savings in column P are already in the bank. What we really need to do is to compare the difference between working at our *average* and working at our *best*. Column Q does this. By subtracting the number of manhours it will take to complete the job working at the best unit rates (column N) from the manhours needed at the average unit rates (in column L), we get the real potential worth of improving each item from average to exemplar.

Item A, which showed a potential overrun of 1161 MH in column P, now displays a potential worth of 2839 MH. This worth is the number of manhours we could gain by bringing the unit rate for item A up from average to best. Referring back to Table 3.1, we see that the average rate to date for item A is 1.00 unit per manhour, only three-fourths as high as the estimate, yet the best weekly rate is 1.55 units per manhour, a considerable improvement over the estimate. And since only half of item A has been installed, bringing the unit rate up closer to the exemplar for the remainder of the job would add up to a substantial savings.

Table 3.2 therefore tells us that the job is coming in about 3900 MH below the estimate (based on current average unit rates) but that it could come in nearly 11,900 MH below the estimate if the remainder of the work could be accomplished at the exemplar unit rates. While it is highly unlikely that we can capture all the extra 8000-MH savings, by concentrating on item A we could pick up as much as 2839 MH.

Relating worth to PARs

While the analysis so far has pointed out the potential worth of bringing each item up from average to exemplar, we have not yet looked at the potential cost of doing so. Refer back to column I in Table 3.1. Here we have calculated each of the PARs for the five work items. Item A, our largest potential worth, also has a large PAR of 1.6. A large PAR means a large difference between average and best. And the larger the variation between average and best, the easier it is to improve, to bring the average up closer to the best. A large PAR usually means that one or more exemplar crews are employing superior work methods that can be effectively transferred to the average performers. (In a later chapter we will discover how to identify superior methods and how to transfer them to other crews.) Note, however, that item D has the largest PAR of 1.9. It also has a fairly high worth of 1488 MH. Here is another good candidate for improvement. Item C, which shows a higher worth than item D, has a PAR of only 1.1, indicating a very narrow gap between exemplar crew performance and average crew performance. It will be very hard to squeeze this gap much closer.

Checking for inaccurate numbers

Although our analysis so far appears straightforward, we must be careful never to be misled by looking only at the numbers. We must also apply a great deal of common sense and look behind the numbers to see where they have come from and what they really represent. It may be, for example, that the best unit rate recorded for item A does not reflect a sustainable rate. Or, with only half the amount of that item installed so far, the low average unit rate may reflect unusually poor productivity rates during startup, and so the best rate may indeed be closer to the current rate of production. Only a more careful analysis of the job can give the true picture behind the numbers. The numbers only point to areas of potential savings, areas to which management should first turn its attention.

If the worth for item A turns out not to be a true picture, then turn to item D. Actually, it ought to take less effort to improve item D than item A, since the PAR of 1.9 indicates a very large variation in unit rates, with the average unit rate well below the best. Something on the job is holding the average unit rate well below the best that the crews are able to achieve. It should not take much effort to discover the cause of the problem and to eliminate it, thereby raising the productivity for item D. *The greater the difference between the average and the best, as measured by the PAR, the greater the potential for improvement and, in general, the easier to capture the improvement.*

Projecting Current Performance

We have seen how to calculate the potential worth of productivity improvements at a single stage of a project. But no job stands still. Each week, further progress changes the amount of work completed and the number of manhours expended and thus requires new calculations to update the numbers.

Four weeks later

Table 3.3 looks very similar to Table 3.1. In fact, columns A through D are identical; columns E through G, however, show new numbers that reflect four weeks' further progress on the job. Thus all the numbers in columns E through G have been updated by four additional weeks' work over the numbers shown in Table 3.1. In addition, two of the exemplars in column H, those for items C and D, have changed to reflect that, during the past four weeks, the unit rates for these two items hit new weekly bests—0.78 unit per manhour for item C (up from 0.70 recorded in Table 3.1), and 0.58 for item D (up from 0.50).

TABLE 3.3 Summary of Unit-Rate Performance to Date, Four Weeks Later

	A	B	C	D	E	F	G	H	I
1	Item to	Estimate			Actual to date			Best-week	
2	install	Amount	MH	Unit rate	Amount	MH	Unit rate	unit rate	PAR
3									
4	*Formula*			*(B/C)*		*(E/F)*		*(H/G)*	
5									
6	Item A	16000	12000	1.33	11200	10200	1.10	1.55	1.4
7	Item B	18000	18000	1.00	6400	5200	1.23	1.40	1.1
8	Item C	15000	30000	0.50	6000	9300	0.65	**0.78**	1.2
9	Item D	1250	5000	0.25	500	1700	0.29	**0.58**	2.0
10	Item E	4000	2000	2.00	800	900	0.89	1.30	1.5
11									
12	Total		67000			27300			

TABLE 3.4   Analysis of Job to Date, Four Weeks Later

	J	K	L	M	N	O	P	Q
1	Item to	Amount to	MH at av	MH at est	MH at best	MH left in	Potential	Potential
2	install	install	unit rate	unit rate	unit rate	estimate	MH savings	MH worth
3								
4	*Formula*	*(B − E)*	*(K/G)*	*(K/D)*	*(K/H)*	*(C − F)*	*(O − N)*	*(L − N)*
5								
6	Item A	4800	4371	3600	3097	1800	− 1297	1275
7	Item B	11600	9425	11600	8286	12800	4514	1139
8	Item C	9000	13950	18000	11538	20700	9162	2412
9	Item D	750	2550	3000	1293	3300	2007	1257
10	Item E	3200	3600	1600	2462	1100	− 1362	1138
11								
12	Total		33896	37800	26676	39700	13024	7221

How is the job going now, as compared to the month before? Table 3.4, similar to Table 3.2, gives us some of the numbers for further analysis. Once again, dividing the amounts left to install (column K) by the average unit rates (column G) gives the expected manhours to complete the work in column L (now down to 33,896 MH if the remainder of the work continues at the average rate to date). Subtracting this total from the 39,700 MH remaining in the estimate (column O) shows the job to be 3904 MH ahead of the manhour budget, very nearly the same as the 3922 MH projected in Table 3.2, four weeks earlier. So the job still seems to be coming in ahead of the manhour estimate.

(If we plan to complete the remaining work at the estimated unit rates from column D instead, then column M shows that the job will be completed in 37,800 MH, a savings of only 1900 MH over the estimate. Estimated unit rates, however, provide notoriously poor indicators of actual field productivity. In this case they seem to offer too low a target; we ought to be able to do far better than the estimate.)

Projecting exemplars

Now look at the projections if we assume that we could continue the job at the exemplars—the best weekly rates we have hit so far. Dividing the amounts left to install (column K) by the exemplars (column H) gives the manhour projections in column N. Now the job could finish in 26,676 MH if all the exemplars could be realized, a potential savings of 7221 MH over the 33,896-MH projection from the average unit rates. But as noted above in the analysis of Table 3.2, it is highly unlikely that anyone can improve every unit rate to the best. Usually the most we can hope for is to move the rates with the largest PARs closer to the best. Column Q in Table 3.4 shows us that the largest potential worth now comes from improving the unit rate for item C.

Here we stand to gain 2412 MH if the remainder of the job could be done at the new best unit rate of 0.78 (established sometime over the past four weeks) instead of being done at our average unit rate to date.

Setting priorities

But look at the PAR for item C in column I (Table 3.3). It is only 1.2. Items A, D, and E have far larger PARs and therefore show a greater promise of improvement. *(Remember that, as a general rule, the larger the PAR, the lower the effort required to reduce it.)*

Item A, which showed up as the biggest potential savings in the analysis four weeks ago, looks less promising now. Why is that? It is because we made a big improvement in the unit rate for item A over the previous four weeks, raising our average unit rate from 1.00 to 1.10 units per manhour. (Productivity for item A, counting only the past four-week period, can be calculated by subtracting the new amounts in place and the new MH expended from the original and dividing. This calculation gives 3200 units placed in 2200 MH, or 1.45 units per manhour, very close to the exemplar of 1.55.) The improvement in item A means that the difference in the projection of the average rate against the best rate has narrowed. Thus we have already captured a substantial portion of the potential improvement in item A and can now turn our attention to other items for improvement.

What about item D? Here we have a large PAR of 2.0 and a potential gain of 1257 MH. Certainly item D warrants further investigation. In addition, item D set a new best-week high during the past four weeks, up from 0.50 to 0.58 unit per manhour. Calculating the average unit rate for item D over just the past four weeks, we find that 100 units were placed and 200 MH expended, a four-week average of 0.50 unit per MH, equal to the previous exemplar for a single week. With very little effort we ought to be able to pick up much of the potential manhour savings for item D.

The past four weeks

But aren't we fooling ourselves by assuming that the job will continue at the average unit rates to date? The average unit rates reflect average productivity since the beginning of the job and may thus be a very poor indicator of current productivity. Calculation of the average unit rates over only the past four weeks gives a much better picture of current performance. And this current picture alters the conclusions of our analysis so far.

Table 3.5 extends Table 3.4 yet farther to the right, adding seven additional columns. Column S computes the amount of work installed

TABLE 3.5   Analysis of Performance over the Past Four Weeks

	R	S	T	U	V	W	X
1	Item to	Four-week calculations			MH at	Potential	4-week
2	install	Amt done	MH used	Unit rate	4-wk rate	MH worth	PAR
3							
4	*Formula*			*(S/T)*	*(K/U)*	*(V–N)*	*(H/U)*
5							
6	Item A	3200	2200	1.45	3300	203	1.1
7	Item B	1400	1200	1.17	9943	1657	1.2
8	Item C	1000	1300	0.77	11700	162	1.0
9	Item D	100	200	0.50	1500	207	1.2
10	Item E	300	400	0.75	4267	1805	1.7
11							
12	Total		5300		30710	4034	

over the four-week interval by subtracting the amounts of work in place (columns E) between Tables 3.3 and 3.1. Column T does the same for manhours expended (in columns F). Column U then divides the four-week manhour expenditure (column T) into the four-week units placed (column S) to calculate the average unit rates (amount/MH) over only the past four-week period.

Now common sense tells us that the average productivity over the past four weeks provides a better assessment of the *current* capability of the work force than does the average productivity to date. This is because the average to date extends many weeks into the past. It includes the low weekly productivity encountered during startup. It may also include numbers based on working conditions that no longer exist—the job is further along, the weather may have changed, and the crews may have more experience. Conversely, the most recent four-week unit rates tell us more about how well the work force is *currently* performing. It makes better sense to *use measurements of current performance, not historical averages, to project future performance potential.*

Projections of job performance, based on the four-week unit-rate averages, are shown in column V. Here we see the amounts remaining to be installed (from column K, Table 3.4) divided by the four-week average unit rates from column U. We see that if the job continues at the latest four-week unit rates, it will be completed in only 30,710 MH, shaving almost 9000 MH off the estimate.

Finding a new worth

A comparison of the manhour projections at the exemplar rates (column N of Table 3.4) with the projections at the four-week rates (column V of Table 3.5) should give us a more accurate projection of the potential savings we could realize from unit-rate improvements. These projections are shown in column W, which subtracts the numbers in column N from those in column V. Now we see that the potential savings for bringing all the current productivity rates up to the exemplars has dropped to 4034 MH, down from the 7221-MH projection given in column Q (Table 3.4). This is because the difference between our best unit rates and our current four-week average unit rates is not as great as the difference between our best rates and our average-to-date unit rates. We also see that only items B and E offer substantial MH savings. And by calculating new PARs based on dividing the four-week average into the exemplar, as shown in column X, we see that only item E has a large enough PAR to offer promise of immediate gains.

Using unit-rate averages over the past four-week period changes the conclusions of our earlier analysis, which was based on average-to-date unit rates. There our calculations pointed to item D for priority management action, while now we see that item E offers a better starting place for improvement. While no set rule governs which unit rates to use in figuring where the greatest potential worth lies, experience dictates that averages based on the most recent two to five weeks provide the greatest accuracy for projections.

Our analysis of the numbers so far points out those work items which promise the greatest potential gains. By comparing the projections of average and exemplar unit rates, we immediately see where the biggest payoff lies for productivity improvement. But what about the cost of this improvement? Better unit rates do not just happen; it takes considerable management effort to gain consistent improvement. Merely pushing field supervisors for better numbers usually results in just that—better numbers, but without the completed work to show for it. Months later the endless pages of punchlist items reveal the real price paid by focusing only on the numbers and not on the work methods behind them. How to make real improvements in methods will be the subject of the next chapter. Before we get to improvement methods, however, we first need to look further into the reality behind the numbers we will be using.

Giving Excuses or Taking Responsibility?

Chuck Carefield worked as a senior project manager and troubleshooter for UMCC, a large mechanical subcontractor with projects across the country. UMCC had called Chuck the afternoon before and asked him to fly out to Colorado and look into the problems on a power plant they were building. Low productivity and missed schedules the past month seemed to point to a need for drastic changes. Chuck arrived at the jobsite in the early morning after a long trip and little sleep. After finding a coffee mug without cigarette butts soaking in the bottom and filling it with the remains of last night's coffee warming on the hotplate, Chuck sat down to look over some recent manpower reports while waiting for the project's manager, Hank Hardman, to arrive.

Getting the numbers

During the long and often tense morning, Chuck and Hank went over all the project reports and tried to pinpoint the cause of the problems. A brief walk around the project after a sandwich from the canteen truck did little to clear Chuck's head. By late afternoon, before returning to his motel and some much-needed rest, Chuck asked Hank to give all the time sheets and work-completion numbers to one of the computer clerks to attempt to recalculate the productivity rates. So far, nothing else seemed to make much sense.

Early the next morning Chuck and Hank sat down to go over the new computer reports. Now, some patterns seemed to emerge. One report, in particular, offered a clue. It showed the productivity rates, measured in units of work installed per manhour, for six types of work across six similar work areas (Table 3.6).

In examining the numbers in Table 3.6, Chuck and Hank highlighted the unit rates that were better than the average. Only Area 17 was below the average for all six rates, and only Area 19 was consistently above the average. Although both Chuck and Hank recognized that the gross numbers they were dealing with contained many possible errors and that lumping pipe sizes together probably distorted some of the unit rates, at least it gave them a clue as to where to look

TABLE 3.6 Measured Productivity by Work Item and Work Area

	A	B	C	D	E	F	G	H
1	Pipe work item	Area 12	Area 15	Area 16	Area 17	Area 19	Area 22	Average
2								
3	Small bore, type A	1.52	0.66	0.92	0.88	1.87	1.32	1.44
4	Small bore, type B	2.32	1.88	1.54	1.01	2.71	1.60	1.94
5								
6	Large bore, type A	0.22	0.54	0.61	0.21	0.82	0.58	0.60
7	Large bore, type B	0.34	0.95	0.59	0.48	1.11	0.62	0.55
8								
9	Hangers, small bore	1.22	0.78	0.65	0.24	1.15	0.44	0.73
10	Hangers, large bore	0.74	0.38	0.60	0.20	0.71	0.46	0.44

further for answers. Why was Area 17's productivity consistently poorer and why was Area 19's better?

Tracking the numbers

That morning the two men toured the jobsite again, this time speaking with the general foremen assigned to each of the piping areas and with a few of the foremen as well. They spent extra time in Areas 17 and 19, making sure they spoke with each of the foremen in these two areas. One of the things everyone they spoke with agreed on was that in the past month or so their productivity was down. But the reasons given varied. Some complained of the difficulty in getting the materials; deliveries of the shop-fabricated pipe spools had been erratic. Others complained of the interference and delays caused by the other trades on the job; as the work progressed, they were finding themselves increasingly hampered by lack of support from riggers and operators and, at the same time, boxed in by electricians and civil trades. All pointed to delays caused by quality control inspections of welds. The job was rapidly turning sour, not because of major problems, but because of hundreds of minor ones.

Jobsite delays

The general foreman in Area 19, the exemplary performer, provided the single exception to the litany of complaints. He talked instead about what he was doing to overcome the problems. Sure, his foremen griped as much as the others, but he tried to write down what their problems were and estimate how many manhours it was costing him. He then devoted his time to solving the biggest time-losers, not the loudest complaints.

For example, he pointed out that very little time was actually lost because of waiting for riggers or equipment; maybe 15 minutes for a crew sometimes. And electricians were not a real problem either; they usually got out of the way if you gave them a little notice. But the fitters had to blame someone for their frustrations, and it was always easier to pick on the other trades than to blame themselves.

Yes, spool shortages were a real problem and so was quality control. Both accounted for real manhour losses if he wasn't careful. He tried to schedule work on lines for which he had all the spools and valves so that the crews could work right through and not have to come back and fit in the missing pieces later. But he seldom had all the pieces. It seemed that the delivery trucks waited until they had a full load before making the 170-mile run from the fab shop out to the jobsite. So they often had to work around missing pieces and go back and fit them in later when the pieces arrived. He estimated that working around the lack of materials still cost his crews a good two hours extra each day, even though he had already managed to save nearly an hour by planning the work more carefully.

As for quality control (QC), the inspectors only checked welds when a piping foreman was with them. This tied up a lot of the foremen's time, running from one weld to another and then tagging a welder to come and make corrections as they were needed. By counting the manhours lost waiting for QC inspectors, stopping and starting work to make corrections, and the time other crew members were standing around waiting for the foreman to get to them, he figured QC was good for another hour and a half per crew per day. By saving up all his welds in one area and then notifying QC, he could put one foreman and one welder in the inspection area for a few hours until they were done. This had also saved about an hour a day for each crew.

The cost of lost time

As Chuck and Hank skirted the huge ringer crane on their way back to the trailer before lunch, Chuck mentally calculated the lost manhours on the project. At an average of only three hours per day per crew, and with an average of nine workers per crew and 28 crews—why it came to a minimum of 750 MH per day, over 5000 MH per week! Could it be right?

Back at the trailer, Chuck and Hank decided to conduct a "foreman delay survey" to determine how many hours each foreman was actually losing each day and for what reason. They made up a report form to go to all the foremen every morning for the next five work days.

Chuck and Hank agreed that Hank should reorganize the QC procedure to try to bunch inspections, rather than inspect each weld as it was completed, and should then see if the other foremen thought it saved them time. Chuck would stop by the fab-shop supplier on his way back to the airport that afternoon and look into speeding up deliveries, even if it meant paying extra freight charges for partially loaded trucks. Chuck would phone Hank in a few days and come back out to the site at the end of next week.

As the last flight out lifted off the runway and Chuck settled back to wait for the cocktail service to begin, he pulled out the computer reports he had brought with him. With his calculator, he refigured the piping and hanger unit rates, subtracting estimates of "lost" hours from the performance numbers. Without the lost time added in, productivity in *every* area and *every* work item could be brought up *better* than the performance of Area 19. What was the "real" productivity at the job, Chuck wondered—the productivity you got when you were actually working instead of standing around waiting or running in circles?

Lost Time and Work Time

Lost time is a fact of life at every jobsite. No one can organize a job so well that people never have to wait for anything or spend extra time doing a task inefficiently. But few contractors, and even fewer foremen, look at this time as "lost." To them, it's just an accepted part of every job, something you learn to live with. You do the best you can and work around the problems.

But as Chuck and Hank learned, *measurements of lost time can be useful tools in locating the most important causes of jobsite delays.* And when you know what causes most of the lost time, you can take actions to reduce it.

Figure 3.1 diagrams the amount of paid time a crew spends at a jobsite during a week. This time divides into time spent working at assigned tasks and time spent not working: time lost for one reason or another. Clearly, a contractor who can reduce the fraction of lost time each week will add hours to the work time, thereby accomplishing more for the same number of paid manhours.

Lost time and motivation

On a very large and complicated construction job, such as a large industrial project, the difficulties of coordinating the work of thousands of craftsmen lead to considerable lost time. In fact, on jobs such as nuclear power plants, noted for their cost overruns, the proportions in Figure 3.1 may well be reversed, with lost time far exceeding work time. Whenever a significant fraction of a workday is wasted, for whatever reason, it often causes an individual to devalue his or her own worth to the job. People will reason that if their time is so unimportant to the job that management can afford to waste so much of it, then why should they bother to put out any effort at all? Thus a large

Figure 3.1 Lost time and work time as fractions of a crew work-week.

fraction of lost time not only subtracts from work time, it can also undermine an individual's incentive to work productively even during work time.

The worker viewpoint that attributes lost time to an "I don't care" management attitude also tends to adopt an "I don't care either" attitude toward the job. To combat lost time and its detrimental effects, both to worker attitude and to overall productivity, management must take aggressive steps to minimize lost time.

The first step is to measure it.

Measure the gripes

As we saw above, Chuck and Hank first realized how to get at their lost-time problems when they saw how one of their general foremen used measurements of his lost time to decide what caused the largest manhour losses. As he pointed out, listening only to the loudest complaints often ignores the real causes of lost time. Measurements not only tell us how much time we are losing, they can also tell us where best to put our energy to reduce lost time. Not every jobsite gripe is reason for action. Many people gripe just out of habit. But by collecting the gripes and correlating the manhour losses with them, we find out which gripes are real. We turn gripes into valuable information about jobsite productivity that can help identify actions to improve performance.

Collecting Measurements of Lost Time

Contractors who measure lost time (or delay time, as it is sometimes called) generally rely on three primary methods. Counts of lost-time hours according to these three methods show that jobs typically lose from 10 to 40 percent of all payroll hours. The first method, the foreman delay survey, was used by Chuck and Hank in the story above. The second asks foremen actually to count their lost time on their crews' time sheets each day. Both the foreman delay survey and the modified time sheet provide a means to measure lost time directly. A third method, called work sampling, is discussed in the Appendix. Work sampling relies on indirect means to identify lost time through statistical techniques. Each of the three methods has its merits and drawbacks.

Foreman delay surveys

Figure 3.2 illustrates a typical foreman delay survey form. Typically, every foreman on a job completes the form each day for a week. Man-

Foreman Delay Survey

Date: _____   Foreman: _____

                            Number in Crew: _____

_____ Problems Causing Delay _____

Problem	Number of Hours	X	Number of Men	=	Manhours
Rework for design change	☐	X	☐	=	☐
Rework for field error	☐	X	☐	=	☐
Rework for damage	☐	X	☐	=	☐
Waiting for materials	☐	X	☐	=	☐
Waiting for tools	☐	X	☐	=	☐
Waiting for equipment	☐	X	☐	=	☐
Waiting for directions	☐	X	☐	=	☐
Waiting for other trades	☐	X	☐	=	☐
_____	☐	X	☐	=	☐
_____	☐	X	☐	=	☐
_____	☐	X	☐	=	☐

Comments: _____

_____

_____

Figure 3.2   A foreman delay survey form.

agement then tabulates the results to find the major sources of delay on the job.

Often the most frequent causes of work delay are printed on the form, with space left for the foremen to add additional items. For each delay cause, the foremen write in the number of hours lost due to the delay and the number of craftsmen involved in the delay. Multiplying the two together gives the total number of manhours lost due to the delay.

At the end of each day (or the week) the survey forms are collected and tabulated. For a large job, the results will show the major causes of work delay for each craft and the number of hours lost. By correlating the reported lost time with the causes of delays, project management can take action to resolve the problems and to eliminate the delays.

As its name implies, the survey method is usually conducted only once a month, not as an ongoing count every week (although it may be used more frequently if desired). Management then uses the information collected during one week of each month to spot and correct sources of delay on the job. The survey is widely used because it takes little time; foremen can complete the form in a few minutes at the end of a day and only need to be bothered with it one week a month. However, there is a weakness in the three-week gap between surveys, during which other sources of delay may arise without being flagged (although the surveys can certainly be taken more frequently). The surveys also require a short cycle time between the collection of the information and management actions to eliminate the sources of delay. Unless management acts quickly, foremen may come to discount the value of the exercise. Another potential weakness is found in the survey's reliance on gross estimates by foremen of how much time they actually lose. Such inaccuracies, however, balance against the ease of collection. Any information is usually better than none at all.

In most cases, foremen readily count the hours lost due to delays. Foremen are usually just as anxious as top management to eliminate the delays. Lost time lowers crew morale and undercuts foreman leadership. Nearly every worker prefers a job that minimizes lost time. The key to getting accurate reports on delays is follow-up. Top management must work with field supervisors by taking timely actions to eliminate the causes of delays.

Daily time-sheet counts

The second method uses a modified daily time sheet, such as that shown in Figure 3.3. Foremen report the hours worked every day by each individual in the crew. These hours are charged to specific work items, which are listed across the top of the form. The total hours charged to each work

Time Sheet Foreman:_____ Crew Number:_____ Date:_____ Employee Name	Work Item						Total
Total Payroll Hours							
Work Time Hours							
Lost Time Hours							
Lost Time Causes							

Figure 3.3   Foreman's time sheet showing lost-time hours.

item are summed at the bottom, then broken into work hours and lost hours (if any). Whenever foremen record lost hours for a work item, they also add a note at the bottom, identifying the cause of the lost time. Normally a list of the 10 or so most common causes of lost time are given code numbers in order to make reporting easier.

Obviously the time-sheet method requires more time and care on the part of foremen. Each day they need to keep track of the lost time charged to every work item the crew spends time on. And because the system runs continuously, so does the foremen's paperwork burden.

On the plus side, the time-sheet method produces *much greater accuracy and detail* in reporting. It can pinpoint which work activities experience the most delay. And by including rework as a cause of lost time, management can obtain a comprehensive picture of nonproductive crew time. However, because the method offers so much information, some contractors think that foremen and their crew members will resist using it due to a fear that the information, if reported accurately, will be used against them rather than to help solve their problems. In practice, however, most foremen do not find lost-time reporting threatening. Just the opposite. Reports of lost time, if used effectively by higher management to troubleshoot a project and to solve problems, actually help foremen do their jobs better.

Although counting lost time on time sheets may seem at first glance like overkill, it offers both management and the work force a not-inconsiderable additional benefit: It is the only method that can identify "true" unit rates.

True Unit Rates

Lost-time hours occur on every job. And these hours are charged to the job, usually buried in one or more work items where they are least likely to be noticed. But isn't there a better way to cope with lost time? By explicitly counting lost-time hours separate from work time, contractors finally have the means to exercise real management control over their jobs.

Who's responsible?

Now if construction crews lose so much time each day due to rework, waiting, and other reasons not directly connected with the crews' capacity to do the work, how can we compare measurements of performance in order to calculate PARs and exemplars? Clearly the crew foreman who faces continued delays in getting needed materials and equipment will not willingly be judged by productivity rates that include all the crew's lost time in the manhours charged to the crew. As foremen see it, lost time due to causes beyond their control is not their fault; *it's management's fault.* How many times have we heard foremen complain about their problems on the job? They seize on everything they can find that offers an excuse for diminished productivity. And why not? In nearly every instance their crews do lose time because of problems outside of the foreman's control. (Of course, the crews also lose time because of foreman mismanagement and crew slack time, but foremen seldom blame themselves for continued productivity loses.) Essentially, because most on-site management systems hold foremen responsible for crew productivity, foremen naturally look for excuses just in case someone criticizes them. (Many foremen even carry around a little notebook in which they carefully record the problems that hurt their productivity.)

Any measurements of crew productivity that lump lost time together with work time will undoubtedly be met with resistance on the part of foremen and their crews. And rightly so. They should not be held responsible for poor productivity rates caused by factors over which they have no control. Confronting foremen with evidence of low productivity inevitably produces a host of excuses, most of them true. Foremen understandably refuse to take responsibility for someone else's shortcomings.

But if foremen cannot be held responsible, who can? Management does not pick up the tools each day to install the work, so how can it be held responsible for slack crew performance? Each side blames the other for poor productivity.

Separate measurements

By separating work time from lost time, however, we can place responsibility, not blame, where it belongs. Management, indeed, must accept responsibility for time lost on the job due to delays over which foremen have no control. And foremen must accept responsibility for crew productivity for time spent actually working at the task at hand. By counting manhours lost each day and identifying the causes of lost time, management has all it needs to take appropriate action to minimize further lost time. And by subtracting lost time from total payroll hours, the work force can be credited with only the time spent on actual accomplishments.

Removing lost-time hours from work hours allows us to calculate the "true" unit rates for work items. *Counting how much work a crew has accomplished and dividing it by the number of manhours actually worked on the item provides a true measurement of crew productivity.* This measurement, called a *true unit rate*, shows what crew productivity really is after removing all the excuses for delays and lost time.

This is the rate at which the crew could work all day if management could only eliminate all the reported causes of lost time.

Separate reports

Figure 3.4 diagrams the relationship between lost time and true unit rates. Suppose that crew foremen use a weekly time sheet similar to the one shown in Figure 3.3. They charge all work time to preset work codes and charge all lost time to predefined causes (such as waiting or rework). Each week, management reports the total lost-time and work-time hours. Lost-time hours are summarized according to the problems that caused them. Work-time hours are summarized according to the work codes, and then the manhours actually worked are matched to the counts of work accomplished to compute the true unit rates.

Such a system of measurement offers management nearly everything needed to troubleshoot job performance and to improve it. But it is not cost-free. The collection, processing, and analysis of the numbers needed to make the system work well require investments of time, training, money, and effort. But the benefits, in terms of improved productivity and tighter job control, offer management a tremendous payback. Every dollar spent on providing better feedback to management returns many more dollars in field savings. A later chap-

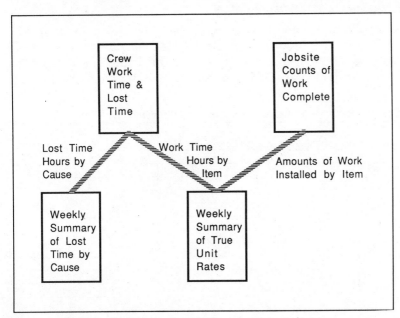

Figure 3.4 Splitting lost time and work time gives true unit rates.

ter will address the practical issues of implementing such alternative productivity and performance management methods. For the moment, the important thing here is to see the value of distinguishing lost time from work time on project jobsites. A case study underscores this potential value.

CCA Chemical

Carol Cando recently joined the Human Development Department of a large construction firm. The HD Department supports field operations through productivity studies, offers foreman training courses, and writes after-action reports on all projects. Carol's boss, Hal Halstorm, assigns her to study past reports from the CCA chemical plant under construction in Ohio. Hal will be flying out to visit the jobsite next week and wants an update on the project's status.

Carol begins sifting through the reports, trying to make some sense out of them. Eventually she turns to her computer to help her organize the numbers. Not all the numbers she needs are available, but she is able to build a picture of the job from nine of the major work items. In putting the numbers onto a computer spreadsheet to compute true unit rates in a search for PARs, she carefully excludes all the lost time, which has been reported separately on the CCA project.

Estimated versus actual performance

Table 3.7 shows numbers for nine of the major work items on the project (work codes 1200 through 1700). Carol compares the estimates for amounts, manhours, and unit rates to the actual amount of work completed to date, the number of manhours used, and the average

TABLE 3.7   Comparison of Estimated to Actual Performance

	A	B	C	D	E	F	G	H	I
1	Work code	Est amt	Amt in	% Done	Est MH	MH used	% Used	Est rate	Av r
2									
3	Formula			C/B			F/E	B/E	C/F
4									
5	1200	15000	8600	57%	14220	8540	60%	1.05	1.
6	1300	12300	5400	44%	14580	7120	49%	0.84	0.
7	1360	5600	2150	38%	8750	3220	37%	0.64	0
8	1380	4580	1080	24%	9200	2880	31%	0.50	0.
9	1400	23050	6430	28%	40300	13210	33%	0.57	0.
10	1420	12400	2300	19%	28450	6230	22%	0.44	0.
11	1540	3200	1050	33%	10460	3960	38%	0.31	0.
12	1600	6800	2800	41%	31100	21020	68%	0.22	0.
13	1700	900	300	33%	7500	3080	41%	0.12	0.
14									
15	Total MH				164560	69260	42%		

unit rates to date. Comparing the percentage of work done (column D) to the percentage of manhours used to date (column G) shows that a slightly higher percentage of manhours has been used for most items than the percentage of work completed. Comparing the estimated unit rates (column H) with the average rates to date (column I) shows that most of the rates are slightly below the estimate. However, since the manhours charged during startup probably accomplished very little finished work-in-place, the slight lag between hours charged and amounts completed may not be serious. By subtracting the manhours expended (column F) from the estimate (column E), Carol notes that only 95,300 MH remain in which to complete the job.

(The original estimate included a total of 193,600 MH for the project, of which 15 percent, or 29,040 MH, was expected to be charged to lost time. So far, 51 percent of this 29,040 MH, or 14,810 MH, has been expended on lost-time items, leaving only 14,230 MH in the project's lost-time manhour budget. So instead of running at only 15 percent of the total payroll hours, lost time accounts for 17.6 percent of the 84,070 MH spent on the project to date.)

The past three weeks

On her computer, Carol skips down to row 17 and builds a second spreadsheet below the first to show the numbers for just the past three weeks, as shown in Table 3.8. A review of the unit rates over the latest three weeks (columns D, G, and J in Table 3.8) shows the weekly unit rates for nearly all work items, except 1380 and 1400, to be very near to the estimated unit rates. (Remember, all of Carol's numbers are

TABLE 3.8   True Unit Rates for the Latest Three Weeks

	A	B	C	D	E	F	G	H	I	J
17		Week ending 3/25			Week ending 4/1			Week ending 4/8		
18	Work code	Amt in	MH used	Rate	Amt in	MH used	Rate	Amt in	MH used	Rate
19										
20	*Formula*			*B/C*			*E/F*			*H/I*
21										
22	1200	410	365	1.12	320	285	1.12	400	380	1.05
23	1300	180	220	0.82	200	225	0.89	320	400	0.80
24	1360	240	395	0.61	320	544	0.59	120	210	0.57
25	1380	40	140	0.29	60	150	0.40	60	160	0.38
26	1400	350	722	0.48	510	966	0.53	450	950	0.47
27	1420	280	466	0.60	100	203	0.49	140	250	0.56
28	1540	40	147	0.27	30	110	0.27	30	100	0.30
29	1600	210	923	0.23	150	780	0.19	180	840	0.21
30	1700	40	388	0.10	50	450	0.11	10	200	0.05
31										
32	Total MH		3766			3713			3490	

TABLE 3.9   Crew Productivity Rates Averaged for the Latest Three Weeks

	A	B	C	D	E	F	G	H	I
35	Work code	Crew 01	Crew 02	Crew 03	Crew 04	Crew 05	Crew 06	Crew 07	Crew 08
36									
37	1200	1.12	0.86	0.66	1.09	1.22	**1.31**	0.92	0.86
38	1300	0.84	0.76	0.52	1.01	1.08	**1.09**	0.55	0.80
39	1360	0.57	0.64	0.61	**0.91**	0.84	0.80	0.44	0.67
40	1380	0.38	0.50	0.51	**0.87**	0.72	**0.87**	0.39	0.40
41	1400	0.47	0.57	0.34	0.68	0.84	**0.91**	0.39	0.42
42	1420	0.34	0.47	0.25	0.50	0.48	**0.57**	0.29	0.37
43	1540	0.33	0.31	0.21	0.35	**0.44**	0.42	0.34	0.28
44	1600	0.12	0.18	0.06	0.09	0.10	**0.22**	0.11	0.08
45	1700	0.10	0.04	**0.19**	0.15	0.11	0.14	0.07	0.05

true unit rates and do not include lost time because foremen have charged their lost time separately, not to any of the work items.)

Crew productivity rates

In addition to looking at average unit rates for the job, Carol skips down another two rows on her computer and builds a third spreadsheet, this one giving her the average unit rates for the latest three weeks for each of the company's eight crews. Table 3.9 shows the results. Carol highlights the exemplars on her spreadsheet and notes that Crew 06 seems to do better than the others on most of the work items. On the other hand, Crew 03 and Crew 07 show the poorest productivity rates (except for item 1700, for which Crew 03 is the exemplar).

Manhour projections

Skipping down to row 54, Carol now combines information from each of the three tables above to create Table 3.10. Here she computes in column B the amount of work remaining to install (by subtracting the amount done from the amount in the estimate, columns C and B in Table 3.7). She then copies the two unit rates she calculated in Table 3.7—the estimated and the average-to-date in columns H and I—into columns C and D.

In column E Carol computes the three-week average unit rate by summing the manhours from columns C, F, and I in Table 3.8 and then dividing by the total amount placed for each item over the three-week period. Lastly, she copies the exemplar-crew unit rate from Table 3.9 (using one of the spreadsheet's internal functions to pick out the maximum value for each item from columns B through I).

(Because of the computer's power to copy formulas and to reference other cells, Carol builds Table 3.10 almost entirely by referencing her work in the three tables already on the spreadsheet. By tying all her

TABLE 3.10   Calculation of Manhours Needed to Complete the Job at Different Unit Rates

	A	B	C	D	E	F	G	H	I	J
54	Work code	Amt left	Est rate	Av rate	3-Wk	Best	MH est	MH av	MH 3wk	MH best
55										
56	*Formula*						B/C	B/D	B/E	B/F
57										
58	1200	6400	1.05	1.01	1.10	1.31	6067	6355	5834	4885
59	1300	6900	0.84	0.76	0.83	1.09	8179	9098	8329	6330
60	1360	3450	0.64	0.67	0.59	0.91	5391	5167	5829	3791
61	1380	3500	0.50	0.38	0.36	0.87	7031	9333	9844	4023
62	1400	16620	0.57	0.49	0.50	0.91	29058	34145	33468	18264
63	1420	10100	0.44	0.37	0.57	0.57	23173	27358	17850	17719
64	1540	2150	0.31	0.27	0.28	0.44	7028	8109	7676	4886
65	1600	4000	0.22	0.13	0.21	0.22	18294	30029	18837	18182
66	1700	600	0.12	0.10	0.10	0.19	5000	6160	6228	3158
67										
68	Total MH						109220	135753	113895	81239
69	Total MH remaining in estimate						95300	95300	95300	95300
70	Total MH over (or under) estimate						13920	40453	18595	− 14061

work together on a single spreadsheet, Carol is sure that any changes she makes to her numbers will immediately be reflected in all her work. She will have no need to redo any of it; the computer will automatically recalculate everything for her.)

In columns G through J in Table 3.10, Carol computes the manhours it would take to complete each work item if the remainder of the job were to be done at each of the four different unit rates—the estimate, the average to date, the latest three-week average, and the exemplar. At the bottom, in row 68, she sums the manhour projections. If the remainder of the job were to be completed at the estimated unit rates, it would take 109,220 MH. At the average rates to date, which are generally higher than the estimate, it would take 135,753 MH.

Using the average unit rates of the past three weeks, the projection shows that the job could be completed in 113,895 MH. Finally, projecting the exemplar unit rates gives only 81,239 MH to completion.

In row 69, below each of the four sums, Carol repeats the number of manhours remaining in the estimate, 95,300, and, by subtracting, shows in row 70 a potential manhour overrun for all the projections except the exemplar. If all crews could work at the exemplar rates for the remainder of the project, it would come in 14,061 MH *below* the estimate.

Carol makes the assumption, based on the numbers she has, that the rates obtained over the past three weeks represent the best guess as to how the job will probably continue if no one intervenes to change anything. At these unit rates (column E in Table 3.10) the job will come in 18,595 MH *over* the estimate (column I). The difference between completing the job at the current three-week average unit rates and at the exemplar unit rates amounts to 32,656 MH, a very large difference indeed.

The worth of improvement

The potential worth, therefore, of improving the job from its current average performance to exemplar performance is 32,656 MH. To carry the analysis further, Carol develops Table 3.11 to show the PAR and the potential worth for each of the work items. (Again, she skips a line and enters the new spreadsheet on her computer directly under Table 3.10 above.)

Columns B and C in Table 3.11 recopy the three-week average unit rates and the exemplar unit rates from columns E and F in Table 3.10. Dividing the three-week average into the exemplar gives the PARs, listed in column D. Finally, in column E, Carol shows the worth as the manhour difference between completing the work at the three-week average unit rate and at the exemplar rate. (She got the numbers by subtracting the best manhour projections in column J from the three-week projections in column I in Table 3.10.)

Table 3.11 tells Carol several important facts about the CCA job. First, most of the PARs are quite high, meaning that a large difference exists between the current average performance and the exemplar crew's performance at the site. Carol recognizes that this may be due to different conditions under which the crews work, and she resolves to look into it further. If working conditions are similar for all crews, then it would certainly pay to find ways to improve the average performance.

Item 1400 accounts for a worth of 15,205 MH, nearly one-half of all the potential worth. And it has a high PAR, 1.83, which indicates that efforts to improve the average performance should not be overly diffi-

TABLE 3.11   Calculation of the PARs and Worth for Each of the Work Items

	A	B	C	D	E
72	Work code	3-Wk	Best rate	PAR	Worth (MH)
73					
74	*Formula*			*C/B*	*I − J*
75					
76	1200	1.10	1.31	1.19	948
77	1300	0.83	1.09	1.32	1999
78	1360	0.59	0.91	1.54	2038
79	1380	0.36	0.87	2.45	5821
80	1400	0.50	0.91	1.83	15205
81	1420	0.57	0.57	1.01	131
82	1540	0.28	0.44	1.57	2789
83	1600	0.21	0.22	1.04	655
84	1700	0.10	0.19	1.97	3070
85					
86	Total MH				32656

cult. Looking back at Table 3.9, Carol sees that the exemplar for item 1400—0.91 units per manhour—was set by Crew 06 but that Crew 05's average is not far below at 0.84. The close comparison of the two productivity rates from different crews means that Crew 06's exemplar may not be a fluke, but actually a performance achieveable by the other crews as well.

Item 1380 shows the highest PAR—2.45—and a large potential worth—5821 MH. Again, Table 3.9 shows Carol that the exemplar is likely to be real; both Crew 04 and Crew 06 have achieved unit rates of 0.87 units per manhour for this work item.

Lost-time hours

Finally, Carol turns to an analysis of the lost time on the job. Although the CCA time sheets seem reasonably complete, Carol is not sure that anyone has ever done anything with the lost-time information. At least she can find no evidence in the files of follow-up or actions based on the lost-time reports. Carol fears that if no one has followed up on the reported lost time, foremen may have stopped reporting it in order to save themselves the trouble. If so, the lost time could be even higher than the 14,810 MH reported.

Using reports from the past three weeks, Carol constructs Table 3.12. It shows the number of manhours reported as lost time for each of the nine lost-time codes. The total lost time for each week seems consistent—over 600 MH per week. Code 10, rework for design changes, and Code 20, waiting for materials, account for the majority of the lost time, over 60 percent.

Next, Carol uses Table 3.13 to analyze the distribution of reported lost time among the eight crews.

TABLE 3.12   Lost Time by Cause for the Past Three Weeks

	A	B	C	D	E	F	G	H	I
89	Lost-time code and cause				3/25	4/1	4/8	Total	Percent
90									
91	10 Rework, design changes				233	154	251	638	34%
92	11 Rework, error				21	34	18	73	4%
93	12 Rework, QC				101	85	32	218	11%
94	20 Wait for materials				124	210	184	518	27%
95	21 Wait for equipment				58	66	42	166	9%
96	22 Wait for directions				12	38	26	76	4%
97	23 Wait for other trade				78	14	24	116	6%
98	24 Wait, other reason				22	6	19	47	2%
99	30 Other				13	10	28	51	3%
100									
101	Total MH				662	617	624	1903	100%

TABLE 3.13   Lost Time as Reported by Crews for the Past Three Weeks

	A	B	C	D	E	F	G	H	I	J
108	LT code	Crew 01	Crew 02	Crew 03	Crew 04	Crew 05	Crew 06	Crew 07	Crew 08	Tota
109										
110	10	52	110	24	65	84	154	69	80	63
111	11	0	0	4	42	13	8	4	2	7
112	12	14	24	10	55	42	37	24	12	21
113	20	46	59	20	77	104	97	31	84	51
114	21	16	4	17	25	64	20	14	6	16
115	22	14	0	0	2	41	18	0	1	7
116	23	0	4	5	34	29	20	14	10	11
117	24	6	16	0	8	7	0	4	6	4
118	30	0	2	8	0	11	22	3	5	5
119										
120	MH totals	148	219	88	308	395	376	163	206	19
121	Percent	8%	12%	5%	16%	21%	20%	9%	11%	100

Productivity versus lost time

Comparing Table 3.13 with Table 3.9, she sees that the crews with the best productivity—Crews 04, 05, and 06—are the same crews with the greatest percentage of lost time. Conversely, Crew 03 not only has the poorest productivity but also has reported the fewest lost-time manhours. Suddenly Carol is suspicious of her analysis of worth so far. If the 300 to 400 MH of lost time per crew for the past three weeks reported by Crews 04, 05, and 06 is accurate (and she has no reason to believe that it is not), then perhaps the other crews are *underreporting* their lost time. Maybe Crew 03 isn't so bad after all; maybe the foreman just doesn't report the lost time. If so, then more hours would be charged to work time than were actually worked, thereby hurting the crew's productivity rates. Carol makes a note to be sure to check the accuracy of the lost-time reports with the foremen at the jobsite. Because crews reporting exemplar lost time (fewest lost hours) also have the poorest productivity rates, Carol suspects that the exemplars for lost time are phony, so she skips trying to calculate the lost-time PARs, since they would probably not give her accurate information.

The worth of lost time

Carol proceeds to calculate the worth of correcting the lost-time problems, however. Assuming that the lost time reported in Table 3.13 is real (even if too low), can it be reduced? Carol doubts that the time lost due to design changes can be reduced; engineering problems have plagued the job from the start, and there is no reason to believe that the drawing errors will suddenly go away. However, if design changes cost the job 638 MH every three weeks (or 213 MH every week), how much more time will be lost before the job is completed? At the three-week average productivity rates, the job will take another 113,895 MH to finish (from Table 3.10). If the crews work an average of 3650 MH per week (from Table 3.8), she calculates that the job will take another 31 weeks to complete. Thirty-one weeks times 213 MH per week gives 6600 MH of lost time to be expected from design changes alone! Of course, Carol reasons, as the job moves toward completion the number of errors in engineering ought to be fewer. But she guesses that at least another 4000 MH will be lost.

Multiplying 31 weeks times 634 MH—the average lost time per week (1903 MH divided by three weeks from Table 3.13)—gives an incredible 19,654 MH of projected lost time. Scanning down the numbers in Table 3.13, Carol notes that code 20, waiting for materials, is the second-highest lost-time cause; it costs an average of 518 MH every three weeks (or 172 MH every week). All crews show code 20 as either the largest or second-largest cause of lost time. But if some crews are underreporting, perhaps even more time is lost here. Solving the waiting-for-materials problems would be worth 173 MH per week times 31 weeks, or 5353 MH, not an inconsiderable amount. Again, as the job nears completion, the materials problems ought to diminish, but here it is hard for Carol to guess whether it will. Materials problems could even get worse if continued delays keep key items from reaching the jobsite. In any case, materials shortages certainly cost the job a lot of manhours.

In her analysis of the remainder of the lost-time items, Carol finds that item 12, waiting for QC, is worth 2253 MH (73 MH per week average times 31 weeks). But looking at the trends in lost manhours over the past three weeks (Table 3.12), this and some of the other higher lost-time numbers seem to be going down, not up. Is this a real trend, or is it due to a failure of crews to continue reporting their lost time? At this point it's hard to say, although she suspects that the QC problems will probably increase, rather than decrease, as the job moves toward completion.

Priorities for action

Carol sums up her analysis by making a priority list of the four areas in which management stands to make the biggest gains in saving manhours on the CCA project.

Area for action	Worth (in MH)
1. Bring item 1400 up to exemplar rates.	15,205
2. Bring item 1380 up to exemplar rates.	5,821
3. Eliminate lost time waiting for materials.	5,330
4. Bring item 1700 up to exemplar rates.	3,070
	29,426MH

Relying on Numbers

Many contractors avoid relying on numbers in managing their jobs. They prefer to leave the "number crunching" to the accountants and the data processing department. Only when the bottom line begins to indicate a loss do they sit up and listen. In the past, such an attitude was justified because no one could afford the time to collect and process all the data. But with the power of personal computers available on every desktop and in every trailer, the numbers have become affordable. But in turning to numbers to help them manage their jobs, contractors must be sure that they get the right numbers and that they train their people to use the numbers to improve their projects.

Checking the numbers

Based on the numbers Carol had to work with, she has done an outstanding job of pinpointing the most critical problems on the job, those areas in which management stands to gain (or lose) the greatest number of manhours, and those which also offer the greatest promise of solution. However, we can see many possible flaws in the numbers. What about errors in crew reporting? Are the past three weeks really representative of current job conditions? At what phase is the work, and are projections based on the current phase reasonable? Are the crew exemplars real? We could go on and on, questioning the validity of the numbers, and we are right to do so. We want to check the sources of the numbers continually to make sure that the information we get is as accurate as possible. But given Carol's analysis, *we now know what numbers to check first*—the crew exemplars for items 1380 and 1400 (from Crew 06) and for item 1700 (from Crew 03), plus the lost-time reporting from Crew 03. A 10-minute meeting with both foremen ought to resolve the matter. If the numbers are good, Carol's list tells us where to start working first. If the numbers are bad, we know we have failed to keep our feedback reporting system operating properly and can take steps to improve it. We can also reexamine Carol's analysis to find other priority areas for management action.

Adopting an analytical method

Without measurements of jobsite performance, we fall back on experience and guesswork in locating major opportunities for performance improvement. Measurements provide a means for moving management toward increasingly competent performance. Carol has shown us the power of using numbers to set priorities for management action. How else could one so easily and quickly spot the key problems? Certainly years of on-site experience can also lead one to the same conclusions, but how many of us can afford to wait those years? Most contractors need help now. Carol's method offers that help.

Not every job is the size of the CCA project or promises as much in the way of savings if priority problems can be pinpointed and solved. Yet every job, no matter what its size, can be improved. One carpentry contractor, doing repetitious interior trim on a series of similar apartment buildings, took the time to start measuring the number of manhours required to complete a single unit. Much to his surprise, he found that the number varied quite a bit, almost by a factor of 2. On the average, his crew always met his estimate, but the daily amounts of work completed jumped up and down. Upon looking further into it, he discovered that when all the materials needed to complete an apartment were placed in the units before his carpenters arrived, they zipped right through the work. But when materials were missing, carpenters interrupted their work to search through other units to find the materials they needed. This, in turn, left other units short of materials later. By simply overordering and making sure that every unit had more than enough materials, he cut his labor hours for each of the remaining units 40 percent below his estimate. The extra materials, picked up after the units were completed, were saved for reuse on other jobs. Without the numbers to guide the way, however, the contractor would have remained quite content knowing that his crews met the estimate.

In the three chapters so far, we have learned two important skills—how to measure construction performance and how to set priorities for improving that performance. We now know what we want to improve. The next step is to learn the techniques for making the improvements we want. It is time to turn our attention from collecting and calculating numbers to the methods that will improve the numbers.

Chapter

4

The Methods Engineering Model

The first three chapters emphasized accomplishments, not the methods for achieving them. However, the competence of management in performing construction tasks depends on the ability to create valuable accomplishments while, at the same time, holding down the costs of the methods required to achieve them. This chapter develops a model for analyzing and altering jobsite methods in pursuit of improved performance. But keep in mind that our concern with method follows only after we have properly analyzed measurements of accomplishments. Until we know that a performance is deficient, we have no reason to concern ourselves with the methods employed to achieve it.

One critical aspect of creating competent jobsite management is to establish practical performance goals—goals which are clear, which are measurable, and which reflect accomplishments we value. In addition, the goals must be achievable. To reach performance goals, we must learn to develop efficient methods.

Imagine the "world's greatest" construction crew, a highly trained team of master craftsmen, working together smoothly to build a beautiful model home of highest quality at the lowest possible cost. Is the crew competent? The difference between competence and efficiency becomes clear if we are told that the world's greatest crew built the house on the wrong homesite! Efficient methods may not always lead to competent performance. Efforts to alter methods, while essential to engineering high performance, always follow *after* an analysis of accomplishment. Efficient methods are not an end in themselves.

Management and Methods Improvement

Suppose a general contractor employs a general foreman to oversee the work of several carpenter crews in the remodeling of a small retail mall building. Under the general foreman's guidance and direction, the carpenter crews do very well, at least according to the company's performance measurements. The crews tear out unwanted walls and counters in lightning speed and rapidly frame new walls, windows, doors, and counters. Unfortunately for the general contractor, the carpenter crews, in their haste to complete their own work, provide only minimal support for the other trades on the job. When asked to move equipment and materials to make room for scaffolding for the sheet-metal and ceiling subcontractors, the general foreman makes promises that he later breaks. The general foreman refuses to let electricans and plumbers into areas where their work may interfere with the carpenters' progress. The subcontractors on the job soon realize that the delays caused by the general foreman are costing them money in overtime and out-of-sequence work. In the future, any bids they submit to the general contractor for work will carry a high markup to cover the extra costs of working with little or no support. Over time, the higher bids will diminish the amount of work the general contractor will be able to get, and the company may go out of business.

In spite of the high marks gained by the general foreman in managing the carpenters' work, he is incompetent. Although he utilizes work methods for his crews that could produce a competent job for the contractor, he fails because he misses an important goal—fostering cooperation and good will among the many subcontractors on the job. If the contractor redefines the general foreman's role to include cooperation with other trades, the foreman may become a very competent performer, generating good will on the job through work methods that incorporate cooperative behavior while only slightly diminishing crew efficiency. In such a case, the contractor can change the general foreman's performance from incompetent to competent not by direct manipulation of his behavior, but by supplying him with information about another measurement of his performance—the relative number of complaints (or praise) from subcontractors on the job.

Here, the contractor can take responsibility for the methods used by the general foreman by finding a way to change them to improve performance. Yet in many construction situations, management places the responsibility for methods change on the work force rather than accepting the responsibility for engineering better performance. How many times has management claimed, "The workers don't care," or "They have no motivation," or "They're too dumb to do it right the first time"? Such judgments put the blame on the other side. Seldom, if ever, does management turn the judgment around on itself by saying, "We haven't provided the right incentives to get our workers to perform better," or "We haven't trained them very well in how to do the work correctly," or "The feedback we've given our workers has been inadequate." To admit that management may be at fault hurts. That's why many contractors find it easier to blame their labor force for poor performance.

Competent management, however, accepts responsibility for engineering jobsite performance. After all, this is presumably what management gets paid for. To do so, it needs a means to identify and measure jobsite competence along with a means to identify the causes of deficient performance. Management needs a performance engineering model, a model that will guide it in troubleshooting work methods and in arriving at effective strategies for changing methods to raise overall performance.

Elements of Work Methods

What influences jobsite methods? Suppose I wish to start a small masonry contracting business, doing residential work. To succeed and make money, I must engineer competence among my work force. The accomplishment end is easy: I set objectives for performance and develop measurements of accomplishment. I know the quality of work expected in laying up brick walls, and I know the amount of work a mason can be expected to accomplish in a day. But how do I ensure that a mason working for me will meet my standards for quality and will work productively?

Behavior and environment

I start by hiring a mason, Mr. Will Martter. Mr. Martter is an ordinary person in most every way except one—he possesses a unique set of masonry skills. He can follow general instructions, as well as detailed plans and specifications, to create brick walls. To accomplish this, he takes many specific actions, such as setting up level lines, mixing mortar, laying bricks, and finishing joints. Mr. Martter has worked for more than 30 years as a mason, and he continues to work in the trade because he likes it; he finds the work both challenging and satisfying. As is the case for other people, Mr. Martter's work skills have become part of his personal characteristics, part of what he brings to the job each day. His inherent skills, combined with those actions he takes on the job which display his skills, are what we generally call his *work behavior*. A person's work behavior is how we see the person act and what we see the person do on the job. I shall designate this work behavior B.

But Mr. Martter alone, even with all the experience and skill of his masonry work behavior, is not sufficient for me to get the results I need for my business. I also need a *work environment*. This work environment, which I shall designate *E,* is just as fundamental an element of the work methods on the jobsite as Mr. Martter's behavior repertory. I must provide Mr. Martter with the information he needs, such as the plans and specifications for a wall and the feedback he needs to direct his performance toward the accomplishments I seek; I must also make sure he has the tools and equipment he needs as well as the necessary materials for the wall; and, of course, I must supply the incentives he desires, in the form of wages, recognition for good work, flexible work hours, and such. If I miss any one of these three elements, Mr. Martter will fail to accomplish any work at all.

Work methods

So I find that the behavior *B* brought to the job by the mason, plus the opportunities and limitations placed on the work by the site environment *E,* combine to create on-site work methods *M* that will produce the finished wall, the accomplishment *A* that I want. Thus the construction method *M* employed on the job is a combination of two elements, behavior plus environment:

$$M = B + E$$

Now Chapter 1 developed a relationship between work methods *M* and accomplishment *A* that defined performance *P*. Performance, we saw, is equal to accomplishment divided by methods:

$$P = \frac{A}{M}$$

Combining the two relationships and substituting our new definition of methods (*M* = *B* + *E*), we see that:

$$P = \frac{A}{(B + E)}$$

That is, performance *P* is equal to what I am able to accomplish *A* divided by the work methods, where these methods are a combination of work-force behavior *B* and the work environment *E*.

Performance deficiencies

As defined in Chapter 1, the worth *W* of the performance is represented by the ratio of value *V* to costs *C*, given as:

$$W = \frac{V}{C}$$

This definition of worth parallels our definition of performance; worth W is the performance P we desire. Accomplishment A provides the value V to the job, and the methods M represent the costs C. So we see that both the behavioral and the environmental aspects of the work methods are included in the job costs. The lower the cost of either, the greater the worth (and the higher the performance) I can produce.

Now, of course, I must pay the costs of the methods I have chosen for constructing brick walls—the costs of hiring a mason possessing a desired behavior repertory and then of providing him or her with an adequate work environment. If the methods are my costs and the brick wall is the accomplishment I value, then the overall worth of the performance depends upon how high a value I am able to create for a minimum cost.

The definitions above tell me that I must pay for both the behavior of my labor force and for their supporting work environment. Further, the relationships tell me that *for any given accomplishment, a deficiency in performance can always be traced to a deficiency in behavior or to a deficiency in the work environment, or both.* And, because management exerts considerable control over both behavior and environment, performance ultimately reflects management competence. Thus, if I wish to improve my performance as a contractor, I will look to correcting deficiencies either in the behavior of my labor force or in the working environment I provide for them, or both. But in order to discover where faults lie concealed in my methods, I require a systematic means of investigating performance deficiencies.

The Methods Engineering Model

Upon closer examination of the story about Mr. Martter, we find that we have identified all that we need to know about work methods in order to construct a model of the requirements for superior jobsite performance. First, in looking at the work environment E, we see that management must provide three elements essential to establishing the work-accomplishment methods to be used at the jobsite:

Environmental requirements

1. Management is obligated to provide *information,* normally the plans and specifications, necessary for doing the work plus feed-

back, (in the form of ongoing direction and approval), necessary to keep the work on track.

2. Management is obligated to provide the *resources* (in the form of tools, equipment, and materials) necessary for doing the work.

3. Management is obligated to offer the *incentives* (primarily in the form of wages) necessary for doing the work.

Second, in looking at Mr. Martter's work behavior, we see that he also possesses three behavioral elements *B* required for working efficiently at the jobsite:

Behavioral requirements

1. He possesses a body of *skills* (in the form of his training and experience) necessary for doing the work.

2. He possesses the physical and mental *capability* (in terms of his health and intelligence) necessary for doing the work.

3. He possesses the *motives* (in his desire to continue in the masonry craft) necessary for doing the work.

Each of these six elements is an essential requirement for establishing efficient work methods at the jobsite. If any element is totally missing, no work can be accomplished. At the same time, at no jobsite is every element totally present; no job is so perfect that its work methods cannot be improved. Every jobsite is made up of a mix of the six elements, each interacting with the others to produce the resulting work methods.

An example of incompetence

To understand the importance of each of the six elements, suppose we set out to engineer *incompetent* construction performance by creating the most inefficient work methods. Table 4.1 lists some of the actions we might take.

While these rules for engineering incompetent performance may strike some contractors as ridiculous, *many contractors follow one or more of them regularly.* It doesn't take much to imagine situations in which these rules are commonly applied at construction projects.

Creating competence

If we reverse the rules in Table 4.1, however, we can arrive at a more sensible model for engineering performance. Any construction job characterized by the rules in Table 4.2 would certainly reveal a high

TABLE 4.1   A Model for Engineering Incompetent Construction Performance

Environmental Elements

1. Information
- Give people incomplete plans and poorly written specifications.
- Change the plans frequently as the work progresses.
- Never plan the work ahead or tell people what they will do next.
- Provide little or no guidance as to how to perform well.
- Do not tell people what is expected of them.
- Don't let people know how well they are performing.
- Make misleading statements about how the job is progressing.

2. Resources
- Use equipment that is unsuited to the task.
- Fail to have tools available when they are needed.
- Use inferior materials.
- Avoid following safety rules.
- Overwork equipment so that it either breaks or is unavailable.
- Deliver materials only after they are needed.

3. Incentives
- Make sure that poor performers get paid as much as good ones.
- See that good performance gets punished in some way.
- Don't reward people for good performance.
- Fail to tell people when they have done a good job.

Behavioral Elements

4. Skills
- Leave the training to chance.
- Hire unskilled people and do not train them.
- Give new workers experience working next to poor performers.
- Put the burden of acquiring skills on the workers.
- Provide training that is irrelevant to jobsite conditions.
- Permit foremen to skip holding regular safety meetings.

5. Capability
- Understaff the crews for physically demanding tasks.
- Fail to provide protection from adverse weather.
- Provide inadequate toilets and washup facilities.
- Select people for tasks they find difficult to perform.
- Do not insist on safety protection.

6. Motives
- Make sure the job has no future.
- Avoid making working conditions more pleasant.
- Give empty pep talks to pressure people to work harder.
- See that good performers work themselves out of a job quicker.

degree of competence in work methods.

In reading down the list, it is clear that performance engineering is not free. It costs money to engineer more efficient work methods. Yet since no construction job employs perfect work methods and since improvements are therefore always possible, the question is not how much it will cost to improve the work methods but whether this improvement will raise the *worth* of the job. If the cost is lower than the value it produces, the overall worth increases. The key concept here is

TABLE 4.2   The Methods Engineering Model

Environmental Elements

1. *Information*
   - Provide clear and correct plans and well-written specifications.
   - Avoid changes to the plans as the work progresses.
   - Plan the work well ahead and keep people informed as to plans.
   - Provide frequent feedback as to how well people perform.
   - Tell people exactly what is expected of them.
   - Show people how to perform well.
   - Keep the work force informed as to progress against schedule.
2. *Resources*
   - Use equipment that is well-suited to the task.
   - Have tools available when they are needed.
   - Use adequate materials.
   - Follow all safety rules.
   - Provide equipment when it is needed.
   - Make sure materials are available as needed.
3. *Incentives*
   - Make wages contingent upon performance.
   - Provide nonmonetary incentives.
   - Reward people for good performance.
   - Tell people when they have done a good job.

Behavioral Elements

4. *Skills*
   - Design the training to fit jobsite conditions.
   - Use only exemplary performers to train new workers on the job.
   - Remove obstacles to continued training.
   - Ensure that competent people teach jobsite safety.
   - Draw on individual experience whenever possible.
5. *Capability*
   - Fit the crew staffing to the tasks.
   - Protect workers from adverse weather.
   - Provide acceptable toilets and washup facilities.
   - Select people for tasks they perform best.
   - Insist that all workers wear safety protection.
6. *Motives*
   - Hire individuals who enjoy construction work.
   - Make people feel good about working on the job.
   - Keep good performers on the job.
   - Offer career opportunities.

leverage. We need to use the methods engineering model to find those improvement strategies which offer the greatest leverage for improving jobsite performance.

Glassman Glaziers, Inc.

Gunther Glassman started his glazing company just after the war and quickly prospered. His hero was Ludwig Mies van der Rohe, the German-born architect who practically invented the all-glass skyscraper. Gunther's daughter, Judy, received all the benefits her father never had, including an expensive college education, a graduate degree in sociology, and a well-heeled lifestyle. But when a sudden stroke killed Gunther shortly after Judy's second marriage fell apart, she decided to make something of herself by taking over the family business. Judy is a very smart lady; she kept all the senior management people and stayed well out of their way while she applied herself to learning everything she could about the glazing business.

Management and motivation

People tell her that the only unknown in the business is the labor force. Management can engineer glass walls and get the materials and equipment to install it. But management cannot get labor to work, certainly not the way they did "in the old days after the war." Nowadays you never know if the workers on the job will make money for you or lose it. They just don't have any motivation. They do sloppy work and can't follow directions. It is a risky business. Profits sure aren't what they used to be.

Judy listens carefully to such statements. But she doubts that they're all really true. In school, her subjects had included the study of behavior in the workplace. Her old college texts emphasized the psychological aspects of behavior, stressing how different every individual is in terms of motivation and behavior. But to Judy's way of thinking, it hadn't made sense then and it still doesn't make sense now. Everyone she sees on her jobs behaves pretty much the same, and she can't believe that they all show up for work every morning for completely different motives. She thinks their motives aren't all that different—they all want to make a living working as glaziers. Trying to improve jobsite performance by changing the workers' motives would be silly. So, true to her academic background, Judy decides to do "field research"; she goes out and asks the workers themselves how they feel about their jobs and what they see as deficiencies in their work methods.

Categorizing gripes

For several weeks Judy interviews workers (they couldn't believe she was actually paying them to stand around and talk to her). Once she gets them talking, Judy finds the workers interesting to listen to and willing to tell her a great deal about the work. They seem to take pride in their skills and like their work. However, they all complain about something. Judy's notes turn out to contain every major gripe she has heard on 22 different jobsites, ranging in size from 4 to 47 workers. As she compiles her notes, she groups similar gripes under three problem headings:

1. Knowledge problems

   - No one spends time at the beginning of a job showing workers how to install novel glass and frame designs they have never seen before.
   - New workers at the site are not shown how to do the work but are left to learn by watching others.
   - Management never asks experienced workers for suggestions.
   - No one is ever told exactly what is expected of them, so everyone just does what others do.
   - No one is ever told how well they have performed, so they never know when they have done well (except that no one criticizes them).
   - Plans and directions are frequently confusing, and time is wasted getting clear answers.
   - Work is seldom planned ahead of time, so workers are unsure what to do next when they reach the end of a task.
   - Work must sometimes be redone because of inadequate directions as to how it should have been done the first time.

2. Capacity problems

   - People often waste time waiting for deliveries of glass, yet glass stored at the site is often damaged or broken.
   - The lifting equipment is old and often inadequate; to place heavy panes correctly requires considerable time and effort.
   - The safety harnesses are old and worn, and workers often feel scared working at heights.
   - The company refuses to purchase expensive, "state-of-the-art" vacuum-powered handgrips for holding glass panes.
   - Not enough equipment is assigned to large jobsites working several crews.

3. Motivation problems

   - No matter how well workers perform on a job, their pay is locked into a contract wage scale that is the same for everyone.
   - While they are working on one job, workers are never told if they will be needed on another job.
   - Project management is quick to criticize slack performance and never acknowledges superior performance.
   - Workers feel that management "looks down on them."

Looking over her list of problems, Judy feels both a sense of accomplishment and a sense of discouragement. She feels that her list provides a valuable guide to improving productivity, but she doesn't know where to start. All the problems seem formidable. All the solutions seem too time-consuming, too expensive, or too contrary to company traditions. But, she decides, that won't stop her from trying.

The missing pieces

Judy's efforts to locate the causes of her company's problems are commendable. Her list of problems (with its three categories) appears promising. However, she missed two critical steps. First, she failed to define and measure the accomplishments she values. While she assumed that profitability was her overall goal and improved jobsite productivity a subgoal, she needs specific measurements of jobsite performance in order to locate deficient performance. Where are the largest performance ability ratios (PARs)? Without measurements of what it is she wants to accomplish on the job, she cannot easily design solutions that will address the largest sources of incompetence. Second, Judy cannot set priorities among alternative problems since she has no way of judging which solution will most likely offer the greatest leverage—that is, which will provide the greatest value relative to its cost. Let us look at a way to resolve this question of priorities.

Priorities in Work-Methods Analysis

To set priorities to improve work methods, we first need to locate tasks that promise a large return for a minimum of effort. (To do this, we have learned how to compute PARs and calculate potential worth.) We next need to know exactly what actions to take to improve the work methods and in what order to take these actions. The methods engineering matrix satisfies this second need.

A matrix of categories

Turn back to the methods engineering model in Table 4.2. Notice that Judy's three categories of problems include all six of the elements identified in the model, but grouped differently. We can use Judy's three categories to help structure the six elements of the methods engineering model into the matrix shown in Figure 4.1. The methods engineering matrix permits us to pigeonhole any jobsite methods problem into one of six boxes. Each box is identified as either an environmental problem or a behavioral one. Further, each box falls into one of Judy's three categories—knowledge, capacity, or motivation.

A sequence for analysis

In what sequence do we attack the problems identified in the matrix? Let us start with the last one. We have already seen that individual

	Knowledge	Capacity	Motivation
Environmental Elements	1. Information	2. Resources	3. Incentives
Behavioral Elements	4. Skills	5. Capability	6. Motives

Figure 4.1 The methods engineering matrix.

motives in construction cannot vary too greatly, for if people did not want to work at construction, they would work elsewhere. So it is unlikely that variance in motives causes large jobsite PARs. The same is true of *capability*. Nearly all workers are physically fit for the job, and all crews working at similar tasks encounter more or less similar physical conditions. And, although individual *skills* may vary considerably, most crews contain a mix of experienced and less experienced workers. So unless crew assignments consciously separate the most skilled workers from the least skilled, crew skills are also unlikely to be a source of large PARs on the job. We see, therefore, that the behavioral elements of the matrix are unlikely to be the starting place for finding worthwhile improvements to work methods.

In fact, the matrix in Figure 4.1 lays out the elements in the most likely order of discovering the causes of deficient performance. All elements are equally important in engineering efficient work methods. But solutions to correcting deficiencies in the environmental elements promise a greater payoff for less cost and effort. In general, it is usually far easier for management to make changes to the work environment than to change the work behavior of the labor force. Therefore, it pays to follow the sequence in Figure 4.1 in a search for improvement strategies, looking first to the least expensive and least difficult solutions.

Begin with *information*. Ask if crews have the information they need to do the work properly. Do they know how it should be done? Do they know how well it can be performed (the exemplar)? Poor direction and lack of feedback concerning how well they are doing their jobs may well be the single largest source of jobsite incompetence at all levels.

Next, look at *resources*, the tools, equipment, and materials required to do the job. Do workers have the resources they need in order to perform well? Large measurements of lost time on jobs due to waiting come primarily from management's consistent failure to provide resources when they are needed.

Then examine *incentives*. How can incentives be improved and made more contingent upon good performance? If wage scales are fixed by contract, what nonmonetary incentives might be offered? And how can one eliminate negative incentives that discourage good performers and reward poor ones?

Finally, if a large PAR still persists after manipulating the environmental elements, decide whether any training to improve job skills will help. While worker skills are an extremely important aspect of jobsite performance, contractor-run training programs can prove to be very expensive. If training is used, it should be directed specifically to the tasks on the job.

The methods engineering model and the matrix, then, provide a performance troubleshooting sequence. Once we know that a problem exists, the model gives an orderly way to discover cost-effective strategies for improving deficient work methods. Remember, however, that the model does not pretend that one element is more important than another. It merely orders the elements so that solutions with the greatest worth are more likely to be discovered first.

Applying the model

Suppose we now apply the model to Judy's problems. In doing so, we quickly develop a checklist of questions (given in Table 4.3) that lead us directly to priorities for attempting solutions.

In reading down Table 4.3, one thing stands out immediately. While the sequence of questions leads generally toward more expensive solutions, the single question and answer in item 5, "Capability," calls for immediate attention. Safety is not an "expensive" solution. Instead, *failure* to provide a safe workplace may be one of the most expensive decisions a contractor can make. The search to find and remedy unsafe conditions never stops; worker capability on the job can be drastically reduced by accidents, sometimes serious enough to halt further work. So always pay attention to safety issues first.

Besides the safety issue, we see that the first deficiency on the list turns out to be information. Here the problem turns out to be with the foremen and project supervisors who do not spend enough time planning the jobs. Poor planning results in confused directions, lack of coordination, and unforeseen problems with plans and installation. Workers also fail to get adequate feedback concerning how well they are doing, particularly on rush jobs where management always seems too busy to pay attention to the work being done. Improving jobsite information is usually the least expensive way to improve performance. Judy needs to review the workload on her foremen and project supervisors and make sure that they alter their priorities. Planning the jobs and providing clear direction and feedback should be their primary responsibility.

TABLE 4.3   The Methods Engineering Model—Troubleshooting Checklist

Variables	Solutions
Environment	
1. Information	
• Are plans and directions clear?	No. Field supervisors must learn to plan
• Are work standards clear?	ahead, anticipate problems, give clear
• Is work planned ahead?	directions, and provide feedback.
• Is performance feedback offered?	
2. Resources	
• Is equipment adequate?	No. New equipment and tools must be
• Are tools adequate?	purchased and methods found to deliver
• Are materials available?	early and protect glass.
3. Incentives	
• Are nonmonetary rewards used?	No. Good performance must be
• Are workers treated with dignity?	recognized, acknowledged, and rewarded.
Behavior	
4. Skills	
• Do workers know how to install?	No. Training must begin for novel instal-
• Are new workers trained?	lations and new hires.
5. Capability	
• Can workers perform well?	No. New safety equipment must be pur-
	chased to allay workers' fear.
6. Motives	
• Do workers want to perform well?	Yes.

New equipment and tools may represent a significant expense for the company. But failing to provide workers with the resources they need to do the job tells them that management doesn't really care about them, only about saving money. If the company cannot afford to reoutfit all the crews at once, then new equipment, as it is purchased over time, might be used to reward those crews whose work is most outstanding. Giving vacuum-powered handgrips to the crews that do the best work each month, for example, may provide an excellent incentive for crews to improve. Recognition for a job well done, even if it is only a token reward, fosters a sense of pride in accomplishment and encourages crews to continue to do well in the future.

Setting up a training program for new hires and for crews faced with difficult or novel installations can become another source of recognition for exemplar performers. Judy can use her exemplar performers to teach others how to do the work. Pulling several of the best workers and foremen off a job for half a day or so to figure out the best way to install glass on an upcoming job solves two problems: It gives recognition to individuals who have demonstrated superior work skills, and it anticipates potential installation problems beforehand, giving management time to develop work methods to avoid the problems.

Once Judy (or any contractor) uses the work-methods engineering model to analyze a job, the solutions become obvious. Repeated application of the methods model to many jobs will soon eliminate the most common problems and, in the process, improve the performance of both work crews and management.

Jobsite Motivation

The methods engineering model distinguishes two aspects of motivation: incentives and motives. *Incentives refer to the work environment,* the wages, rewards, and recognition offered by management. *Motives refer to the personal attitude toward the job that an individual brings to work each morning.* Combined, the two define the motivation that drives someone to try to accomplish a construction task. If either incentives or motives are missing, motivation also disappears.

The final question in Table 4.3 assumes that the workers' motives are not a problem, that the people want to work and will do so if the other environmental and behavioral elements are met. Yet, on some jobs, worker motives may indeed be questioned. Workers may no longer want to work on jobs that have "gone sour." Some projects, suffering from incompetent management, experience jobsite conditions that greatly reduce workers' desire to accomplish anything at all.

Motives can change

It ought to be apparent that working conditions at the jobsite can affect individual motives, and hence motivation. An unskilled apprentice who receives no encouragement for his or her efforts, but hears only criticism, will find the job less and less satisfying. Although the pay remains the same, the desire to do the work diminishes. Other inner motives, such as the desire to learn a trade and earn a living, the comradeship of other craftsmen on the job, and the pleasure of working with one's hands, may not be strong enough to compensate for the misery of daily hassle and rebuffs. Motivation fails, and either the apprentice quits the job or the work falls off so much that he or she is fired. Because management has failed to provide a positive work environment, the worker suffers. In such a case, the lack of positive feedback (information), the absence of recognition for work accomplished (incentives), and the lack of assistance in learning (skills) affect motives and undermine motivation.

In fact, there is no way to alter one element of the model without having at least some effect on other elements, sometimes a very large effect. Lighter tools (resources) may make it easier for women to use them (capacity). Training (skills) and feedback (information) can provide powerful personal reasons for wanting to do a good job (motives). This interrelationship among job elements and motivation demonstrates how useless the word *motivation* is when discussing jobsite problems. When a contractor says that the work force is not motivated, it does not tell us anything about *why* motivation lags. Is it because the contractor does not pay enough (incentives), or because the equipment on the job continually breaks down (resources), or because directions are confusing and make little sense (information)? One thing we do know, however, is that the alleged lack of motivation is very unlikely to stem from the workers' own motives. They probably want to work and like construction work; so why has management failed to tap that feeling and reinforce it? The answer is nearly always to be found in the incompetence of management. A competently run job seldom experiences a "motivation" problem.

Focus on results

So how does one separate motivational elements from knowledge and capacity in designing better work methods? Suppose we find a deficiency caused by confusion over unclear shop drawings. After we have an engineer redraw portions of the plans to clarify the installation details, we find that we get exemplary performance. Obviously, part of the reason for the improvement is informational; the better drawings make the work easier. But part of the improvement may also be motivational; by removing a source of frustration, we have made the job more pleasant. How do we tell the difference? In such a situation, we cannot tell the difference. But there is no reason to worry over which effect, information or motivation, caused the performance improvement. We are concerned only with the results.

The methods engineering model cannot tell us if the information on the job is adequate or if the workers' motivation is high. It can only tell us where to look first for obvious flaws. First we look at information. If we find nothing there that we can correct, we go on to look at resources, and so on. The model cannot find every defect in jobsite work methods; it can only help us search for observable defects in an orderly fashion. It prompts us to ask the "obvious" questions (the ones we so often forget to ask) with the sole aim of improving performance.

Every solution will have a crossover effect on the other elements of the model. We need not concern ourselves with quantifying this effect, for we are not behavioral scientists. We are construction contractors, managers, and field supervisors, interested only in raising on-site job performance.

The methods engineering model offers us a way out of the "motivation" and "attitude" trap that so frequently leave contractors helpless in their desire to improve productivity. The model provides a simple method for discovering the real reasons for performance deficiencies. In the next chapter we will examine its application in troubleshooting a job to improve performance.

Troubleshooting
Construction Performance

When experienced individuals look over a construction job, they often spot problems and recommend improved work methods. They attribute their ability to troubleshoot jobs to their familiarity with a wide range of construction projects. Such individuals seldom rely on a methods engineering model or any other formal analytical process. They just "know" what is right and what isn't.

The methods engineering model is not a substitute for experienced judgment. Rather, it is a supplement that can help people do a better job of troubleshooting. The more experience one has, the more quickly one ought to be able to use the model to pinpoint the causes of problems and to design workable solutions. *The value of the methods engineering model lies in its capacity to summon our knowledge of construction performance in an orderly and systematic way.* In doing so, it helps us avoid wasting time and effort following unprofitable improvement strategies. Instead, in combination with an analysis of performance ability ratios (PARs) and worth, we can focus our attention on the most promising strategies for methods improvements.

The construction industry employs a vast variety of work methods, and somewhere among them there may be an alternative method that could improve a job. Which method is best will depend on the specific conditions of each job. Sometimes conditions make it nearly impossible to use an obviously "better" method; less efficient methods remain in use because the cost of change (in terms of money, delays, or hassle) far exceeds the worth of the immediate payback. Troubleshooting jobs and discovering the worth of better methods, even if strategies for their sucessful implementation temporarily elude us, will build pressures for future change. Yet even if the "best" solutions seem beyond our immediate grasp, some improvement of current performance is always possible. We must always remember that performance engineering is first and foremost a pragmatic science. We aim only for what we can do, not for the impossible.

Levels of Performance Measurements

In our search for more productive work methods, the previous chapters have limited our analysis to the jobsite; we have learned to measure and analyze performance at the crew and project level. But what about individual performance? And what about all the off-site factors that affect on-site productivity? At what level should our analysis start and where should it stop?

Placing blame

Because we can find different answers to these questions depending upon whom we talk with, we may be tempted to throw up our hands in despair. The work force blames mismanagement for poor productivity. Contractors blame poor design drawings for inept performance. Designers blame owners for indecisiveness and continuous changes. Owners blame changing market conditions for altering projections of corporate needs. The government points to foreign competition, new knowledge, and political pressures to justify their meddling in the market. Where does it end? Trying to discover who is to blame for poor jobsite performance is a fruitless effort. On the other hand, trying to improve jobsite performance is a rewarding effort. If our goal is to improve jobsite performance, therefore, where should we start?

Individual performance

Some professions find measurements of individual performance appropriate. Brokers count shares sold, detectives count cases solved, and golfers count birdies scored. But in most professions, accomplishments and performance are seldom individual efforts. Exemplary performance most often results from cooperation and teamwork. In such instances, measurements of individual performance are not only difficult to get, but the very effort to quantify individual accomplishment may encourage competition among team members, thereby destroying the teamwork required to achieve superior performance. If a basketball coach only started those players who scored the most points the night before, the team might soon find itself at the bottom of its league.

In many ways, construction also depends on a team effort, not on individual stars. A construction crew might be thought of as a team—each member contributing toward aggregate crew performance. Attempts to measure the performance of each individual within a crew might soon lead to chaos. Either competition between individuals would interfere with cooperation or, more likely, the individuals would quickly find effective ways to frustrate the measurement efforts. Most measurements of individual performance, because they rank people from best to worst, necessarily put someone at the bottom of the ladder. In sports, where competition is the name of the game, players accept a ranking system (while protesting their position at the bottom). People never want to be at the bottom if they can help it. It hurts their pride, opens them to criticism, and, in the world of work, may cost them their jobs. People will go to extraordinary lengths to avoid being measured and to undermine the validity of such measurements if they wind up at the bottom. Construction workers are no different.

Crew performance

Measurements at the crew level encounter the same potential problem of ranking. However, because the leadership and skill levels of each crew vary, as do the working conditions and methods, attempts to rank crews seldom appear credible, even to the people doing the ranking. While efforts to identify exemplar performers among crews can provide valuable information for setting goals and finding PARs, efforts to identify the "worst" crew are usually counterproductive. Inexperienced foremen, less skilled craftsmen, slightly different circumstances, and a host of other reasons can contribute to low performance. Ask the crew at the bottom the reasons for their poor showing and they will give a thousand excuses, none of which admit to personal responsibility. On the other hand, ask the crew at the top why they do so well and they will recount a dozen reasons why they personally excel, never attributing their success to accident or forces beyond their control. To the performance engineer troubleshooting a job for methods improvement, exemplar crews offer a wealth of untapped knowledge concerning techniques and tricks for improving performance. The crews at the bottom offer only excuses, not positive examples for others to copy.

Thus it makes little sense to measure crew performance in order to rank crews, but it makes a great deal of sense to measure crew performance in order to find exemplars whose work methods provide suitable examples for imitation by others. Measurements at the crew level can quickly lead the performance engineer to identify exemplar work methods. Conversely, measurements at the individual level tend to be resisted, distorted, and inapplicable.

Aggregate performance

Aggregate measurements at levels higher than the crew (the craft, the project, or the company) often fail to pinpoint exemplar performance in a way that can be readily analyzed. Unless we can zero in on the work methods that produce exemplar performance, we miss one of the strengths of the methods engineering model—*comparing the environmental and behavioral elements of average performers to those of exemplar performers.* Such comparisons can help us quickly identify appropriate actions that will increase the efficiency of the work methods of average performers.

Aggregate measurements of craft or project performance, obtained by averaging the performance of many crews, provide the performance engineer with valuable information from which to compute PARs among similar craft accomplishments and similar projects over time. But aggregate measurements that bury the richer details of crew and work-item performance are seldom helpful for troubleshooting and improving performance on current jobs, except to the extent that they provide a baseline against which to judge current performance. Knowing that project A is performing better than project B does not immediately suggest where to look for the causes of project A's success or of project B's shortcomings. Comparison of such aggregate project measurements as schedule, profitability, and manhour expenditures can confuse troubleshooting efforts. In such cases where detailed measurements of crew performance and work-item productivity are unavailable, the project manager may take credit for success or may blame others for failure. In either case, company management may learn little of immediate use.

Measurements of overall company performance (other than profitability, which may bear little relationship to construction performance) also provide useful information for computing and comparing trends. But such longer-term measurements, while valuable in establishing goals against which to judge further improvement, seldom translate directly into procedures for improving jobsite work methods.

Start at the jobsite

All of this is not to say that we should ignore opportunities for improving the performance of such off-site activities as design and engineering, office record keeping, estimating, and labor relations. But the reason to make improvements in off-site activities lies in the effect of such improvements upon on-site performance. If measurements of jobsite performance reveal large amounts of time lost because of faulty design drawings, then we must look for methods to improve the quality of the drawings if we wish to cut down on the lost time. (The methods engineering model can apply off-site as well as on-site: Designers may persist in producing faulty drawings not because they cannot do better, but because they do not get feedback from the jobsite as to the impact of their work on the productivity of the work crews.) But in every case, *the first place to look to locate the sources of poor field performance is in the field.* And the place to measure the results of changing off-site procedures is in the field. Measurements of performance at the jobsite reveal our true competence as managers of construction; measurements of company profitability, on the other hand, only tell us how competent we are as business people, a completely different (yet extremely important) arena of performance.

Noonan Constructors, Inc.

As a design-build firm, Noonan Constructors failed. The firm switched from construction contracting to design-build four years ago and immediately hit it big with a large contract for a municipal housing project for the elderly, two college dormitories, and a private condo development. Noonan hired lots of engineers and began successfully marketing a prefab apartment of its own design. Noonan also added some hotshot salespeople, and soon orders were pouring in faster than the firm could build them. As the rate of growth soared, company officers turned to a form of management by objectives (MBO) to increase productivity in the face of rising overhead costs. Sales, engineering, accounting, and construction departments set goals for increasing monthly output while holding down costs.

As department goals trickled down to specific targets for individuals, engineers found themselves working within a system that counted the number of drawings completed each month. Because design work continued right up to the start of construction (and often beyond), mechanical engineers began turning out "completed" drawings that contained such cryptic notes as "see structural drawing for exact location of wall." They couldn't wait for final dimensions from the structural people, they claimed. They had to get the drawings done. With rising pressures to hold down costs while increasing the number of drawings, all the engineers soon began referencing each other's drawings instead of taking the time to develop a single, integrated drawing set. While this practice of referencing other drawings boosted engineering productivity, it sure hurt productivity in the field. In order for field foremen to put in ductwork, for example, they might need to refer to five or six different sheets to make sure they had the right dimensions.

With more and more "referenced" drawing sets reaching the crews, field productivity began to plummet. Behind schedule on several projects, over budget because of overtime, and losing frustrated foremen faster than they could be hired, Noonan Constructors lost the race between cash inflow and cash outflow.

Narrow measurements

Noonan Constructors dramatizes the pitfall of overly narrow performance measurements. High performance in the field should be the overriding goal of any construction firm, yet many firms fail to emphasize jobsite performance. Instead, they look only to profitability, assuming that if the firm turns a profit each year, it must be performing well in the field.

Such an assumption can be dangerously false. Suppose, for example, that a mechanical subcontractor wins a multimillion-dollar job with a low bid that errs in underestimating the job but that the sub then turns around and more than makes up the difference by purchasing the needed pipe at a better price than the sub expected to pay. As the job proceeds, it becomes clear that the original labor estimates were wrong. Yet the sub shows little concern for poor jobsite productivity since the savings on the pipe have guaranteed a profitable job. Is the subcontract profitable? Yes. Does the sub perform well in the field? No. Similar stories could contrast poor field performance with high profits gained from stock turnovers, mergers, changes in accounting methods, overestimates, equipment sales, favorable subcontracts, lucky bids, real estate appreciation, and a dozen other sources of income unrelated to competence in managing construction at the jobsite.

Measurements of management competence in construction will ultimately be found at the jobsite. The *causes* of incompetence may be found on-site or off-site (or both). Strategies to improve jobsite performance will lead to changes in on-site or off-site work methods (or both). But the effectiveness of the strategies will ultimately be found in their impact on measurements of jobsite performance.

Troubleshooting and the Performance Audit

Earlier chapters have developed the fundamental tools we need to engineer superior jobsite performance. It is now time to learn to combine those tools into a troubleshooting sequence. We can think of construction projects that need improvement. But what do we do first? How do we apply what we have learned so far? We need a simple guide to follow in order to troubleshoot a project and identify the actions that will lead to improvement. Successful troubleshooting of jobsite performance follows six steps, called a *performance audit*.

The performance audit

1. *Identify accomplishments.* Make sure the items of work describe measureable accomplishments, not merely jobsite activities. We want to identify and measure work-in-place. Vague task categories such as "wiring" and "framing" describe activities, not measureable accomplishments.

2. *Identify requirements.* Here we apply the questions for the performance measurement requirements of quality, quantity, and resources from Table 2.3. Asking and answering the questions identifies the key measurements and units to use for each of the accomplishments identified in step 1.

3. *Define exemplary performance.* Having identified the accomplishments and requirements, the next step is to define what constitutes exemplary performance for each of the accomplishments and measurements. How do we distinguish exemplars? For measurements of productivity, we look for higher amounts installed per manhour. But what about measurements of work quality and jobsite safety?

4. *Measure exemplary and average performance.* Collecting the numbers for each of the accomplishment measurements may require considerable time and effort. The numbers, however, provide the basis for locating significant variations in performance.

5. *Compute the PARs and worth.* Analysis of the measurements leads to finding the greatest opportunities for improvement and the biggest potential paybacks.

6. *Apply the methods engineering model.* Only after we have completed each of the five steps above are we ready to apply the model as a guide for developing strategies to improve performance. In applying the model, pose these questions:

INFORMATION: Do people know what accomplishments are expected of them and what the standards are? Do people get regular feedback as to how well their performance meets the standards? Do they know how well they perform relative to the exemplar? Do they get information on where their deficiencies are so that they may improve? Is the feedback complete, accurate, intelligible, and timely?

RESOURCES: Are the drawings, tools, equipment, and materials suited to the job? Are they available when needed? Can people reach exemplary performance with the resources available to them?

INCENTIVES: Are the incentives sufficient to encourage exemplary performance? Are they contingent upon good performance? Are there competing negative incentives that inhibit good performance? Are all the available incentives used?

SKILLS: Do people have the necessary knowledge and training to perform well? Could they reach exemplary performance if their lives depended on it?

CAPACITY: Do people have the physical capacity to perform well? Do weather, hazards, health, and personal conditions make it impossible to achieve exemplary performance?

MOTIVES: Is the work so unrewarding and punishing that no one will want to perform well even if provided with excellent incentives?

Answers to these questions help us devise strategies to improve work methods. To see how the troubleshooting sequence might be applied in the field, let us follow an example in detail.

Busten Poure Company, Inc.

The Busten Poure Company specializes in paving replacement. Each winter it submits bids to the county for sidewalk- and street-repair work. The bids are unit-price bids; Busten Poure bids so many dollars per square yard for various types of work. This spring, the county hired Mike Nickles, a student in construction management at a local university, as a summer intern. Mike will work as a project engineer, inspecting the work of four of the Busten Poure crews on three of the county street-replacement jobs in residential neighborhoods. In addition, to get course credit for his internship, Mike must write a detailed report on some aspect of his experience. Mike chooses to investigate the productivity of Busten Poure's paving crews.

Applying the performance audit

1. Mike begins by *identifying accomplishments*. He lists six:

- Locate and mark paving areas for replacement.
- Break and remove existing paving.
- Prepare and grade subsurface for new slab.
- Prepare formwork.

- Place and finish new slab.
- Clean up.

In reviewing the list of accomplishments with the full-time project engineer for the county, Mike finds that the first accomplishment, locating and marking the paving areas to be replaced, has already been done by the county. Engineers identified, and marked with spray paint, all substandard squares to be replaced. (A *square* is the area between expansion joints in the concrete streets, normally measuring 13 ft by 20 ft, one-half the width of a 26-ft-wide residential street.)

Breaking and removing the existing 6-in concrete road surface requires a paving breaker, a loader, and one or more dump trucks for hauling away the pieces. After the old slab has been removed, along with any "spongy" soil beneath, crews add gravel aggregate to fill holes and to provide a firm foundation for the new concrete. Because each new slab needs to meet county requirements for minimum thickness, crews take care in raking out the gravel to maintain the correct depth for the finished slab. A 1-ton roller then compacts the gravel.

Crews then place the formwork for the new slab, making sure to maintain the correct slopes for proper drainage. After these preparations, Mike, in his role as a county engineer, must inspect the work and approve the next step, placing the concrete. Placing and finishing the slabs then proceeds quickly. Finally, crews clean up the area before leaving it, backfilling and resodding along the curbs as well. (As crews normally work on three or four locations on several streets at the same time, Mike can see that just keeping track of the work will be a big job.)

2. Next, Mike must *identify the requirements* of the job. For this, he turns to the *performance measurement requirement* questions (refer to Table 2.3). For each accomplishment, Mike asks as many quality, quantity, and resource questions as he can think of, followed by the measurements (and units) he will use. He comes up with the following list:

Requirement	Measurement (and unit)
ACCURACY. It seems unlikely that crews would break out the wrong slab. However, the depth of each new slab must be at least 6 in. Subsurface fill must be firm. Also, slabs must slope properly to drain. The concrete mix must meet strength specifications and must be finished properly.	Depth (inches) Gravel fill (OK, Not OK) Slope (OK, Not OK) Mix (OK, Not OK) Finish (OK, Not OK)
WORKMANSHIP. Mike finds no requirements here.	None

Requirement	Measurement (and unit)
PRODUCTIVITY. Because some of the slabs vary in size, Mike decides to use square yards divided by manhours (SY/MH) as his primary productivity measurement. Since nearly all the slabs are 6 in deep, the area measurement can be easily converted to cubic yards (CY) in order to measure the amount of material removed and hauled and the amount of concrete placed per manhour. Formwork placement can be measured in linear feet per manhour (LF/MH).	Break (SY/MH) Remove (SY/MH) Haul (SY/MH) Prepare (SY/MH) Formwork (LF/MH) Place (SY/MH) Finish (SY/MH)
SCHEDULE. Mike is unsure how schedule affects the contractor. Her contract requires her to replace several hundred thousand square yards of pavement before November 1. No other interim-schedule deadlines affect the work. However, since the contractor intends to work only the four crews on the three contracts Mike will oversee, Mike assumes that tracking the progress against the time remaining will be important to avoid either putting on more crews or working overtime near the end of the project.	"Progress ratio" (percentage of work done divided by percentage of working days used)
MANPOWER. The number of people in each crew and their craft skills affect jobsite performance. Differences in wage scales for crafts affect costs. Also, the amount of overtime, if any, affects the hourly wage scale.	Crew size (#/crew) Skills (craft) Wages ($/MH) Overtime (MH)
MATERIALS, TOOLS, AND EQUIPMENT. Until Mike knows better, he decides to keep track of all the materials, tools, and equipment at each site.	Concrete (CY/slab) Gravel (CY/slab) Tools (type) Equipment (type) Equipment (condition) Equipment (hours used)

3. Mike talks to the other county engineers to *identify exemplary performance*. This turns out to be relatively easy for some of the measurements. Exemplary performers always meet the depth requirement exactly and never fail to get approval on the other measurements of accuracy. Exemplary performers must have good productivity rates (although Mike has no idea what *good* means in numerical terms) for the firms to make money. And exemplary performers always finish before the schedule deadline.

But no one knows what exemplary performance means in terms of crew size or mix of craft skills. Every crew seems to vary. And they use different tools and equipment some of the time. Exemplary performers, however, could be expected to waste a minimum of concrete and gravel.

4. Ready with his performance measurements, Mike sets out to collect the numbers he needs to *measure exemplar performance* and to

measure average performance. Over the next six weeks on the job, Mike gathers the numbers shown in Table 5.1.

The numbers in Table 5.1 show that Mike's measurements of accuracy turn out to be relatively unimportant, since they show no variation. Most of the measurements of productivity show substantial variations; Mike could not collect manhours for the formwork since it is normally done while preparing and grading. He combines placing and finishing since both of these tasks are done at the same time, usually by the same people. The schedule ratio, figured by calculating the percentage of work completed and dividing it by the percentage of workdays used out of the total workdays in the contract, shows the job staying slightly ahead of schedule. Manpower measurements prove more difficult, since the number of people working varies from week to

TABLE 5.1   Busten Poure's Performance Measurements

	A	B	C	D
1	Work measurement	Unit	Average	Exemplar
2				
3	*Accuracy*			
4	Slab depth	Inches	6 in	6 in
5	Gravel fill	OK, Not OK	OK	OK
6	Slope	OK, Not OK	OK	OK
7	Concrete mix	OK, Not OK	OK	OK
8	Finish	OK, Not OK	OK	OK
9				
10	*Productivity*			
11	Break	SY/MH	170	220
12	Remove	SY/MH	60	75
13	Haul	SY/MH	18	30
14	Prepare	SY/MH	19	25
15	Formwork	LY/MH	NA	NA
16	Place and finish	CY/MH	11	15
17				
18	*Schedule*			1
19	Progress ratio	%	1.06	1.08
20				
21	*Manpower*			
22	Av crew size	#/crew	10	NA
23	Foreman	#/crew	1	NA
24	Finishers	#/crew	3	NA
25	Drivers	#/crew	2	NA
26	Laborers	#/crew	4	NA
27	Overtime	MH/week	12	2
28				
29	*MTE*			
30	Concrete	CY/slab	5	4.9
31	Gravel	CY/slab	4.1	2.3
32	Tools	Type	NA	NA
33	Pavement breaker	Hours used	3	NA
34	Loader	Hours used	3	NA
35	Backhoe	Hours used	1	NA
36	Dump trucks	Hours used	20	NA

week among the crews, as does the craft makeup of the crews. Mike collects numbers for the average crew size and makeup but knows that more detailed numbers are needed. He wants to calculate productivity rates for different crew sizes and makeups in order to study the effect of crew size and makeup on productivity.

Lastly, in the category of materials, tools, and equipment (MTE), the measurements of materials show little wasted concrete (more or less is used in the curbs in order to empty the trucks) but substantial variation in gravel used. Tool use does not vary among the crews, but the number of hours they use their equipment does vary. Again, Mike decides that he needs to measure equipment usage for each crew in order to examine its effect on productivity.

5. Mike combines what he believes to be the important measurements from Table 5.1 in Table 5.2 to *compute the PARs* and *calculate the worth* of improved performance for each item. He obtains the PARs by dividing the average into the exemplar, except in the cases of overtime and gravel where, because of the units chosen for measurement, the exemplar is the *lower* number. In those two cases he must divide the lower number into the higher to get the PAR.

To compute worth, he estimates that about 200,000 SY of concrete remain to be replaced and that the job will run another 30 weeks. For rows 4 through 10, worth is calculated as the difference between completing the remaining 200,000 SY at the average and at the exemplar. In row 4, for example, it will take 1176 MH to break 200,000 SY working at 170 MH/SY but only 909 MH at the exemplar of 220 MH/SY.

TABLE 5.2   Busten Poure's Performance, PARs, and Worth

	A	B	C	D	E	F	G
1	Work measurement	Unit	Average	Exemplar	PAR	Worth	Unit
2							
3	*Productivity*						
4	Break	SY/MH	170	220	1.3	267	MH
5	Remove	SY/MH	60	75	1.3	667	MH
6	Haul	SY/MH	18	30	1.7	4444	MH
7	Prepare	SY/MH	19	25	1.3	2526	MH
8	Place and finish	SY/MH	11	15	1.4	4848	MH
9							
10	Average productivity	SY/MH	3.2	3.9	1.2	11218	MH
11							
12	*Manpower*						
13	Overtime	MH/week	12	2	6.0	1200	MH
14							
15	*MTE*						
16	Gravel	CY/slab	4.1	2.3	1.8	12414	CY

The difference is only 267 MH. The worth of overtime, in row 13, is calculated by figuring 30 weeks times 4 days per week (no overtime on Fridays) to get the days remaining. At 12 MH per day, overtime will amount to 1440 MH; at only 2 MH per day it will run only 240 MH, a difference of 1200 MH. The worth of gravel in row 16 comes from dividing the remaining 200,000 SY by 29, the number of square yards in a typical 13-ft by 20-ft square, and then multiplying by the number of cubic yards of gravel per square (the 4.1-CY average and the 2.3-CY exemplar). The difference between the two is very high, 12,414 CY.

Among the productivity items, the PAR and worth for hauling the broken slabs away stand out. So, too, do the PAR and worth for placing and finishing.

In row 10, column C, Mike computes an average overall productivity for both crews by dividing the total amount of concrete placed by the total number of manhours expended. He also goes back over his data to find the best performance by each crew in any one day. He averages the best from each of the four crews to get an "average exemplar" and enters this number in row 10, column D. From this he computes an overall job PAR of 1.2.

Overtime hours per crew per week offer a large PAR and enough potential manhour savings to make it worth looking into. He is also startled by the potential savings in gravel—over 12,000 CY. In watching the work during the day, he had not noticed such a large difference in gravel use.

6. Now Mike is ready to *apply the methods engineering model* to try to find the causes of the large PARs. He decides to start with the gravel since it seems less likely to be controversial. He asks the foremen at each of the three jobsites questions about how they decide how much gravel to use. They all tell him that they normally excavate about 6 in of the soil beneath the removed slab and replace it with compacted gravel. When he asks why, he is told that once, just as one crew started a pour, a county engineer walked across the foundation gravel and told them the foundation was too spongy and that he could not allow them to place concrete over it. So they had to stop the pour, excavate all the wet concrete along with the mud and gravel underneath, and replace it with compacted gravel. It was such a pain that, from now on, they almost always take out an extra 6 in to be on the safe side. Mike is aghast. For not only does it cost more for the gravel and the time spent moving and raking it, but at 8 yd of gravel per dump truck, Mike figures it will take an *extra* 1500 trips just to haul gravel to the jobsites! At an average of six trips per truck per day, it comes to 250 extra truck-days. With only 150 workdays remaining in

the contract (30 weeks times 5 days per week), this means that the jobs will need two more trucks—with drivers—to haul in all the extra gravel. All this just to "be on the safe side."

Applying the methods engineering model

Organizing what he is told about the gravel use into the format of the methods engineering model, Mike writes:

Questions	Findings
1. *Information*	
Do foremen know how much it costs to overexcavate the depth of the hole beneath the slabs?	No.
Do foremen get feedback on how deep the hole is?	Yes, they see it.
2. *Resources*	
Do foremen have the tools and equipment needed to excavate to the correct depth?	Yes.
3. *Incentives*	
Are foremen judged on how much gravel they use?	No.
Does the balance of incentives favor overexcavation?	Yes, foremen want to avoid underexcavation.
4. *Skills*	
Do foremen know how to control the depth of the excavation to avoid overexcavation?	Yes.
5. *Capacity*	
Are foremen able to control the operator running the excavation equipment?	Yes, normally they run the equipment themselves.
6. *Motives*	
Would foremen want to control excavation and gravel use if they knew how much it cost the job?	Yes.

Even though his formal write-up looks a little silly to him, it gives Mike confidence that he has not missed anything. It appears to him that foremen only need information concerning how much the overexcavation costs to get them to alter their work methods. (Along with a reminder, perhaps, from the contractor, telling them that she will start judging the foremen's performance on how well they can control costs and that it is better to risk reexcavation once in a while than to continue to waste gravel. Or better yet, test the gravel for sponginess *before* starting a pour.) At a conservative estimate of $15 per hour for each of the two extra drivers and another $50 per day per truck plus $20 per yard for gravel, Mike figures a potential savings of about $75,000. The cost to the contractor to get this savings? No more than five minutes with each foreman to explain the situation.

(Mike learns later that the contractor is not nearly so dumb. Overexcavation is the exception, not the rule. However, no real controls are used to minimize overexcavation, and Mike guesses it still costs the contractor tens of thousands of dollars each year.)

A second model application

Although Mike feels that he has made a dramatic discovery in improving work methods, his real aim is to study productivity, not material and equipment costs. So he constructs another formal methods engineering model, this time to troubleshoot crew productivity.

Questions	Findings
1. *Information*	
Do crews know what is expected of them?	Yes. Crews pour 300 SY/day.
Do foremen plan crew work ahead of time?	Yes. But work is very repetitive.
Do crews know how to perform as well as the exemplar?	Yes. Every crew has had exemplary days.
Do crews know how well they are performing relative to the exemplar?	Yes. They compare themselves to their past performances.
2. *Resources*	
Do crews have the equipment they need to perform well?	Yes.
Do crews have materials when they need them?	Yes. Waits for gravel and concrete are short.
Is equipment operated in a safe manner?	Yes.
3. *Incentives*	
Are wages contingent upon how well the crews perform?	No. Wages are set by contract.
Do crews receive nonmonetary rewards or recognition for exemplary performance?	No.
Do negative incentives operate against exemplary performance?	Yes. If crews seem to be finishing early, the foreman orders more concrete.
4. *Skills*	
Do crew members have the training and/or experience necessary for exemplary performance?	Yes.
5. *Capacity*	
Is the crew size optimum for best performance?	No. Crew sizes vary.
Does the mix of crafts promote exemplary productivity?	No. Craft mix varies.
Is weather protection necessary for exemplary productivity?	No.
Does traffic interfere with crew performance?	No.
6. *Motives*	
Do crews want to perform as well as the exemplar?	Yes. Crews take pride in doing well.

Crew methods

Mike's second model doesn't give the easy answers of his first. Here he must consider the relationship between the overall productivity of the crews (in terms of total square yards of output divided by total manhours of input) and the productivity of each phase of the work (such as breaking, hauling, grading, and finishing). Maximizing the productivity of any one of the subaccomplishments (breaking, for example) might lower the productivity of a related task (removing, for example). Therefore, Mike's analysis of work methods must take into account how each subaccomplishment relates to getting the whole job done.

To study overall crew performance, Mike makes charts of what each worker on the job does during a typical day. Table 5.3 shows one of Mike's charts analyzing the activities of the two 9-person crews, A and B. (Crew C, with 20 persons on Mike's third jobsite, is nearly a composite of A and B.) Crew A is composed of three finishers and three laborers, while Crew B has only two finishers and four laborers. Both crews work from 7:00 a.m. until 3:30 p.m., placing 300 SY of concrete paving. They normally form and grade in the afternoon, ready to place and finish the next morning when the air is cooler. (Also, by the time the crew leaves the job in the afternoon, the fresh concrete placed in the morning has usually set up enough to discourage neighborhood kids from writing in it.)

TABLE 5.3 Daily Activities for Two Paving Crews

	A	B	C	D	E	F	G	H	I	J
1		7:00	8:00	9:00	10:00	11:00	12:00	1:00	2:00	3:00
2	Crew A									
3	Foreman	Break and remove					Break and remove			
4	Finisher 1	Forms	Pour				Form			
5	Finisher 2	Forms	Pour				Form			
6	Finisher 3	Forms	Pour				Form			
7	Driver 1	Haul					Haul			
8	Driver 2	Haul					Haul			
9	Laborer 1	Grade	Pour			Grade	Grade		Clean up	
10	Laborer 2	Grade	Pour			Grade	Grade			
11	Laborer 3	Tractor	Pour			Tractor	Grade			
12										
13	Crew B									
14	Foreman	Break and remove					Break and remove			
15	Finisher 1	Pour					Form			
16	Finisher 2	Pour					Form			
17	Driver 1	Haul					Haul			
18	Driver 2	Haul					Haul			
19	Laborer 1	Pour					Grade		Clean up	
20	Laborer 2	Pour					Grade			
21	Laborer 3	Pour					Grade			
22	Laborer 4	Tractor					Tractor			

Crew differences

Mike then computes the productivity for each of the operations using an average of 300 SY per day per crew. He notes that the three finishers in Crew A do not usually work the full day. Two of them lose about an hour at the end of the day, while the third loses about a half-hour. Sometimes they stretch out the task of forming for the next day's pour, but more often than not they just work steadily to get it done, then knock off and sit in the shade watching the others complete their tasks. On both crews, the foreman operates the pavement breaker and the loader intermittently throughout the day. However he frequently must interrupt one task to give directions to drivers who are hauling away the broken pavement and returning with gravel. Or he jumps down from the pavement breaker to run the loader to fill a dump truck when it arrives, then resumes breaking. Mike notes that in both crews, the foreman-operator stays very busy, even helping out on the pours whenever an extra hand is needed.

The extra laborer in Crew B spends most of the day bringing gravel from stockpiles on the street to the holes and doing rough grading with the tractor. Crew B uses the tractor far more than Crew A, but much of the time the Crew B tractor operator sits waiting for other crew members to complete some other task. With only two finishers in Crew B, both must work steadily throughout the day in order to complete their assigned jobs.

Observations

Over the next six weeks, in collecting further measurements of crew productivity and in probing further the causes of variation, Mike makes the following observations:

- Crews work faster when concrete trucks are backed up, waiting to unload.

- When the foreman is busy elsewhere, workers waste much more time.

- Workers who are fast but do not care about quality have lower productivity than slower workers who make fewer mistakes and therefore have less rework to do.

- Crews always pace themselves to complete the pour (regardless of when they start) just before lunch. (By limiting themselves to 300 SY in the morning, there is no chance that they will have to do more in the afternoon, although they can do the 300 SY in less than two hours when they push it.)

- Crews lose time when drivers do not bring gravel when it is needed.

- As long as most of the crew members are working, no one wastes time, but if several people must stop to wait for something, then others will slow down or stop too.

- Drivers waste about a quarter of their day serving as taxis for the foremen, who must check on crew activities spread out over several streets. Drivers also lose time searching up and down streets for the foreman and the loader in order to pick up a fresh load of rubble.

The ideal crew

With this information and his measurements, Mike tries to design an "ideal crew" that he believes could always achieve exemplary productivity rates. After many false starts, he finally settles on a 15-person crew pouring 600 SY per day (3000 SY for the week) plus a 4-person crew working Saturdays to backfill and sod. Table 5.4 shows each task, the number of people assigned to it, and the hours per day each will work. Overtime hours (column D) count the Saturday work at time and a half. The total manhours for the week (column F) divided into the total amount placed for the week (column G) gives the expected average productivity rates in column H. Comparing column H with his measured exemplars in column I, Mike sees that the expected rates represent achievable goals.

Mike predicts that his ideal crew would regularly achieve a productivity rate of 4.6 SY/MH, *18 percent better than the measured exemplar*. This improvement is possible because Mike has redesigned the

TABLE 5.4 The Ideal Crew's Exemplar Productivity Rates

	A	B	C	D	E	F	G	H	I
1	Task	Persons	Hours/day	OT ?	Days/week	Total MH	Amount	Av unit rate	Exem
2									
3	Break	1	3	1	5	15	3000	200	
4	Remove	1	8	1	5	40	3000	75	
5	Haul	3	8	1	5	120	3000	25	
6	Place & finish	6	7	1	5	210	3000	14	
7	Formwork	6	1	1	5	30	3000	100	
8	Formwork	1	8	1	5	40	3000	75	
9	Grading	3	8	1	5	120	3000	25	
10	Cleanup	4	8	1.5	1	48	3000	63	
11	Supervision	1	5	1	5	25	NA	NA	
12									
13	Total					648	3000		
14	Average productivity (amount/MH)					4.6			
15	Crew size						15		

work methods to take maximum advantage of the individually recorded exemplars and to avoid the lost time normally experienced by crew members. Table 5.5 lays out the typical workday for the crew members.

Task assignments

In developing his ideal crew, Mike gives the following reasons for the number of people and their task assignments:

- *Supervision and breaking* would be the foreman's sole responsibilities. Since supervising a nine-person crew took up several hours of the foreman's time and, even then, the foreman was not always available when needed, Mike feels that the foreman needs more time for supervisory activities but could still operate the pavement breaker at least three hours each day. According to Mike's field measurements, the foreman could easily break up 600 SY of pavement in less than three hours, even with interruptions.

- *Removing* the broken pieces would require a full-time operator on the loader who could remove 75 SY per hour, or 600 SY per day. Operating the loader all day would also eliminate the time lost by drivers returning empty and searching for the foreman in order for him to reload their trucks.

- *Hauling* 300 SY per day required two drivers, but they did not work

TABLE 5.5 The Ideal Crew's Task Assignments

	A	B	C	D	E	F	G	H	I	J
1		7:00	8:00	9:00	10:00	11:00	12:00	1:00	2:00	3:00
2	Ideal Crew									
3	Foreman	Supervision		Break			Supervision			
4	Operator	Remove					Remove			
5	Finisher 1	Pour					Pour			Form
6	Finisher 2	Pour					Pour			Form
7	Finisher 3	Form					Form			
8	Driver 1	Haul					Haul			
9	Driver 2	Haul					Haul			
10	Driver 3	Haul					Haul			
11	Laborer 1	Pour					Pour			Form
12	Laborer 2	Pour					Pour			Form
13	Laborer 3	Pour					Pour			Form
14	Laborer 4	Pour					Pour			Form
15	Laborer 5	Grade					Grade			
16	Laborer 6	Grade					Grade			
17	Laborer 7	Grade					Grade			

all of the time, often waiting an hour for the loader to fill them. Therefore three drivers, with the full-time loader operator, should be able to haul 600 SY each day.

- *Pouring and finishing* 300 SY consistently took six people 3.5 hours (including cleanup). Therefore, the six ought to be able to do 600 SY in seven hours, leaving each an hour at the end of the day to help complete the formwork for the following day. In the event that all six were not needed for formwork, the four laborers could be reassigned to grading or some other end-of-the-day task (such as repositioning traffic barrels).

- *Forming* 300 SY usually took about one man-day: less if one person worked on it straight through, and more if the job was split up with interruptions for other tasks. One person working full-time on forming should be able to set the majority of the forms for 600 SY in a day, relying on help from others at the end of the day to complete the job. This task might rotate among the three finishers.

- *Grading,* plus backfilling, sodding, and street sweeping, normally kept three workers (including one with a tractor) busy for half a day (about 15 MH). Extending their task for the full day should complete the grading for 600 SY if they do not spend too much time on the backfilling and sodding tasks. Because of interruptions and the press of other work, crews seldom finished all the necessary backfilling and sodding by the end of each day. Often several people would stay overtime to complete it. Instead, Mike proposes to bring in a crew of four (a foreman who would double as a tractor operator, plus two laborers and a truck driver) on Saturdays to do all the backfilling and sodding for the past week's work. By postponing the backfilling and sodding during the week, the laborers and the tractor would be able to perform the grading and their other tasks more efficiently. In addition, the drivers would not be interrupted with sod requests during the week. Devoting Saturdays to this work would also permit the crew to do a better job and to deal immediately with any complaints from homeowners. Mike figures that the 32 hours of overtime for the extra day, although more than the 10 overtime hours per week that the crews now experience, would more than pay for itself by making the other operations during the week more efficient.

Productivity gains

Mike also considers that the labor agreement may require a second foreman for a 15-person crew, but at $1 per hour more in wages (making the operator a foreman), it is a relatively small cost for the anticipated gains. If Mike's ideal crew could really achieve an average weekly productivity of 4.6 SY/MH, it would be a 44 percent jump over their present average of 3.2 SY/MH. With 200,000 SY of concrete left to complete, it would take 62,000 MH at 3.2 SQ/MH and only 43,500 MH at 4.6 SY/MH, a savings of 18,500 MH. At an average wage rate of $15 per hour, the potential savings could reach $277,500. No small change.

Altered Incentives

Mike's analysis of crew size and makeup holds considerable promise for Busten Poure, Inc. In order to achieve the potential productivity gains, however, the crews may need additional environmental support in the form of altered incentives. Currently, the crews limit their production to 300 SY per day by pacing themselves. Placing concrete in the cooler mornings allows more rest time in the hotter afternoons. The proposed change in crews would extend concrete placement into the hottest part of the day, something crew members might be expected to resist. After all, what's in it for them? It seems that the change would only make their jobs harder without any offsetting gains. To achieve the expected high productivity, therefore, we must also look to altering the balance of incentives on the job so that crew members would *prefer to place 600 SY per day* rather than only 300.

Since, by contract, neither the work hours nor the pay scales can be changed, Busten Poure must look to on-the-job incentives. Two potential incentives come to mind. First, Mike noted that regardless of the time a pour started, concrete placement always finished before lunch. Crews took anywhere from 2 to 4.5 hours in the morning to place 300 SY. Their incentive for working faster in the morning was to avoid working in the heat of the afternoon. Suppose that Busten Poure's policy allowed the crew to quit working as soon as they met the 600-SY quota. In other words, as long as the crew could average 600 SY per day, no more would be asked of them. They would be free to relax in the shade for the rest of the day once the work was completed. With such an incentive to get the work done, it would not be surprising to find crews placing the entire 600 SY some mornings before lunchtime. In practice, however, there would be many additional tasks to complete in order to ready the site for the next day's pour—formwork, grading, and sweeping up loose gravel would continue throughout the afternoon, but perhaps at a much more relaxed pace. Such an "early quit" policy might not work, but at least it might be tried.

The second incentive lies in the scheduled Saturday overtime work. Many people like to work overtime because of the increased wage scale. Therefore, overtime work might be assigned to those people who both want it and who work well during the week. Overtime could be treated as an additional incentive, provided crew members desired the overtime work.

The larger picture

The performance engineering viewpoint adopted by Mike led him far beyond the traditional management analysis of jobsite performance. Mike discovered that in order to get the improved productivity he wanted, he would need to offer something in return. This balancing of costs and benefits frequently occurs when one attempts to engineer better performance. But even if Mike is unable to create his ideal crew, he has gained a very real sense of control over the job; he knows exactly the accomplishments and the methods that define jobsite performance.

A balance of consequences

While each job may require its own unique set of incentives, contractors must not overlook the importance of altered incentives in developing productive work methods for their crews. Increased productivity generally means doing the same job in fewer manhours. This saves the contractor money but costs the work force, in that they lose the work represented by the manhour savings. When the opportunity for increased productivity presents itself, contractors need to think in terms of how to share the potential savings with the labor force in order to be sure of getting the productivity increase. In other words, before changing work methods, ask, "What's in it for me?" from labor's point of view and then look for that new combination of incentives that will offset any new disincentives. Mike asks his ideal crew to produce more, but he also permits early quits and offers Saturday overtime. Is it enough? Will the work force gain enough to offset the pressures of higher productivity expectations? We do not know until we try it. But it is always this *balance of consequences* resulting from both positive and negative incentives that affects the workers' willingness to perform well—their motivation.

Job control

The performance audit provides a very powerful tool for job control. Contractors who institute a system of performance measurement, including calculations of worth, backed by the regular application of the methods engineering model, find that they gain increasing control over jobsite performance. Job control translates directly into higher profitability for the contractor and better construction for the owner. Job control also benefits the work force, for it places the onus of responsibility for performance where it belongs—directly on management. In the longer term, as management competence rises and construction becomes an attractive investment alternative, labor will benefit from both the increased work and the increased wages that result from continuing productivity gains.

Measurements and Estimates

Most contractors who track their productivity on a job do so by comparing their actual unit rates against their estimate. *Such comparisons can frequently mislead because of two common problems: errors and troubleshooting dead ends.* Errors arise if the estimate is wrong, the measurements of work progress and hours charged are wrong, or (as is often the case) both the estimate and the measurements are wrong. The second problem is more serious—what to do with the productivity comparisons. Finding that a task is taking more manhours than expected does not automatically lead to corrective actions. When a report shows excessive manhours charged to a task, it is not always easy to discover if the estimate is off, if the hours were incorrectly charged, or if productivity is really down. And if it is down, what should be done about it? Tracking job progress against estimates gives managers information about the work, but if estimates are used as comparison standards for controlling work, then contractors should understand the limitations of the information on which they base their decisions.

Measuring Productivity against Estimates

Since so many contractors use their estimates as a basis for judging field productivity, it seems worthwhile to review briefly some of the most common methods for comparing estimates to actual performance. Regardless of what method a contractor may use, however, estimates rarely provide good standards by which to evaluate job performance. Estimates normally reflect average performance over past jobs.

Rather than use their averages, contractors ought to set their performance goals according to their exemplars.

Estimated versus actual productivity

Table 6.1 shows a simple job report that compares estimated to actual productivity. Calculations of the percentage of manhours expended against the percentage of work completed are also included.

Table 6.1 tracks 10 classes of carpentry work items on a 192-unit condominum project consisting of 16 identical three-story buildings, each containing 12 condo units (four to a floor). Columns B, C, and D show the estimated amounts, manhours (MH), and unit rates for the job. Note that, on this project, the unit rates are figured as manhours per unit of installation, not as units per manhour as in earlier examples. Many contractors use estimates of manhours per unit in computing their bids; it is natural to continue using the same convention in the reports. Since one is the inverse of the other, using MH/units or units/MH makes no difference—except to remember that when using MH/units, as in Table 6.1, the *lower* the rate, the *more* productive the work. Therefore, as in the first item in row 4, "Floor joists and floor," because the *actual* rate of 18.2 MH/amt (column E) is *lower* than the *estimated* rate of 20.0 MH/amt (column D), the actual rate is *more* productive than the estimate.

The two central columns, D and E, directly compare estimated to actual productivity rates. Columns F and G show the actual manhours and amounts used to calculate the rates in column D. Columns H and I compute the percentage of work completed and the percentage of

TABLE 6.1 Comparison of Estimated to Actual Productivity

	A	B	C	D	E	F	G	H	I
1	Carpentry work item	Estimated				Actual		Percent compl	
2		Amount	MH	MH/amt	MH/amt	MH	Amount	Amount	MH
3									
4	*Formula*			*(C/B)*	*(F/G)*			*(G/B)*	*(F/C*
5									
6	10 Floor joists and floor	16	320	20.0	18.2	218	12	75%	6
7	20 Frame exterior walls	96	576	6.0	6.4	435	68	71%	7
8	30 Frame interior walls	384	1152	3.0	3.1	775	250	65%	6
9	40 Trusses and roofs	16	1344	84.0	68.0	612	9	56%	4
10	50 Stairs and decks	64	768	12.0	14.8	414	28	44%	5
11	60 Drywall	384	768	2.0	2.2	396	180	47%	5
12	70 Windows	672	672	1.0	0.9	378	420	63%	5
13	80 Exterior trim finish	32	256	8.0	5.0	80	16	50%	3
14	90 Interior doors & trim	96	1344	14.0	12.7	178	14	15%	1
15	00 Other	96	2304	24.0	29.1	1571	54	56%	6
16									
17	Total		9504			5058			5

manhours expended for each item. Comparing the numbers in columns D and E or in columns H and I shows how well the job is going for each of the 10 items, relative to the estimate.

Earned manhours

Another common method for reporting job progress against the estimate uses the concept of *earned manhours;* manhours are "earned" for completed work in place (or for the percentage of work completed). Table 6.2 provides an example of calculations of earned manhours. Multiplying the estimated unit rates (in manhours per unit) in column D by the amount of work completed (units) in column G gives the number of manhours earned for that particular task to date (in column H). Subtracting the actual number of manhours charged to a task in column F from the number of earned manhours in column H provides a ready indicator of job productivity in column I. If fewer manhours have been charged than have been earned, the task shows a positive number, indicating that the job is ahead for this task. Conversely, a negative number indicates productivity below the estimate. Adding all the earned hours and all the charged hours gives an overall indicator of job productivity relative to the estimate. In this case, the job is behind by 168 MH.

Table 6.2 uses the same information as shown in Table 6.1, but it calculates the earned manhours for each of the completed tasks instead of the percentage completed. Note that calculating earned manhours adds no new information to the report—it just provides a

TABLE 6.2   Comparison of Earned Manhours to Actual Manhours

	A	B	C	D	E	F	G	H	I
1		Estimated				Actual		Earned	MH
2	Carpentry work item	Amount	MH	MH/amt	MH/amt	MH	Amount	MH	diff
3									
4	*Formula*			*(C/B)*	*(F/G)*			*(G*D)*	*(H−F)*
5									
6	10 Floor joists and floor	16	320	20.0	18.2	218	12	240	22
7	20 Frame exterior walls	96	576	6.0	6.4	435	68	408	− 27
8	30 Frame interior walls	384	1152	3.0	3.1	775	250	750	− 25
9	40 Trusses and roofs	16	1344	84.0	68.0	612	9	756	144
10	50 Stairs and decks	64	768	12.0	14.8	414	28	336	− 78
11	60 Drywall	384	768	2.0	2.2	396	180	360	− 36
12	70 Windows	672	672	1.0	0.9	378	420	420	42
13	80 Exterior trim finish	32	256	8.0	5.0	80	16	128	48
14	90 Interior doors & trim	96	1344	14.0	12.7	178	14	196	18
15	00 Other	96	2304	24.0	29.1	1571	54	1296	− 275
16									
17	Total		9504			5058		4890	− 168

different (and perhaps easier) way to compare progress against the estimate.

Bogey standards

Other variations on the same measurement method calculate "bogey" manhours. A *bogey* is an estimated standard—as in golf, where one over par (a bogey) on every hole is the expected average. Par on every hole is closer to the exemplar for most serious players.

Depending on how they are calculated, bogey manhours tell how many hours a task should take to complete (essentially the estimate), how many hours the task ran over or under the estimate (actual manhours subtracted from estimated manhours), or how many manhours should be required to complete the task (the amount of work left to do multiplied by the estimated unit rate in manhours per unit). Some firms have developed their own variations on such measurements. Some even compute bogeys for the amount of work being placed rather than for the manhours charged or earned. None of the alternative methods produces any greater accuracy than the accuracy of the original estimate combined with the accuracy of the field counts of work completed and manhours charged. (Some contractors estimate and measure in great detail, hoping that, by using many numbers, the errors will tend to cancel each other out so that the resulting aggregate measurements will be accurate indicators of overall job progress.)

Weighted work units

Rather than giving credit for *manhours earned* for each unit of completed work, some contractors give credit for *work units earned* instead. Weighting factors convert measurements of each work item into a standard measurement of work accomplishment. Converting estimated and completed amounts of work into standard work units is usually more complicated than using an earned-manhours system. Table 6.3 shows how the information in Table 6.2 might be displayed as weighted work units instead.

In Table 6.3, the estimated amounts, manhours, and manhours per amount in columns B, C, and D, respectively, remain unchanged from Table 6.2. The numbers for actual manhours per amount, manhours, and amounts (now in columns G, H, and I) also remain unchanged. Two new columns, E and F, have been inserted to show a *weighted amount* and a *manhours per weighted amount* in the estimate. The weighted amount in column E is simply the actual amount in column B multiplied by the estimated unit rate in column D. Note that, in this simple case, the resulting number exactly equals the manhour esti-

TABLE 6.3 Using Weights to Convert Amounts of Work into Standard Units

A	B	C	D	E	F	G	H	I	J	K	L
1			Estimated						Actual		
2				Weighted	MH per					Weighted	MH per
3 No.	Amt	MH	MH/amt	amount	wtd amt	MH/amt	MH	Amt	Weight	amount	wtd amt
4											
5			(C/B)	(B*D)	(C/E)	(H/I)				(I*J)	(H/K)
6											
7 10	16	320	20.0	320	1.0	18.2	218	12	20	240	0.91
8 20	96	576	6.0	576	1.0	6.4	435	68	6	408	1.07
9 30	384	1152	3.0	1152	1.0	3.1	775	250	3	750	1.03
10 40	16	1344	84.0	1344	1.0	68.0	612	9	84	756	0.81
11 50	64	768	12.0	768	1.0	14.8	414	28	12	336	1.23
12 60	384	768	2.0	768	1.0	2.2	396	180	2	360	1.10
13 70	672	672	1.0	672	1.0	0.9	378	420	1	420	0.90
14 80	32	256	8.0	256	1.0	5.0	80	16	8	128	0.63
15 90	96	1344	14.0	1344	1.0	12.7	178	14	14	196	0.91
16 00	96	2304	24.0	2304	1.0	29.1	1571	54	24	1296	1.21
17											
18		9504		9504	1.0		5058			4890	1.03

mate in column C. Column F then computes the weighted unit rates for each item by dividing the estimated manhours in column C by the weighted amounts in column E. *All the weighted unit rates are equal,* in this case equal to 1.0. In every case, the real amount of work to be accomplished has been converted into standard units of work (given as weighted amounts) by a weighting factor (here the estimated unit rate).

Now, as the job progresses, actual measurements of work accomplished are collected (as shown in column I). For each item, the actual amounts are multiplied by the weighting factor for that item (repeated in column J) to give the number of standardized work units "earned"—the weighted amount shown in column K. Thus, for example, a crew that has completed 12 floor joists and flooring (row 7, column I) would be credited with 240 units of work in column K (12 times the weighting factor of 20). A crew that completed framing 68 exterior walls (row 8, column I) would be credited with 408 units of work in column K (68 times their weighting factor of 6). Now it becomes a simple matter to compare the relative productivity of work on different items. Divide the weighted amount of work that each crew completed by the actual number of manhours charged to each crew to get their weighted productivity rate (shown in column L). A rate in column L that is higher than the "standard" rate of 1.0 (given in column F) means that the crew is less productive than expected; conversely, a rate below 1.0 means that the crew is doing better than the estimate. (If unit rates are calculated by dividing manhours into units instead of units into manhours, then, of course, a rate above 1.0 would mean better-than-expected productivity.)

The apparent complexity of a weighted-amount system may be justified in circumstances where a contractor finds it desirable to "equalize" workloads among crews doing vastly different tasks. A "work point" system that credits standardized work units for completion (or, frequently, for partial completion) of complicated, highly varying, or intermittent tasks can help management track productivity and make useful comparisons among tasks. In Table 6.3, for example, one may add all the actual manhours charged to date (column H) and add all the weighted amounts of work completed to date (column K) and then, by dividing the amount into the manhours, determine an overall productivity rate for the job as a whole—given as 1.03 at the bottom of column L. In addition, by dividing the total weighted amount of work in the estimate (column E) into the total weighted amount of work completed (column K), one can quickly get the percentage of work completed on the job. (In this case it is 4890/9504 = 51 percent, which can be directly compared to the percentage of manhours expended to date, 53 percent, given in Table 6.1.)

Limits of accuracy

The often convoluted calculations of a weighted-amount system, however, offer no more information than the earned-manhours system, just a different way of arriving at the numbers in Table 6.2 or the straight reporting system in Table 6.1. For example, from the earned hours shown in column H of Table 6.2, one can also calculate the percentage of work completed by dividing the estimated manhours into the earned manhours (4890/9504 = 51 percent). One can also get an overall productivity factor for the job by dividing the earned manhours into the actual manhours to date (5058/4890 = 1.03). Both systems give the same numbers.

The success of either system, however, depends upon the accuracy of the numbers used to weight each work item or to compute the number of earned hours. Rarely is the estimate good enough to provide credible numbers that will withstand the criticism of field crews. When an earned-hours or weighted-amount system is used to provide feedback to the field, contractors need to take extra care in chosing the conversion numbers. Advice from experienced people, averages from other jobs, or even asking crew foremen how to assign different weights to their work will help produce believable (and therefore useful) reports.

Graphing the trends

However one chooses to measure the unit rates, collecting these measurements weekly and comparing them to the estimate will soon reveal trends in the work. These trends may be graphed in order to convey a visual history of job progress. Suppose, in the example above (row 9 of Table 6.1), that we have computed the actual unit rates for trusses and roofs each week for the past 10 weeks. Figure 6.1 graphs the weekly rates to show the trend relative to the estimate.

The straight horizontal line at 84 MH per unit represents the estimate; the dropping weekly rate shows the actual productivity on the job. Note, however, that because productivity rates are measured in manhours per unit of completed work, the *lower* the rate, the *better* the job; therefore, the downward trend in the weekly rate is good. However, because many people associate improving productivity with a rising graph line, some graphs of productivity use rates measured in units placed per manhour (as used throughout the earlier chapters). Graphing the units per manhour will show improvements in productivity as rising trends, and losses as downward trends. In reading graphs of productivity trends, be careful to check whether good means up or down.

Estimates as performance standards

In spite of the recognized shortcomings of estimates, many contractors use their estimated productivity rates as standards for field performance. Yet think about how average productivity rates are established for use in estimating. Measurements of actual performance are collected from many jobs and averaged. When a contractor uses this average as a performance standard and falls below it, pressures build to improve field performance. Conversely, when field rates exceed the

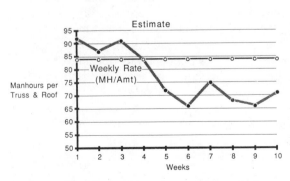

Figure 6.1   Weekly trend in unit-rate measurements.

estimate, everyone believes the job is going well. Because contractors tend to focus their efforts on bringing poor productivity rates up to the average (as represented by the estimate) rather than on pushing some good rates far up beyond the average, chances are that, over time, more rates will fall below the average than will exceed it. This means that field unit-rate averages will tend to be lower than the baseline estimates. But because contractors use measurements of their current performance to update their baseline rates, over time their *average rates will worsen*. And so will their performance based on using the estimates as standards. This feedback between field measurements and estimating can spiral downward, sometimes far enough to put contractors out of business.

Some contractors use cost estimates as standards for performance. They believe (and with considerable justification) that if the weekly or monthly costs charged to a job fall within the estimate, then the work is going well and the job will result in a profit. But job costs must not be confused with job productivity. Actual costs can vary from the estimated costs as a result of many factors that have no bearing on jobsite performance. Materials prices, for example, may be lower than estimated. Or unusually fine weather may speed progress ahead of schedule. If contractors look only at the cost data from such jobs, the jobs may appear to be in good shape *even if productivity is terrible*. Tracking job costs is important for accounting purposes, but comparing the actual job costs to the estimate seldom gives enough detailed information to permit field supervisors to troubleshoot for productivity improvements. Too much attention given to job costs loses sight of productivity—and of the methods to improve it continually.

Remember just what the estimate represents. It is the expected *average* performance. Whether the estimated unit rates are based on handbooks or past experience or a combination of both, average performance is seldom an acceptable performance standard. Only exemplar performance provides a useful standard. And estimates rarely identify exemplar-performance expectations. We applaud jobs that come in on time and under budget, but such applaudable results may conceal the true, underlying performance. On-time and under-budget jobs frequently tell us more about the fat in the estimate than they do about how well management and labor worked together to produce an exemplar performance.

To illustrate the difference between estimated, average, and exemplar productivity rates, let us examine how one estimator measured all three.

Condo Constructors, Inc.

Condo Constructors, Inc., a carpentry general contractor, specializes in multiunit apartment construction. One project, Riverside Manor, includes 16 identical three-story frame buildings, each with 12 apartment units (four to a floor). After 20 weeks of work on Riverside, Condo was over the estimated manhours (but still on schedule). Looking at the high number of repetitive tasks on the project, Jim Johnstone, Condo's aggressive president, decided to try to measure field productivity for the first time. Maybe, he thought, if he knew where the problems were he could do something to pull the project out of the red.

Mr. Johnstone also wants to try giving feedback to his field foremen but is afraid to share the estimates with them. He fears that if his crews learn what the estimate is, they will only work to meet the estimate and never do any better. Besides, if the estimates get to the field, who knows where they will go from there. He shudders to think of his competition (or even the project owner) getting hold of his manhour estimates. Mr. Johnstone discusses what he wants with Jerry Albume, one of Condo's estimators and the one who did the Riverside Manor estimate. He gives Jerry the task of measuring and tracking productivity at Riverside Manor in a way that will provide the project crews with feedback yet not reveal sensitive estimating information. Jerry takes the job with some misgiving; he thinks Mr. Johnstone's real reason in having him measure productivity may be to prove Jerry's estimate wrong.

The job to date

Jerry first looks through his files for the estimates he did for Riverside. He lays out the eight work tasks and codes on an electronic spreadsheet as shown in Table 6.4. In column B he enters the number of work items in each task for a single building; for example, each

TABLE 6.4 Tasks and Manhour Estimates for Riverside Manor

	A	B	C	D	E	F
1	Code and task	Amt/bldg	Total amt	Est MH/amt	Total est MH	Av MH/bldg
2						
3	*Formula*		*(B*16)*		*(C*D)*	*(E/16)*
4						
5	10 Floors	3	48	30.00	1440	90
6	20 Exterior walls	72	1152	3.50	4032	252
7	30 Interior walls	96	1536	6.25	9600	600
8	40 Roofs	2	32	160.00	5120	320
9	50 Exterior trim	4	64	57.50	3680	230
10	60 Interior trim	12	192	54.00	10368	648
11	70 Decks & stairs	24	384	26.00	9984	624
12	80 Doors	12	192	9.25	1776	111
13						
14	Total				46000	2875

building has three floors and 72 exterior-wall panels. Multiplying the number of items times 16 buildings gives the total number of work items in column C. Jerry enters his estimate for the number of manhours required to complete a single work item in column D and, multiplying it by the total number of work items from column C, gets the total estimated manhours for each item in column E. Jerry had previously estimated a total of 46,000 MH for the Riverside project. Dividing the total estimated manhours in column E by the number of buildings (16) gives the average estimated manhours per building for each of the eight tasks.

Next Jerry turns to the file for the daily time sheets that Condo's foremen at Riverside turn in for their crews. They charge all manhours to one of the eight company cost codes for this job and to the specific building on which the work was done. Thus the past time sheets record the manhours on each task for each building. Jerry goes through all the past time sheets and gathers the hours charged to each task and each building so far. Table 6.5 shows his work as an extension of Table 6.4. He includes in column I the field count of the number of buildings completed so far and, by multiplying this count by the number of work items per building (column B), gets the number of items completed (column J). Dividing the amount in column J by the total number of items to do from column C gives the percentage of work completed so far (column K). As he glances down the numbers in column J, it seems to Jerry that the job is about half-finished.

Going through the time sheets, Jerry totals the manhours charged to each of the eight tasks by the foremen. They have expended a total of 22,826 MH on Riverside, 50 percent of the manhour estimate. Jerry notes that tasks 20 and 50 have already expended nearly all their es-

TABLE 6.5   Amount Completed and Manhours Expended to Date

	H	I	J	K	L	M
1	Task code	Bldgs done	Amt done	% done	MH to date	% MH used
2						
3			(B*I)	(J/C)		(L/E)
4						
5	10	10.0	30	63%	652	45%
6	20	9.0	648	56%	3961	98%
7	30	8.5	816	53%	3882	40%
8	40	9.0	18	56%	3157	62%
9	50	7.0	28	44%	3298	90%
10	60	6.0	72	38%	3419	33%
11	70	6.0	144	38%	3545	36%
12	80	7.0	84	44%	912	51%
13						
14	Total				22826	50%

timated manhours yet are only half-completed, while tasks 10 and 30 appear to be ahead of his estimate. How could he have been so far off, he wonders?

Finding worth

Next Jerry extends his spreadsheet farther to the right (Table 6.6) to calculate the average number of manhours spent on each of the eight task codes so far (column P). He figures the average manhours per task for a single building by dividing the manhours to date (column L) by the number of buildings completed (column I). By carefully examining the time sheets, Jerry finds the single example of each task done in the fewest number of manhours (column Q). (In nearly every instance, the exemplar performance occurred on different buildings; Jerry notes in column R the number of the building that showed the exemplar.) The sum of the numbers in column Q is 2225 MH, the time it would take to finish one complete building if all the work could be done at the exemplar unit rates.

Table 6.6 gives the results of Jerry's calculations as he figures the worth and PAR for each of the tasks. In column S, Jerry subtracts column Q (the best) from column P (the average) to get the difference between the crews' average and their best. This represents the number of manhours that they *might* save on each building *if* they could do the work at their best rates instead of at their average rates. The potential savings comes to 850 MH per building.

Comparing his estimate of 2875 MH per building (row 14, column F, in Table 6.4) to the average to date of 3075 MH per building tells Jerry that either his estimate was low or else jobsite productivity is

TABLE 6.6   Manhour History and Projections for Riverside Manor

	O	P	Q	R	S	T	U	V
1	Task	Av	Best	Best	MH dif	Bldg	MH	PAR
2	code	MH/bldg	MH/bldg	bldg	ference	left	worth	
3		(L/I)			(P–Q)	(16–I)	(S*T)	(P/Q)
4								
5	10	65	45	3	20	6.0	121	1.45
6	20	440	250	4	190	7.0	1331	1.76
7	30	457	410	2	47	7.5	350	1.11
8	40	351	250	5	101	7.0	705	1.40
9	50	471	340	2	131	9.0	1180	1.39
10	60	570	475	6	95	10.0	948	1.20
11	70	591	385	5	206	10.0	2058	1.53
12	80	130	70	7	60	9.0	543	1.86
13								
14	Total	3075	2225		850		7237	1.38

not as good as he expected. But looking at the exemplar performance of only 2225 MH per building (row 14, column Q) suggests that his estimate may actually have been too fat; the crews can obviously do better.

Column T lists the number of buildings for which tasks remain to be done; column U multiplies the manhour difference in column S by the number of buildings in column T to get the total number of manhours that *might* be saved *if* the remainder of the buildings could be completed at the crews' best rates. The total potential savings comes to 7237 MH.

The last column, V, shows the performance ability ratio (PAR), which is simply the best performance (column Q) divided into the average performance (column P). The higher the PAR, the greater the difference between average and best, and therefore the greater the chance of finding methods to improve the average and bring it closer to the best. (If the PAR were close to 1, meaning little difference between average and best, it would be far harder to squeeze the gap smaller. A large PAR points to a larger gap and therefore to a greater ability to improve performance.)

In comparing columns U and V, Jerry sees that the highest PAR, 1.86 for code 80, doors, has a potential worth of only 543 MH. The largest worth, 2058 MH for code 70, decks and stairs, has a relatively high PAR of 1.53, so it offers a good target for improvement. The next best bet for improvement efforts appears to be code 20, exterior walls, with a worth of 1331 MH and a high PAR of 1.76.

Walls and decks

Jerry highlights the two primary work tasks that appear to offer the biggest opportunities for improvement: task 20, exterior walls, and task 70, decks and stairs. Both would afford considerable manhour savings if the remainder of the work could be done at exemplar rates, and both exhibit high PARs. Jerry next visits the jobsite to observe the work at all tasks more closely and to look specifically for reasons for the large variations in the performance of tasks 20 and 70. Task 20, exterior walls, requires a work crew with a crane to unload prefabricated wall panels from a truck and place them on the foundation walls. (Another subcontractor places the concrete foundations; Condo frames the floors over the basements before setting the exterior walls.)

In looking over the past time sheets, Jerry had kept note of the number of people employed on each task during each day. The number working on exterior walls varied considerably; the average was between five and six, but eight had worked on the walls the week the best record was set on building 4. Jerry watches as a six-person crew unloads and sets exterior walls on building 10. One person operates the crane, two work on the truck attaching walls to the slings, and three work to set and brace the walls. While these three maneuver the wall into place and nail up temporary bracing to hold it before releasing the slings, the other three wait. Then, while the crane picks another panel, the three on the foundation wait. Jerry sees only about 50 percent productivity with a six-person crew. He wonders, how can eight people be *more* productive?

Next Jerry watches the carpenters framing the cantilevered decks. Each unit has two decks, one serving as an entrance porch (with a stairway to it) and the other serving as a private outdoor space off the kitchen and dining area. Usually a single carpenter works to build a deck from precut lumber supplied to the site by Condo. But not all the lumber fits exactly right, Jerry notices. In fact, nearly half of it needs to be cut to fit; the irregular edges of the exterior walls do not line up evenly with the L-shaped decks. Now he sees why task 70 seems to have overrun his estimate so much. He expected that all the precut lumber would fit exactly.

Looking for exemplar performance

Later, talking with the project superintendent, Jerry learns that the five foremen on the job not only run their crews but also work alongside them. This means that foremen prefer smaller crews, since it means less time spent on giving directions and overseeing someone else's work. The two more experienced foremen on the job regularly work crews of only two or three people; the younger foremen often get "stuck" with six or eight people working under them. Every morning the foremen tell their carpenters what to work on and then let them go off and do it with little supervision. Sometimes, when the foremen need an extra hand, they grab whichever worker is handy to help.

"What about setting the exterior walls?" Jerry asks. "How many people do you use for that?" The superintendent describes the operation Jerry had watched this morning, then adds, "If we have two or three extra guys, then we do it differently. We have them hold the wall in place as soon as we set it so the crane can let go and swing back for another panel. By the time the crane gets back with the next one, the five or six guys on the floor have the last one set and braced. But this means we've got to pull guys off other jobs, which slows us down." Jerry understands now why productivity is so much higher with eight people; the work proceeds more quickly without the time spent waiting for the crane between panels. Pulling workers off the task-oriented individual work to set panels should not slow the job at all. It seems to Jerry that foremen only decide in the morning, after they have gotten their crew for the day, what work they will do. It all appears very informal and unplanned.

"Well, how about decks and stairs?" asks Jerry. "How do you normally do those?" The superintendent patiently explains that decks and stairs are "fill-in" work. "Anybody can do those by themselves anytime they haven't got anything else to do that requires a crew. Walls, partitions, and roofs, for example, require several guys to work together. Decks don't," he emphasizes as he grabs his lunch pail to leave for the day, thinking the real reason the estimator is out on the job is to prove the estimate correct and the work force lazy.

The next day Jerry again pays particular attention to the deck work. (Jerry thinks the superintendent seems to be avoiding him but can't figure out why.) In most instances, the carpenters do work alone, seemingly at random around the buildings. Feeling the cold wind, Jerry realizes that they all pick decks on the sunny side of the buildings to stay warmer in the chill late-winter weather. In one case he sees two people working on a single deck. A woman with a power saw cuts lumber and hands it up to a carpenter working on the first level. The man on the deck is busy, measuring and nailing. But the woman with the saw works less than half the time, standing and waiting for the man up above to call out the next dimension. Since the symmetrical building plans have at least two sets of decks right next to each other, Jerry can see that one person with a saw could easily support two carpenters working side by side on adjacent decks. Maybe that's how they set the low best record of 385 MH for all the decks on building number 5, he thinks. But to keep it up means assigning a crew with a foreman to organize the work instead of doing decks on a hit-or-miss basis as fill-in work.

Building a composite building

After observing the work in the field, Jerry realizes that his estimate does not provide a very good basis for judging the weekly performance of the crews. In some cases his estimate is wrong, and in other cases the crews are regularly doing better than he had estimated they could. If he compares their average productivity with his estimated productivity, the crews will look so far behind that they may just give up trying to improve. Although their current productivity is better than their average, it is still not nearly as good as their exemplar. To show the superintendent and his field work force that they are improving but that they need to continue to improve, Jerry must compare their current weekly performance to their best performance.

To make this comparison, Jerry needs three numbers for each of the past eight weeks. First, he gets the average-to-date manhours per building from row 14, column P, in Table 6.6. The second number is the average manhours per building for each week. To get this, Jerry must count the manhours and amounts installed for each of the eight items for each week and compute the average number of manhours it took that week to complete each task. (These numbers look very similar to the numbers in columns P and Q in Table 6.6.) By adding them together, he calculates how long it would have taken that week to have completed a single building at that week's unit rates. Lastly, Jerry takes the best weekly average manhours per building from row 14, column Q, in Table 6.6. The three numbers represent the manhours required to complete a single building working at three different rates—the average-to-date, the current week's, and the exemplar. Table 6.7 shows his electronic-spreadsheet layout for the numbers.

In Table 6.7, Jerry tracks the average number of hours per building (starting with week 15) in column B. Column C records the number of hours per building for the current week. In column D he keeps track of the best building records, made up of a composite of the best records for each of the eight individual tasks. He then calculates a performance index for current and best performance in columns E and F. The index is merely the current or best divided by the estimate (2895 MH per building).

Plotting the results

Back in the office at the end of the day, Jerry gets ready to report to Mr. Johnstone in the morning. According to his measurements and his on-site observations, he thinks he can build a convincing case for a potential savings of 3000 MH on the job, enough to pull it back into the

TABLE 6.7   Records of Current and Best Performance

	A	B	C	D	E	F
10		Average	Current	Best	Current	Best
11	Week	building	building	building	index	index
12						
13	*Formula*				*(C/2895)*	*(D2895)*
14						
15	15	3233	3111	2572	1.07	0.89
16	16	3254	3157	2572	1.09	0.89
17	17	3218	3098	2466	1.07	0.85
18	18	3169	2877	2441	0.99	0.84
19	19	3199	2923	2362	1.01	0.82
20	20	3125	2755	2296	0.95	0.79
21	21	3075	2612	2225	0.90	0.77
22	22	3092	2689	2225	0.93	0.77

black (and save his estimate). He believes that if foremen on the job get feedback each week as to how well they are doing relative to the best that they have ever done, it would help them think about finding more efficient methods to get the work done. They *can* do productive work, it's just that they never know *which* of the many methods they use are the most productive. So Jerry designs a simple graph on which he plots the current week's productivity index and the exemplar (as measured by manhours charged divided by the estimated manhours). To make sure that none of the numbers reveals any sensitive information to "outsiders", he decides to subtract 0.6 from his performance indices to get the numbers he will graph. The result is a number that fits on the graph easily between 0 and 0.5. Figure 6.2 shows his results.

The chart in Figure 6.2 plots the current week's performance and the best recorded performance against an index number that represents actual manhours per building divided by the estimated manhours. The lower the lines on the chart go, the better the job. Jerry wants the foremen to see how well they have performed at times (their exemplar) as compared to how well they do each week. The narrower the gap between their best and their current, the better they are doing.

After seeing Jerry's work, Mr. Johnstone decides to send the graph of weekly performance out to the foremen at the Riverside site. Knowing how well their crews are performing relative to how well they can do will provide valuable feedback without giving away any of the numbers in the estimate. Mr. Johnstone never even comments on the possible shortcomings of Jerry's original estimate, much to Jerry's relief.

However one compares actual productivity measurements to estimates, whether by tables or graphs, the same fundamental problems

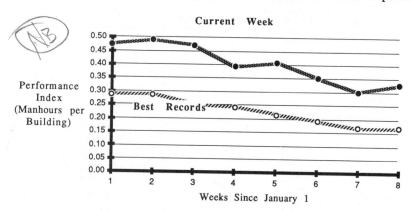

Figure 6.2 Current and exemplar productivity at Riverside Manor.

arise: How good are the estimates, and how does one find the cause of the problem in order to take corrective action? To see the problem a little clearer, let us reexamine the lost-time and work-time distinction discussed in Chapter 3.

Lost-Time Accounting

As noted earlier, every job experiences some lost time. No foreman can run a crew without losing some time somewhere. It may be caused by extra minutes spent unloading a truck because no one else was around to do it. It may come from work interruptions caused by letting another trade gain access to a restricted work space. Or a change order may cause it by forcing people to rework an item they thought was finished. In whatever form lost time appears, foremen must account for it in some fashion. After all, they must fill out (or sign off) regular time sheets for their work force. Each individual will charge the full number of hours spent at the jobsite, whether the time was worked or lost. Now if foremen (or individual craftsmen) are required to charge these hours to the type of work they did, such as the work-code items in Tables 6.1 and 6.2, then where do the lost hours go? If there is no explicit code for charging lost time, it will, of necessity, stay buried in the work time and be charged to one or more of the work items. But which one?

Flexibility in accounting

Now most foremen are smart enough to recognize that although they must account for the lost time somewhere, they don't necessarily have to account for it exactly as it occurred. A certain amount of leeway exists. After all, if a craftsman is called away from work while hanging doors to help unload a truck, does the hour spent unloading the truck need to be charged to hanging doors? Or can it be charged to, say, windows or drywall or any of the other items the craftsman works on during the week? The option is usually open, and foremen take advantage of it to charge lost-time hours to whatever work codes will do them the least harm.

For example, suppose a foreman is behind on hanging doors. Over the past several weeks, the manhours charged to doors have exceeded the estimate relative to the number of doors actually installed. Crew productivity on doors looks terrible, and the project superintendent has let the foreman know how bad it is. So, if the foreman has an option as to where to charge lost hours, will they go to doors? No way. The lost hours will be charged against the work that is going well, for which the foreman appears to be ahead. Only hours that must be charged to doors (because they were actually spent working on doors) will be charged to doors. Hours that can be charged elsewhere (because they were not spent working on doors and it is unclear just what item they were spent on) will be charged elsewhere. This shift in manhour charges will *make good rates look worse than they really are and bad rates look better.*

Long-term bias

Now if foremen on every jobsite exercise a small, but noticeable, influence on how the hours are charged on a job, then they insert a bias into the measurements of actual productivity rates from the job. Foremen will tend, over time, to charge their hours in such a way as to make their actual unit rates come out closer to the estimate. Shifting lost hours away from their poor rates will improve these poor rates, but at the expense of hurting their better rates. A sort of balance comes about as all rates tend to converge toward the estimate.

But what do contractors base their estimates on? Why, on their past experience, of course, as recorded in their field measurements of actual unit rates (or in handbooks made up of measured averages from many contractors). So when foremen bias their reporting slightly to avoid looking bad relative to the estimate, over the long run they succeed in confirming the estimate as correct! After all, the estimate must be correct because ongoing measurements from every job tend to confirm the estimate (or close to it).

In fact, the estimate for any single work item may be totally wrong. But, taken together, the errors cancel out and the total manhour estimate may be reasonably accurate for most jobs. The estimating errors go both ways. For every item consistently underreported on a job, a foreman also has an item consistently overreported. Not because anyone knows that one is over and one is under, but just because the errors in the estimate force a bias into the subsequent field reports. (Not only foremen, but even project managers have been known to "doctor" the field reports to get closer agreement to the estimate.)

One result of this consistent bias in reporting and in estimating is that *few, if any, of the estimated unit rates for individual items provide realistic or useful standards by which to judge on-site performance and productivity.* Great care taken in setting up an accurate field measurement system frequently comes to grief when field reports show actual work at wide variance from the estimates. The problem here is neither the estimate nor the field measurements; the problem lies in trying to compare the two.

Troubleshooting from estimates

In spite of the limitations of comparing actual field productivity to estimated productivity, the practice is widespread. Yet, as we have seen, the accuracy of such comparisons may be largely illusory. The second problem, after the issue of accuracy, is how to troubleshoot the job when actual productivity rates lag behind the estimates. When the field measurements do not confirm the estimate, what does one do about it? If top management responds by putting more pressure on foremen to boost on-site productivity without knowing what the problem is, the result may be that foremen merely start reporting the numbers that management wants to see without actually changing any of their work methods. Contractors who play such numbers games on their jobs have little, if any, impact on actual field productivity.

Roads to Ruin

J&J Mechanical Contracting, Inc. decided at the last minute to bid a shopping mall and office complex planned for one of the nearby suburban communities. As with most of their bids, the Office-Mall Project, as it became known, was put together hurriedly in a few days. J&J's experienced estimators worked by hand, not yet having been introduced to the power of computers for assistance in preparing estimates and bids. The final bid, for about $4 million, included 40,000 MH of pipefitter work. When J&J, surprisingly, got the contract, Sid Beckman, a young gung-ho engineer with the company, was named project manager. Sid and the estimators immediately went back over the estimate, double-checking the materials takeoff for ordering. At the time no one thought to recheck the estimated unit rates (figured in manhours per foot of installed pipe according to pipe size).

Lack of detail

Each of the four piping subsystems had been estimated separately: chilled water, low- and high-pressure steam, and gas lines. The unit-rate figures came right out of the handbook, modified according to J&J's past-experience factors. Although the estimate was typical, it lacked several details that Sid found critical later in the job:

- The amount of off-site prefabrication expected to be done in J&J's fab shop was not calculated separately.
- The quantity takeoffs and the expected unit rates for the mall and the office building were lumped together as average unit rates for both.

• The manhours for supervision and overhead were included in the gross unit rates for each pipe size rather than figured separately.

Job layout

Figure 6.3 diagrams the plan of the job. The 1000-ft length of the mall contained long ground-level chases at the rear for the piping. Placing piping in long runs at grade normally requires far fewer manhours than does more complicated horizontal or vertical work. Thus the competitive unit rates for all pipe sizes used by the estimators reflected an assumption that work would proceed smoothly in the long chases.

At the pre-job conference with the general contractor, Sid discovered, to his despair, two job conditions that could significantly undercut the expected high productivity of the piping work. First, the phasing of the civil work (due to demolition of an existing structure) required starting at both ends of the mall and working toward the center. Sid saw that this would split his work force in two, causing problems in communication, materials storage, supervision, and coordination. Second, as shown in Figure 6.3, two roadways through the building were required to be kept open during construction to allow passage of U.S. Postal Service vehicles to and from the existing building behind the mall. (The post office would later move into new quarters at the end of the mall building.) As these two roadways cut directly across the mechanical chases, Sid's vision of long, uninterrupted piping runs evaporated. The piping work would have to stop and start at each temporary roadway until the general contractor could complete an alternative access road around the east end of the office. Because of restricted site conditions, this alternative roadway

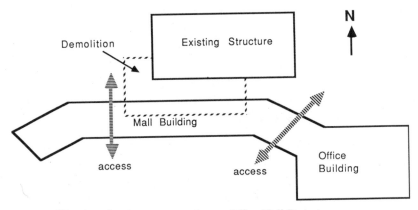

Figure 6.3   Site plan showing access roadways: Office-Mall Project.

could not be finished until the office building's structural frame and exterior cladding were complete. Frantically rechecking the bid documents, Sid found the reference to the two roadways in the general conditions. When he confronted the estimators with the roadway reference, they shrugged it off. Sure they had seen it (so they claimed). It wasn't such a big deal; Sid should be able to work around it.

To manage the pipefitter crews effectively, Sid brought in two general foremen, one for the office area and one for the mall. Since the large boiler and mechanical rooms were located in the basements of the office building, the crews there would encounter more difficult work, hanging pipe high in the air and routing pipe around many bends to reach planned equipment connections. Thus Sid would not normally expect the productivity rates of the crews in the office area to be as good as the rates of crews working in the mall. Yet the estimates showed only a single average unit rate for each pipe size for the job as a whole.

Collecting field measurements

For a major job like the Office-Mall Project, J&J collected daily time sheets from every foreman for their crews. The time sheets included the number of hours charged to each of six pipe-size categories plus two pipe-hanger sizes as well as other work. Each week, a project engineer would walk the job, counting the amount of work-in-place. At the end of the week, the manhours and the amounts of work finished were summarized for major jobs by one of the office secretaries. She normally spotted errors only when someone forgot to turn in either the hours or the amounts. She entered the numbers by hand on a simple form and calculated the unit rates (manhours per foot of installed pipe) for each of the pipe sizes. Table 6.8 shows a sample of a J&J project report form prepared in the office for the Office-Mall Project (but reformatted for the electronic spreadsheet).

The summary report shows six pipe-size categories (A through F), two sizes of hangers (G for small pipe sizes A through D, and H for the larger pipe sizes E and F), and other work not charged directly to pipe or hangers (such as supervision and layout). At this point in the job (a little over half complete), the job has already overrun the estimate by 4269 MH. Sid has done his best to ignore these reports and their rising manhour overruns each week. He (and everyone on the jobsite) knows the job was incredibly underbid. The estimated unit rates are far better than could possibly be achieved under the actual working conditions. However, after seeing the latest report, top management at J&J now believes that perhaps Sid ought to share some of the blame (along, of course, with management's favorite whipping boy, an unpro-

TABLE 6.8   Weekly Unit-Rate Report: Office-Mall Project

	A	B	C	D	E	F	G	H	I	J	K
1	Item	Pipe	Estimated			To date			Earned	MH	Percent
2	code	diameter	Amt	MH	Rate	Rate	Amt	MH	MH	Diff	Done
3											
4	*Formula*				*(D/C)*	*(H/G)*			*(G*E)*	*(I − H)*	*(G/C)*
5											
6	A	½" to 2"	1232	504	0.41	0.90	124	112	51	− 61	10%
7	B	2-½ & 3	6289	4877	0.78	1.20	1188	1426	921	− 504	19%
8	C	4 inch	9906	9255	0.93	1.22	4562	5566	4262	− 1303	46%
9	D	5 to 8"	7017	6127	0.87	1.45	3017	4375	2634	− 1740	43%
10	E	10 and 12"	3335	4944	1.48	1.88	2955	5555	4381	− 1175	89%
11	F	14 to 20"	932	1542	1.65	2.81	890	2501	1473	− 1028	95%
12	G	S hangers	2947	4287	1.45	1.09	1677	1828	2440	612	57%
13	H	L hangers	1844	3225	1.75	1.21	1729	2092	3024	932	94%
14	I	Other	NA	3959	NA	NA	NA	3081	3081	0	NA
15											
16	Total			38720				26535	22266	− 4269	

ductive labor force). Sid is suddenly forced to spend long hours going over the reports in an effort to make the numbers look more encouraging.

Reporting accuracy

In his checking, Sid finds that foremen pay little attention to their division of hours between piping and hangers. Unless the hangers go up well before the pipe, the hours spent on hangers and pipe tend to get mixed together. To Sid, too few hours charged to hangers means that the rates for the hangers may be worse than reported and the rates for the pipe may be better than reported. In addition, the field engineer (sometimes Sid walks the job with him) who counts the amount of work accomplished each week carefully marks up a set of plans with colored pencils indicating completed work. Sid now realizes that because no credit is ever given for partially completed work (such as pipe hung and tacked but not yet welded), the marked-up plans *undercount* the amount of work actually done. Cheered by these two findings, Sid determines to collect and send in more accurate numbers the next week, along with a memo explaining the errors in the summary report.

Office versus mall

In the meantime, Sid decides to try to figure out the difference in productivity rates between work in the mall and office areas. He digs out the original estimates and refigures everything, separating the pipe according to the two buildings. Next, he goes back through all the time sheets on the job to figure out, by work codes, how many hours were charged to the mall and how many to the office building. He then scrutinizes the marked-up set of plans, trying to match counts of work completed each week to the hours charged. After a week of working every evening on the numbers and a long weekend during which his wife threatened to hide his calculator, Sid confirms his guess that the manhour overruns are largely due to the delays and disruptions in the mall portion of the project, and not due to poor productivity in the office portion. In order to show productivity *rising* on his graph, Sid converts the weekly rate measurements from manhours per unit to units per manhour (by simply dividing them into 1 on his calculator). He is pleased with his graphs; pipe size B, for example, given as Figure 6.4, shows a general rise in productivity over the past seven months since the project started.

The graph shows that the job average has remained worse than the estimate of 1.2 ft of pipe per manhour but that the office portion of the project has improved by rising above the estimate and is still improving. Yet the numbers for the last month indicate worsening productivity in the mall and for the job as a whole. The interrupted pipe runs and the split crews in the mall area have clearly hurt the job.

Weighted hours

Over the next two weeks, Sid coaches his foremen to account more accurately for their hours charged to pipe or hangers. In spite of their

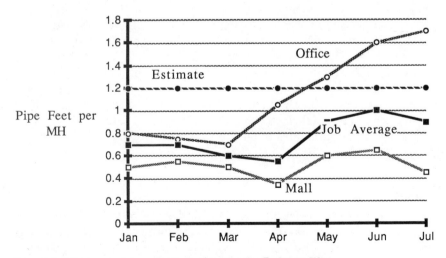

Figure 6.4   The increasing productivity for pipe size B, 2½ to 3 in.

best efforts, Sid realizes that it is relatively impossible to separate the manhours worked on the pipe from those worked on the hangers. Too much of the work is done at the same time, or else mixed together during the day. If he can't get more accurate pipe and hanger numbers, Sid decides that at least he can figure out how to assign weights to the piping and hanger hours he does have so as to get a more accurate accounting of how the manhours were spent. With the help of several foremen, Sid manages to develop a formula that gives a percentage of total hours to pipe and hangers for each of the pipe sizes. The foremen's time sheets should show actual hours charged to pipe and hangers, but the foremen have always simply estimated the split between pipe and hanger hours since it is too hard in practice to track the hours separately. The only reason they even bother to estimate the split is because the time sheets require it. After all this work, Sid is disheartened to discover that his new graphs don't look much different from his first ones. In general, productivity in the mall area is much worse than the estimate, while the office seems to be holding its own.

Prefabrication

For the larger pipe sizes (D, E, and F), the stop-and-start work in the mall has clearly hurt. In tracking the problems with the smaller pipe sizes (A, B, and C), Sid discovers that much less of it has been fabricated off-site in the J&J fabrication shop than the estimators originally expected. Because other J&J jobs have come in, the fab shop has been backed up for months and the foremen on the Office-Mall Project have preferred to fabricate the sections in the field as they need them rather than wait weeks for their job requests to get through the shop. No one ever went through the plans and tried to pick out ahead of time all the prefabrication work; since no one planned ahead, naturally all requests for shop fabrication arise only at the time they are needed, and by then the foremen don't want to hold up their crews waiting for the prefabricated spools. Sid figures it takes crews at least twice as many manhours to do the work themselves in the field as it does in the shop.

Finding leverage

So the lack of prefabrication for the smaller pipe sizes and the lack of clear, unimpeded runs in the chase for the larger pipe sizes have combined to undercut jobsite productivity. By digging into the reports and putting together detailed numbers for each pipe size in the two areas, Sid now feels that he has a handle on what to do about the productivity problem. Even though it is probably too late to turn the job around, Sid looks to where he will have the greatest leverage in making an improvement that will save him field manhours. Table 6.9 shows Sid's effort to locate the greatest opportunities for improvement.

Row 35 in Table 6.9 shows that a total of 29,068 MH have now been charged to the job, 75 percent of the 38,720 MH in the estimate. Counting only the manhours and amounts for the last four weeks, Sid computes in column I the four-week unit rates that reflect current job performance. If all the remaining pipe could be installed at the same unit rates that the job has experienced over the past four weeks (which have been fairly good weeks, Sid thinks), then another 14,461

TABLE 6.9 Comparison of Mall and Office Status

	A	B	C	D	E	F	G	H	I	J	K
1	Mall Area										
2	Item	Pipe		Estimated mall			To-date mall		4-week	MH to	Percent
3	code	diameter	Amt	MH	Rate	Rate	Amt	MH	rate	complete	to do
4											
5	*Formula*					(H/G)				(C-G)*1	(C-G)/C
6											
7	A	½" to 2"	822	321	0.39	1.72	101	174	0.66	476	88%
8	B	2-½ & 3	4231	2844	0.67	1.21	1908	2309	0.91	**2114**	**55%**
9	C	4 inch	6658	6088	0.91	1.14	3711	4231	0.75	**2210**	**44%**
10	D	5 to 8"	4117	3327	0.81	1.25	2281	2851	0.98	**1799**	**45%**
11	E	10 and 12"	2774	3628	1.31	1.42	2233	3171	1.33	720	20%
12	F	14 to 20"	834	1375	1.65	2.62	704	1844	1.87	243	16%
13	G	S hangers	2077	2908	1.40	1.33	1542	2051	1.24	663	26%
14	H	L hangers	1562	2608	1.67	1.54	1217	1874	1.48	511	22%
15	I	Other	NA	2275	NA	NA	NA	1966	NA	800	NA
16											
17	Total			25374				20471		9536	
18											
19	Office Area										
20	Item	Pipe		Estimated office			To-date office		4-week	MH to	Percent
21	code	diameter	Amt	MH	Rate	Rate	Amt	MH	rate	complete	to do
22											
23	A	½" to 2"	410	183	0.45	1.09	165	180	0.56	137	60%
24	B	2-½ & 3	2058	2033	0.99	0.76	1057	803	0.72	721	49%
25	C	4 inch	3248	3167	0.98	1.02	1555	1586	0.77	**1304**	**52%**
26	D	5 to 8"	2900	2800	0.97	1.09	1652	1801	1.06	**1323**	**43%**
27	E	10 and 12"	561	1316	2.35	1.82	233	424	1.42	466	58%
28	F	14 to 20"	98	167	1.70	2.07	98	203	1.69	0	0%
29	G	S hangers	870	1379	1.59	1.88	581	1092	1.42	410	33%
30	H	L hangers	282	617	2.19	2.66	204	543	2.11	165	28%
31	I	Other	NA	1684	NA	NA	NA	1966	NA	400	NA
32											
33	Total			13346				8598		4925	
34											
35	Job totals			38720				29068		14461	

MH will be needed to finish the job. Adding the 29,068 MH to date and the 14,461 MH projected gives 43,529 MH, 4809 MH over the estimate of 38,720 MH.

By computing in columns I and J the rates and amount of work completed for each pipe size, Sid sees that pipe sizes B, C, and D in the mall and pipe sizes C and D in the office building offer the best chance for saving further manhours on the job. Together, the five account for 8750 MH, over 60 percent of the projected manhours needed to complete the job. With the knowledge of where to put his efforts, Sid gets to work pushing as much pipe through the fab shop as possible and doing all he can to boost productivity on the field installation. Of course, his efforts come too late to do as much good as they might have, had he started projecting manhour overruns from the start of the project. Sid learns from the experience that he will need to get involved in collecting and analyzing measurements from the very beginning of his next job. If J&J ever gives him another one, that is.

Estimates—Bids versus Field Supervision?

The J&J story parallels the experience of many contractors who start too late to collect and use measurements of jobsite productivity. Estimators put together a bid based on many variables. Usually their quantity takeoffs and materials prices are accurate. But they must rely on educated guesses of expected productivity as affected by the many jobsite factors that influence construction performance in the field. Estimators normally work under deadline pressures that force them to analyze the job from the point of view of costs, not control. The information generated by an estimate rarely contains the detail necessary for tracking and troubleshooting field performance at the crew and craft level.

In the J&J example, estimators developed the bid by costing out the subsystems on the job (water, steam, and gas). Yet to a field foreman, it may make little difference if the pipe will carry water or steam—it is the pipe size and the number of welds that will affect his or her productivity. In addition, estimates of average overall productivity rates for installation offer little guidance to field supervisors. Supervisors need to know estimated productivity rates for specific areas and particular installations in order to make useful comparisons of their actual performance against expected performance in these areas. Charting progress against the estimate may degrade management decisions if the estimate is too general or too inaccurate to serve as a guideline. Comparisons of actual progress to estimated progress rarely point to where the problems are and what might be done to fix them. In such cases, managers work under the delusion that they actually have control of the job when, in fact, they control only the numbers, not the work.

A detailed estimate

Sid needed a detailed estimate of expected unit rates for pipe sizes and hangers for both the mall and the office portion of his project. He also needed to understand how measurements of manhours and work accomplished were actually being recorded in the field. If foremen cannot distinguish hours charged to hangers from hours charged to pipe, it is foolish to require them to charge the hours separately. They will only guess at the numbers, giving management what it wants to see. If they appear to have poor unit rates for pipe and good rates for hangers, foremen will begin to charge more hours to hangers in order to make their pipe rates look better. If counting methods allow for ambiguous numbers, foremen (and others) will put down the numbers that make them look the best. This is only human nature.

By far the best way to develop a workable counting method is to let the foremen help design it. They know what they can count and what they can't count. (They may resist counting anything, but this, in itself, is a problem for our methods engineering model that will be discussed later.)

In addition, the same units of measurement must be used in both the estimate (perhaps refigured after the bid has been accepted) and in the field counts of manhours and work installed (again, a subject discussed in greater depth later) to make useful comparisons.

Sid's problems with inaccurate and incomplete productivity estimates plague many jobs. No estimate is ever perfect. Worse yet, few estimates provide a one-to-one relationship to easily obtainable field measurements. As Sid discovered, in order to use estimates as a realistic basis for evaluating on-site productivity, the original estimates must normally be refigured to match the measurements that can be collected in the field. Although the extra effort at the beginning of the job can be time-consuming, the superior information available throughout the course of the job pinpoints areas of deficient performance and allows management to remedy productivity problems before they get out of hand. The extra effort required to convert estimates to field measurement units can easily pay for itself by cutting labor costs over the life of the project.

Using the estimate as a target

A good estimate can provide an extremely valuable target for field productivity. However, because the estimate is usually the *average*

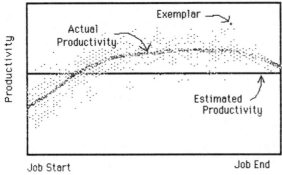

Figure 6.5 Expected productivity variations over time.

productivity expected over the course of the job, it will normally set too high a standard at the start of the job (when productivity is usually lower) and will set too low a standard as the job picks up momentum. Figure 6.5 graphs the estimated (average) and actual productivity over the course of a typical job. The actual productivity is shown as a scatter of points representing the expected range of productivity among different crews, with an exemplar occurring toward the end of the job.

The graph in Figure 6.5 implies that the productivity targets ought to be set about 20 percent higher than the productivity estimates in order to ensure that the standards reflect the best that crews are able to accomplish, not just the average. Whenever possible, however, measurements of *actual exemplar performance* offer even better targets than do estimates.

Recycling Measurements and Estimates

If estimates were accurate enough and detailed enough, they would provide an excellent basis for setting performance standards and developing field productivity targets. Improved accuracy comes from continuous comparison of estimates to actual field productivity. Just as field crews can use regular feedback to improve their performance, so can estimators. Comparing estimated to actual productivity permits estimators to study the effects of job conditions on worker productivity. Over time, the regular feedback provided by comparisons of the estimates to the actual field measurements will narrow the gap between the two, which will result in more accurate and detailed estimates.

Assessing estimating adequacy

Many contractors resist the need to assess continuously the accuracy and completeness of their estimates. Estimating, they may argue, is an art and requires experience and judgment. No one can be expected to get every detail right. An estimate is only that—an estimate, not an infallible prediction. Many contractors also believe that, although their estimates may contain many errors in the details, when the entire job is totaled up the errors cancel each other out and the gross estimate is pretty close to the final cost.

Such reluctance to develop a more accurate approach to estimating may soon disappear as more sophisticated computer estimating programs reach the construction market. Even now, programs prepare materials takeoffs from computerized construction drawings. The power of computers allows estimators to manipulate increasing amounts of detail in preparing their estimates; they can develop many alternative estimates using differing assumptions concerning construction methods and productivity rates in an attempt to find the least costly solution. However, the ease of use of computer programs and canned databases is eliminating the need for skilled and experienced estimators; anyone, it seems, can now develop a job estimate. Yet the increasing use of computer programs by less experienced estimators may lead to less accurate estimates. Loss of accuracy occurs because the greatest risk in estimating now lies in choosing numbers for labor productivity. Equipment and materials prices are relatively easy to obtain, but labor productivity still requires an educated guess from the estimator.

In order to take full advantage of the computer's power, contractors will need to develop detailed databases that record past productivity and job conditions. Estimates prepared from such databases will eventually be accurate enough and detailed enough to serve as performance standards for field supervisors. But to get to that point requires a feedback process for continually assessing the adequacy of current estimates and for collecting detailed measurements of field performance.

However, even the most detailed field measurement system will not provide accurate estimating data until contractors learn to separate lost time from work time. Field reports that charge work hours to installed work and lost hours to the causes of lost time permit contractors to calculate their true unit rates. True unit rates include only the hours actually worked on an item; lost time is charged to management overhead. Estimators can use true unit rates to more accurately choose an expected productivity and then they can add on a percentage of the work hours to allow for the inevitable lost time. For example, an estimate might include 10,000 manhours for productive labor based on a history of true unit rates and then include an additional 1000 or 1500 (10 or 15 percent) manhours for expected lost time based on a history of lost time for similar jobs. With a detailed estimate of expected true unit rates and a separate account for expected lost-time hours, Sid Beckman would have had no problem in staying on top of the Office-Mall Project.

Integrating measurements and estimates

The hypothetical graph in Figure 6.5 displays the expected productivity history of a project. Contractors who collect regular measurements of their jobsite performance can construct such graphs for their own jobs.

Knowing how productivity can be expected to vary over the course of a job provides a valuable reference point for making forecasts of job completion. For simplicity, all the examples used in this book assume straight-line productivity projections (what occurred over the past four weeks, for example, will hold true for the remainder of the job); average and exemplar productivity rates were combined with the amounts of work remaining to project the manhours needed for job completion.

Yet we know that productivity will not remain constant for the remainder of the job. Particularly at the end, when punchlist items require rework, productivity will fall. If estimators had access to a long history of measured productivity, their estimates could show how, over the course of a project, the expected future productivity rates could be expected to vary. Using such nonlinear projections of future productivity would tend to give more accurate assessments of current job status, even from the very start of a job.

Measurements (of lost time as well as of unit rates) offer estimators a sounder basis for estimating than do handbook numbers modified by guesses about past experience. But clearly no contractor can collect measurements of every task and every job condition. The database will always be incomplete. Yet incomplete data do provide a valuable sample, and simple statistical techniques can extrapolate the sample to cover a broader range of conditions. Estimation programs can include such statistical programs to help estimators select the right numbers from among sets of incomplete measurements from a variety of jobs. Over time, as the database grows, the estimates will become more detailed and more accurate. And as the estimates become better, they will point the way to increased accuracy in collecting and interpreting field measurements. Eventually contractors may no longer distinguish between measurement and estimating functions: both will be centered in the same computer system and rely on the same database.

Until such time as estimates improve, however, contractors need to exercise caution before relying too heavily on management systems that depend on comparing reported field productivity to estimated productivity. Neither the field reports nor the estimate may tell the true story.

Feedback to the Field

Every field supervisor needs feedback. *Feedback* means getting back information concerning the results of what you did. Feedback on the jobsite includes finding out how well you did relative to what was expected of you. Did you perform well or not? And why? What caused your exemplar performance? What caused your low performance? And what should you do differently next time?

Perhaps more than any other single factor, feedback has the greatest power to change the way individuals behave. As we have seen regarding the methods engineering model in Chapter 4, feedback is also one of the least costly and most effective means of performance improvement. So far we have discussed methods for measuring field performance and methods for analyzing the results to reach conclusions concerning appropriate management actions. We turn now to a discussion of how these measurements and conclusions might best reach the field supervisors who must act on the information.

Not every number collected and analyzed goes back to the field. In fact, only a few of the numbers ever reach the field. But the important numbers should. Feedback reports to field supervisors—from foremen to project managers—should include only what they *need to know* in order to make informed decisions. Not too many numbers, and not too few. Too many numbers require extra effort in reading and sifting through the reports looking for relevant information. Overly detailed reports tend to be ignored or else ineffectively used. Too few numbers fail to tell the whole story, leaving management to guess how the analysis arrived at the conclusions.

This chapter describes a range of project reports to illustrate the preparation and use of feedback to the field, drawing examples from a reporting system developed by the author. But first, let us look at a situation that illustrates the power of feedback to alter performance.

Dredging for Feedback

It was again time to dredge the coal-barge channel in the river. Every three years or so the Power and Light Company (P&L) had to bring in a dredge to clean out the accumulated mud and silt that threatened to ground the heavily laden coal barges that regularly plied their way up the river to supply fuel to the huge generators. After eight such dredging operations over the past 20 years, the project was considered pretty routine. So Jane Winters, the facilities engineer in charge of all construction and maintenance, assigned the project to Skip Oldman, a new engineering graduate recently hired by P&L. Skip's job involved overseeing the contract performance and writing up a report for the file. Under the terms of the contract, the dredging company was to cut the channel to a specific profile over a course of nearly ½ mile. The coal barges required a minimum depth of 18 ft. Since dredging is an imprecise operation, the power company agreed to pay for any overdredging up to a maximum depth of 20 ft. Any cut deeper than 20 ft. was the contractor's loss.

Jane Winters had already conducted a sonar survey of the channel. A sonar firm had prepared cross-sectional profiles perpendicular to the channel every 100 ft over its ½-mile length. Draftsmen superimposed the desired profiles over the "before" profiles and calculated the amount of dredge material to be removed. During the dredging operation, sonar would be used to prepare weekly profiles of the new channel. Comparison of the desired profiles to the "after" profiles would let both the power company and the contractor track the progress of the job. The actual profiles also served as proof of work done; calculations of the volume of material removed formed the basis for Skip's approval of the contractor's progress payments. Figure 7.1 illustrates one set of the channel profiles.

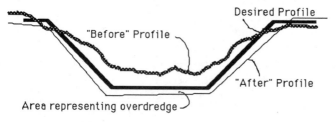

(Area between profiles shows amount of material removed.)

Figure 7.1   Channel profiles.

As Figure 7.1 shows, P&L was required to pay for all material removed between the before profile and the desired profile, including up to 2 ft in additional depth on the bottom. The contractor, on the other hand, could not collect for any overdredge on the sides or for more than 2 ft beneath the desired bottom profile. The amount of P&L's contract exposure could be as low as the difference between the desired and before profiles (if the contractor was exactly accurate in his dredging). Or the contract exposure could be higher by as much as 2 ft times the channel width times the length (if the contractor consistently overdredged).

In looking over the contract, Skip realized it was in P&L's interest to keep the contractor as close to the desired profile as possible without going too deep. And it was in the contractor's interest to stay as close to the desired profile as possible without going too deep either, since too much extra dredging would quickly eat up the profits on the job. But the history of past jobs, as evidenced in the eight previous dredging reports from earlier years, showed a consistent pattern of overdredging. P&L nearly always wound up paying the maximum for the job, and the finished channel was nearly always overdredged, in one instance to 28 ft!

As the job started, Skip soon discovered that the single person most responsible for the performance on the job was the dredge operator. A skilled operator could keep to the desired channel cut rather closely, while a less skilled one would tend to overdredge. Although the contractor had a skilled dredge operator, this operator was not present at the planning meetings, nor was he originally invited to the regular weekly progress meetings Skip held with the contractor.

After the first three weeks of the job, it was apparent that the dredge operator was overdredging, so much so that he was costing both the power company and the contractor money. At this point Skip suggested that he show the dredge operator the new profiles based on the work done. The contractor agreed, and so drawings similar to Figure 7.1 were prepared for the first four week's work.

The following week, when Skip handed the drawings to the dredge operator, he was amazed at the profiles. In all the years he had been a dredge operator, no one had ever bothered to show him the results of his work. Usually the only feedback he received was limited to verbal comments, such as "You're too deep" or "Go a little deeper." Since the water around a dredging operation is extremely muddy, the operator could never see what he was doing. Feedback was critical to the accuracy of his performance.

With the weekly drawings showing exactly how well he was performing, the dredge operator managed to get the channel cut nearly perfect. He anxiously awaited the weekly results of his work and took a great deal of pride in being able to make the fine adjustments necessary to get the profile right where it was supposed to be. After the job was over, the dredge operator commented that it had been the most interesting job he had worked on—*all because he received regular feedback information on his performance.*

It also turned out to cost P&L much less than P&L had anticipated in overdredge charges. In fact, the job came in $200,000 below Jane's estimate based on the long history of previous dredging work. And, best of all, the contractor made a larger profit than he expected, all because he lost very little time in overdredging. Jane gave Skip full credit for the success of the job and instructed him to write up very clear instructions on how to manage the dredging job correctly the next time the river filled in the barge channel.

Effective Feedback

While some contractors may find it hard to believe that people on the jobsite seldom get feedback, the truth is that few contractors bother to provide regular feedback to their work force. This is partly because contractors do not realize the importance of feedback and partly because they do not know how to assemble information into an effective feedback system. Effective feedback can be characterized by the five *TRACI* attributes:

- *T*imely
- *R*elevant
- *A*ccurate
- *C*omplete
- *I*ntelligible

Let us look at each of the TRACI attributes further. *Timeliness* means that we get the information in time to make the right decision at the right time. It does no good to find out two weeks late that we are now two weeks behind schedule. It also means that we get the information frequently enough to provide feedback concerning the impact of earlier decisions. *Relevance* means that the information is exactly what we need to do our job, not too much and not too little. Two-foot high stacks of computer printouts are seldom relevant. We need the *important* numbers, not *all* the numbers. *Accuracy* means that what we have is right; nobody is fooling us (and we aren't fooling ourselves, either). *Completeness* means that we have all the information necessary for decision making. We don't have to guess about any missing facts. Finally, *intelligibility* means that we can understand it. We need numbers in a form that we can read without trouble. Graphs, comparisons, and ratios help convey the real meaning behind the numbers.

Information flaws

No information perfectly fulfills each of the requirements. Worry about missing some important fact from an incomplete report nags contractors decisions. Error and bias in seeing and reporting—inaccurate perception—remains an inherently human characteristic. Managements' desire for intelligibility frequently loses out to the competing urge to amass as much information as possible (even though most of it is worthless and only gets in the way of finding what is really needed). And, since only the people actually watching the job go up can receive instantaneous information, most decisions must be based on information contractors wish had been available sooner.

Information trade-offs

Although we cannot get information of perfect quality, we can upgrade the quality of the information we get by making conscious trade-offs among the feedback's characteristics. As a general rule in construction, it is usually better to stress *timeliness* over the other characteristics, for decisions made too late usually cost much more than decisions made on time. Even if we know that the information may be incomplete or inaccurate, it is still better to get it now and decide to act on flawed information than to get the right information too late to act at all. Stressing timeliness also tends to ensure that the information we get is relevant and intelligible; we can't wait to get too much information, so we focus on the most important and insist that it be understandable. Timely information also permits a faster turnaround in the decision-making feedback loop; receiving continuous feedback, we can quickly spot poor decisions and suggest actions to correct them.

Let us now turn our attention to understanding exactly how feedback reporting can work on a job. Although the following example illustrates a large job with four levels of on-site management, it incorporates the same principles of feedback reporting that apply to all jobs, regardless of size.

The JOB-SIGHT™ Management System

In 1980 the author developed a computer-based on-site performance reporting system for use on several construction projects. The system, named JOB-SIGHT™, has now been effectively employed on many projects. A full description of the system and its operation demonstrates how all the elements of performance reporting and performance management actually interact in the field. The four primary elements are

1. Collection of manhours worked and manhours lost, plus counts of work accomplished
2. Computer entry and record keeping
3. Weekly reports to all levels of field management
4. Troubleshooting procedures

An on-site personal computer processes the data and provides weekly reports for up to four levels of project management:

1. Crew foremen
2. General foremen
3. Superintendents
4. Project manager

Separating lost time and work time

The discussion of lost time and work time in Chapter 3 described a method for collecting crew manhours from a foreman's time sheet. The time sheet (shown there as Figure 3.3 and reproduced here as Figure 7.2) allows foremen to separate their crew time according to the time actually worked on specific work items and the time lost as a result of causes beyond their control. A code (or name) for each work item is entered across the top, and the hours actually charged to each item are listed vertically. At the end of the day each individual's payroll hours are summed to the right, and the same hours are summed by item to the bottom. The foreman then writes in the number of hours actually worked on the item and the number of hours charged to the item but actually "lost" (hours during which no productive work was accomplished). For every lost-time entry, the foreman writes in at the bottom a code or a short description to explain the cause of the lost time. The time sheets are collected daily.

The lost-time manhours are collected each week in a summary report and charged to management; the work time is matched to counts of work completed by the crew each week and is used to compute "true" unit rates. Figure 7.3 diagrams the system (reproduced from

Time Sheet Foreman:_____ Crew Number:_____ Date:_____ Employee Name	Work Item						Total
Total Payroll Hours							
Work Time Hours							
Lost Time Hours							
Lost Time Causes							

Figure 7.2   Foreman's time sheet showing lost-time hours.

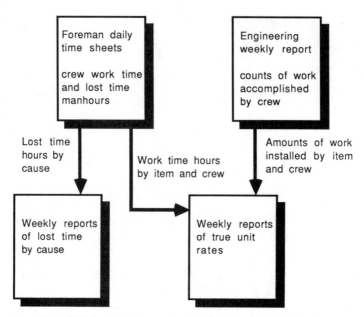

Figure 7.3   Splitting lost time and work time gives true unit rates.

Figure 3.4). JOB-SIGHT™ uses the same method to track lost time and to compute true unit rates for crews.

The feedback cycle

Figure 7.4 illustrates the flow of information at the jobsite. Primary information concerning lost time and unit rates comes from crew foremen and flows up to a central collection point, where it is processed by a computer and turned into performance reports for management. Troubleshooting the reports leads to management actions to solve lost-time problems and to foster improved work methods among crews. The weekly feedback cycle reinforces incentives to foremen to participate and cooperate in the reporting system.

The cycle begins with the collection of time sheets (from foremen) and counts of work accomplished (from engineering), which are entered into the computer for processing (1). The computer prints reports for all management levels (2). The reports serve as the basis for troubleshooting and for an exchange of information among the project management team (3).

Let us now examine each stage of the feedback process in greater detail, using as an example the work of an electrical subcontractor on a power-plant project, Big River Power Plant #2.

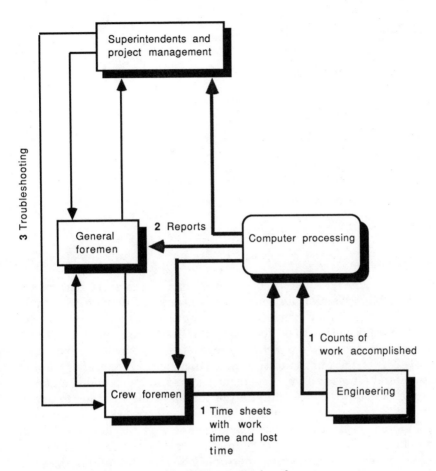

Figure 7.4   Overview of the JOB-SIGHT® feedback cycle.

Lost-Time Manhours

The foreman's daily time sheet (Figure 7.2) charges the work hours on the Big River project to specific work-item codes and charges lost hours to lost-time codes. Discussions with the electrical subcontractor's foremen and crew members have defined the most common causes of lost time on the job, and the simple codes that identify these causes on the reports are as follows:

11 Rework, plan change

12 Rework, damage

13 Rework, design error

14 Rework, other reason

20 Late start/Early quit

30 Travel/Transportation

41 Wait for surveyors

42 Wait for other trade

43 Wait for directions

44 Wait for equipment

45 Wait for materials

46 Wait, other reason

50 Interruption of work

60 Other reason

Rework codes

The first four codes (11 to 14) identify one of the most frustrating causes of lost time on any large job—rework. Craftsmen who must continually redo their work *because of someone else's mistake* quickly lose their motivation to do good work the first time around. *Charging management for rework time* achieves two worthwhile objectives: First, it lifts the burden of rework inefficiencies from craftsmen and crews (and places it on management); second, it gives management a means to count, locate, and analyze the lost time in order to act to eliminate the causes of rework. While not all rework causes can be eliminated, many can be; for example, knowing the lost hours (and therefore the cost) charged to plan changes can justify the added expense of extra engineering personnel to coordinate engineering changes in order to minimize field disruption.

Time lost because of damage to completed work can lead to better methods to protect the finished work. In one instance, electricians on the Big River project reported large amounts of time spent, just before concrete pours, on replacing conduit and termination boxes embedded in the floors. Upon investigation it was found that the termination boxes offered convenient "stepping stones" across floors of open rebar. After a step or two, the upright conduit bent and then soon broke, requiring time-consuming replacement immediately before each pour. The solution? Simple welded rebar "cages" were prefabed in the shop, wired tightly over each box, and removed just before a pour, thereby reducing damage to zero.

Rework charged to design errors (code 13) particularly delighted the electricians but angered the engineers. The dimensioned locations of 4-in conduit required accurate placement, but all too frequently some rebar or other pipe blocked the clearance needed. At this point the craftsman would have to stop work, report the problem, and get reassigned to another task until engineering could resolve the interference the following day. As the hours charged to code 13 mounted, it quickly became clear that hiring an engineer to work directly in the field with the electricians to resolve the problems as they arose would not only save enormous amounts of money but would also boost the morale both of the craftsmen and the engineers.

Codes 20 and 30

Code 20, late starts and early quits, was added as a code item at the insistence of the local union's business agent. He felt his people were being unfairly accused of arriving late and leaving early and, to prove his point, demanded that his foremen record any time lost because of a shortened workday. Not surprisingly, no foreman ever recorded any lost time under this code. But then, too, complaints about late starts and early quits also disappeared as foremen made sure that their crews put in a full day.

Code 30 accounted for the time that workers lost while moving around the large site or waiting for trucks to take them to other areas. Tracking this lost time helped management keep unassigned trucks available for worker transportation in order to cut the amount of time spent walking and waiting.

Waiting time

After rework, waiting time accounted for most of the lost time on the Big River project. Waiting time is unavoidable on any large construction site; too many things can go wrong. By recording the reasons for waiting time, management could offer specific support to foremen to overcome the primary causes of waiting.

Code 41, waiting for surveyors, originally accounted for considerable lost time. Before electricians could run conduit along walls, carefully surveyed dimensions needed to be set to ensure complete accuracy. The general contractor, however, failed to provide sufficient surveyors. Electrician crews frequently waited an hour or more for the surveyors to arrive and set the marks. After recording the lost time for several weeks, the electrical subcontractor confronted the general contractor with a report detailing the cost of electricians' lost time. It didn't take long for the general contractor to figure that he could put on several more surveyor crews for less money than it cost to have the electricians wait. (As this was a cost-plus contract, the general contractor was naturally anxious to avoid being responsible for unnecessary charges to the owner.) Similar problems with other trades were easily resolved once the numbers showed what the lost time was costing the job. Knowing the cost of the problem makes it much easier to devise a cost-effective solution.

Interruptions

Code 50, interruption of work, also needs some explanation. Electricians, besides installing permanent work items, installed temporary power lines for equipment and lighting. As other trades needed power, they called on the closest electrician foreman to provide it. The skyrocketing amounts of time lost because of interruptions was drastically cut by assigning one (later two) crews to do only support work. Their members provided all temporary power and electrical services for the other trades at Big River.

Management follow-up

The lost-time reporting system turns foremen's gripes into valuable information that can help management improve performance. And in reporting lost time, foremen relieve themselves and their workers of much of the frustration that normally undercuts motivation. But the real key lies in follow-up by management. If nothing is done about the lost time, foremen will soon stop reporting it. Only when management aggressively pursues lost time in an effort to solve the problems will foremen continue to report it. In this sense, management must treat a foreman's lost-time report as a plea for help. Something has happened on the job that is beyond the foremen's power to deal with and has cost their crews valuable time. They need help. If, instead, management views the lost time as a reflection of inadequate leadership on the part of foremen, the foremen will very quickly cease to report any lost time at all. Pretending that lost time never occurs and criticizing foremen who experience it is yet another indicator of ineffective and unresponsive construction management.

Counts of Work Accomplished

Work codes are normally established before a job begins. In the example used here to illustrate the JOB-SIGHT™ management system, the Big River project originally contained several hundred codes for distinct work items for electricians. Because the original codes were set up by accountants and estimators for accounting and estimating purposes, they proved to be virtually worthless as measurements of field accomplishment. Thus, with the help of foremen and project engineers, new work items and codes were defined, each one relating to a specific item of installed work easily recognized and counted by foremen and engineers. (The new code system, however, could be "rolled up" into the old system. Adding together certain detailed categories of work gave the hours and amounts required for the old system. Thus management avoided the need to double-count for two different reporting systems.)

Throughout the week an engineer walked the job, keeping track of the amounts of work installed. At the end of the week, the final counts were verified on a separate report for each crew. In the office, a clerk matched the work hours from the daily time sheets with the amounts of work installed for the week for each crew. She then prepared a single summary report for each crew for the week showing amounts of work and manhours along with lost time and causes. Information from these summary crew reports was then entered into the computer. Although preparing an interim summary report by hand for each crew every week may seem like an extra step in the age of computers (why not just enter the numbers directly and let the computer prepare the summary), the extra step provided a very important opportunity to cross-check the accuracy and completeness of the numbers. Foremen's daily time sheets are not always as legible as one would wish. Then, too, missing and mismatched codes needed to be looked up and verified. The summary sheets, neatly laid out and easy to read, encouraged fast and error-free computer entries.

Computer Reporting

For entering the weekly numbers, the JOB-SIGHT™ management system displays forms on the computer screen that look just like the summary sheets. The operator then merely enters the numbers on the screen in the same location as they appear on the summary sheets. (The program automatically checks for typo errors in such entries as work codes, crew numbers, and manhour (MH) totals. During the weekly entry of report information, the operator may also make any changes to the system's administrative files or correct errors from earlier weeks.) After all the numbers have been entered and checked, the program prints out the reports for the week. On the Big River project, when foremen turned in their Friday time sheets at 4:00 p.m., the project manager sometimes had the output reports for the week before leaving the job at 6:00 p.m. Foremen always received their weekly reports on Monday morning. Rapid turnaround in the feedback loop facilitates troubleshooting while events are still fresh in everyone's mind. Timely reporting also ensures that severe problems (and unique opportunities for improvement) do not go unnoticed for long.

Figures 7.5 through 7.10 provide examples of weekly JOB-SIGHT™

performance reports. The first report goes to crew foremen, the second and third to general foremen, and the last three to superintendents and project managers. Each report contains information tailored to the needs of its respective level of management. Further, each report requires two-way communication, both up and down, in order to troubleshoot the numbers successfully. This two-way communication opens up a channel of very useful information to supplement the reports.

The Crew Foreman's Weekly Report

The foreman's report in Figure 7.5 actually fits two reports on a single page. (Never try to give foremen more than one page; they tend to resist paperwork.) The top half shows lost time, and the bottom half shows unit-rate information.

Lost-time report

The numbers at the top of the report reprint the foreman's lost-time history for week of the report, for the week before, and for the last four weeks. Although the foreman can do little with the numbers, printing them serves several purposes. First, it confirms that someone has indeed seen the foreman's lost-time reports and bothered to enter the numbers into the computer. Second, the foreman has the chance to check the numbers for errors. Third, the numbers show how much time the crew is losing, both for specific codes and as a percentage of the payroll, and they also provide a sense of whether the problems are getting worse or improving by giving the trends over time. Lastly, reviewing the lost-time reports serves to remind the foreman of the causes of lost time and of the need to report it whenever it occurs.

Unit-rate report

For the foremen, however, the more interesting part of the report appears on the lower half. Here they see each item on which their crews have worked during the past week, the number of hours actually worked on the item, and the number of units placed. (Again, printing out these numbers gives foremen a chance to check for errors.) Then comes the computation of the unit rates for the week, in this case obtained by dividing the work hours by the units placed. Therefore, the *lower* the unit rate (in manhours per amount), the *better* the productivity. The current week's rates are followed by a computation of a unit rate for the hours and amounts counted over the most recent four

PERFORMANCE CONSTRUCTORS, INC.			WEEK ENDING 09/12/86		
BIG RIVER POWER PLANT #2			CREW FOREMAN WEEKLY REPORT		
			FOREMAN: Williamson, T. J.		

LOST-TIME REPORT

Lost-time code and reason	MH this week	MH last week	MH last four weeks
11 Rework, plan change	27.0	10.0	35.5
12 Rework, damage	12.5	21.0	28.0
13 Rework, design error	42.0	92.5	152.0
14 Rework, other reason	0.0	0.0	6.0
20 Late start/Early quit	0.0	0.0	0.0
30 Travel/Transportation	0.0	0.0	14.0
41 Wait for surveyors	10.0	0.0	9.0
42 Wait for other trade	0.0	20.0	22.0
43 Wait for directions	0.0	0.0	0.0
44 Wait for equipment	11.0	0.0	45.0
45 Wait for materials	1.5	39.0	56.0
46 Wait, other reason	0.0	0.0	16.0
50 Interruption of work	0.0	0.0	0.0
60 Other reason	0.0	8.5	11.0
Total lost time (MH)	104.0	191.0	394.5
Total payroll hours for week	450.0	450.0	1810.0
Percent lost time	23%	42%	22%

Thank you for reporting your lost-time manhours.

UNIT-RATE REPORT (Work hours divided by units placed)

Code and work item	Units	Work hours	Units placed	Unit rate for week	Four-week unit rate	Best 4-wk unit rate
71.4 Metal clad 480 KV	Each	41.0	2.5	16.40	26.82	**26.82**
72.3 Service 4.16–480 KV	Each	138.0	30.0	4.60	5.15	4.64
82.2 RMC 1-½" to 2"	Feet	127.0	400.0	0.32	0.30	0.24
86.1 Wire & conn als	Feet	40.0	100.0	0.40	0.48	**0.48**
Total work hours		346.0				
Total payroll hours		450.0				
Percent work hours		77%				

If you can suggest a better work method or procedure that might improve your unit rates, tell your General Foreman. Thank you for a good job.

Figure 7.5 Foreman's JOB-SIGHT™ report.

weeks of work on the item. This four-week average provides a fairly good indicator of the crew's *current* productivity.

Finally, the report displays the crew's record for the *best* four-week unit rate it ever achieved. This best represents the crew's personal exemplar, its historical best performance. The two numbers in bold type on the report indicate new best records; the current four-week rate has exceeded the old record and has therefore replaced it. Note, too, that current unit rates are below the four-week rates for three of the four items reported. This means that current performance is better than average and, if continued, should soon lead to further improvement in the four-week average rates.

No negative consequences

The system prints only one copy of each foreman's report. True to the principles laid out in the earlier chapters of this book, the JOB-SIGHT™ management system does not attempt to compare unit rates among crews or to spot poor performers. Such negative consequences of feedback would quickly destroy the incentive for foremen to report accurately. On many jobs not all foremen possess equal skills and experience. New foremen, handling crews for the first time, often perform below the average for a while. Ranking the crews or comparing their unit rates can unfairly penalize less experienced foremen, reducing their motivation to improve. (In practice, foremen eagerly show each other their "report cards," vying for top-place honors. Peers can value and promote exemplary performance among themselves without rejecting their hard-working but less accomplished comrades, a fact every schoolchild learns on the baseball field or basketball court.) Rather, the system tracks and spots only exemplar performance, providing positive consequences to encourage continued improvement.

The General Foreman's Weekly Reports

The second and third reports go to the general foreman, who, in this example, has three crews working under him (A2, A4, and A9). The first report covers lost time (Figure 7.6); the second, unit rates (Figure 7.7).

Lost-time follow-up

The general foreman's lost-time report in Figure 7.6 prints all the time that was reported lost by his three crews for the week and for the previous week. The program automatically sorts through all the crew's lost time to find the single largest cause; it then prints the amount of hours lost, the reason for it, and the crew that accounts for most of this lost time. Further, it asks the general foreman to collect additional information about the reasons for the lost time and to suggest what to do about it. General foremen are not in a good position to troubleshoot all the reasons for lost time, but they are in a good position to get detailed information from foremen and crews about the reasons for it and to gather ideas about how to solve it.

JOB-SIGHT™ contains a second, more detailed level of lost-time causes that includes subcategories of reasons. The general foreman's

PERFORMANCE CONSTRUCTORS, INC.
BIG RIVER POWER PLANT #2

WEEK ENDING 09/12/86
GEN FOREMAN WEEKLY REPORT
GF: *Dyson, P. K. Jr.*

LOST-TIME REPORTING
Crews reporting: A2 A4 A9

	Total for week	Total for last week	Percent of payroll manhours
Lost-time manhours	282.0	211.5	19%

This week the largest amount of lost time was:	93.5	MH
This amount of lost time was caused by code:	13	Rework, design error
Most of this lost time was reported by crew:	A4	Williamson, T.J.

Why was this time lost? Check with the crew foremen and mark all the reasons below that apply. Write in any other information you may have that will help identify the cause of the lost time.

13 Rework, design error
Due to: Interference with rebar
         Interference with other pipe
         Interference with other work
         Other reason (write it in)

The best way to keep down these lost hours is by:
(Write in suggestions)

Figure 7.6 General foreman's JOB-SIGHT® lost-time report.

lost-time report shows that for code 13, rework caused by design errors, the real reason may be due to interferences with rebar, pipe, or other work (or some other reason). Rather than require foremen to report lost time in such detail each day, the system only looks into the detailed reasons for lost time when a problem clearly exists. Whenever lost time rises high enough to trigger the printout on the general foreman's report, then more information is collected. Early every week (usually Tuesdays), general foremen meet with superintendents and project managers to discuss the job. One discussion topic is lost time and what to do about it. If the general foremen have followed up on their lost-time reports on Monday, finding out what is hurting the crews and developing suggestions, then participants at the meeting use their time effectively, discussing what to do instead of trying to find out what the problem is.

Unit-rate report

The second general foreman's weekly report is the unit-rate report given as Figure 7.7. This report lists all the items worked on by any of the three crews during the week, including the hours, amounts, and unit-rate calculations for all crews together. Just as the foremen's unit-rate reports offered a "scorecard" for their crews' performance, so,

| Performance Constructors, Inc. | | | Week ending 09/12/86 | | |
| Big River Power Plant #2 | | | Gen Foreman Weekly Report | | |

GF: *Dyson, P. K. Jr.*

UNIT-RATE REPORT   (Work hours divided by units placed)

Crews reporting: A2 A4 A9

Code and work item	Unit	Work hours	Units placed	Unit rate for week	Four-Week unit rate	Best 4-wk unit rate
71.4 Metal clad 480 KV	Each	181.0	8.5	21.29	23.75	**23.75**
72.3 Service 4.16–480 KV	Each	238.5	49.0	4.87	5.01	4.89
73.5 120/280V busway	Feet	191.0	800.0	0.24	0.26	0.24
82.1 RMC 1″ and less	Feet	66.0	240.0	0.28	0.21	0.20
82.2 RMC 1-½″ to 2″	Feet	178.5	610.0	0.29	0.28	0.27
86.1 Wire & conn als	Feet	266.0	500.0	0.53	0.53	0.50

Total work hours 1121.0
Total payroll hours 1380.0
Percent work hours 81%

New records for "Best four-week rates" were set this week by the following crews for the items shown. Check with each crew foreman to make sure their new records are realistic and should remain.

Crew code and foreman	Item code	Item name	Yes, keep	No, delete
A0 Knox, S.N.	73.5	120/280V busway		
A4 Williamson, T. J.	71.4	Metal clad 480 KV		
A4 Williamson, T. J.	86.1	Wire & conn als		

What are these crews doing better that other crews might copy?
If you can suggest a better work method to improve your unit rates, bring it to the next meeting.
Thank you for a good job.

Figure 7.7   General foreman's JOB-SIGHT™ unit-rate report.

too, does the general foreman's report keep a collective score of how well the three crews have done. In the same way that foremen evaluate their own performances, general foremen also look to improve their unit rates.

In this example only one rate, that for the first item, shows up in boldface in the "Best four-week unit rate" column. This indicates that the current four-week rate has hit a new best record, replacing the earlier best record. Compare this best with the foreman's best record for the same item in Figure 7.5. The foreman's best of 26.82 MH per unit is nearly three hours worse than the average of 23.75 MH per unit for the three crews together. How can this be? It appears that the other two crews must be doing much better but that the new best of 26.82 MH was sufficient to bring the average unit rate low enough to set a new record. Now look at the current week's unit rate in Figure 7.5. The 16.40 MH per unit is well below the average. Such a low number may mean that the crew is doing much better this week, well enough to have brought the four-week average down to a new best record, or it may be the result of an error in the reports or records that will need to be corrected.

The bottom part of the general foreman's report lists the new best records set by any of his crews. It asks the general foreman to check with each crew to determine if the new record is real (and not due to an error in the numbers or to an unusual circumstance). If it is real, then a little praise is in order (positive reinforcement to encourage further good work). If not, then the error will be corrected on next week's report.

In addition, the general foreman is asked to observe the crew's work methods in order to discover if there is something to be learned from the exemplar that other crews might copy. The innovative work method developed by Bonnie Redon in the story "A Foreman at the End of Her Rope" in Chapter 2 was discovered this way. Again, all information on work-methods improvements and suggestions are brought to the regular weekly meeting and discussed. Reserving a spot on the agenda for methods improvement ensures that the topic is covered each week; providing the unit-rate reports and requiring follow-up ensures that whatever is said about methods improvement is relevant to the job.

The Superintendent's Weekly Reports

Superintendents (or whatever higher level of management a project has) also receive both a lost-time report and a unit-rate report each week. The top part of the lost-time report in Figure 7.8 summarizes lost time by code for all crews, and the bottom part then summarizes all codes for each crew. The information at the top shows the causes of the biggest lost-time problem, and the information at the bottom shows the crews that need the most help in solving their problems. With this information, senior management can follow up on the lost-time troubleshooting efforts by general foremen. Superintendents can also use the information to direct their general foremen to investigate specific crews or reasons in greater depth. This two-way communication helps ensure that adequate problem-solving efforts are being made in the field.

Focus on improvement

The top part of the superintendent's unit-rate report in Figure 7.9 looks much like the other unit-rate reports except that it adds all hours and all amounts for the five crews under the superintendent.

Performance Constructors, Inc.	Week ending 09/12/86	
Big River Power Plant #2	Superintendent Weekly Report	
	Name: *McLaughlin, R. M.*	

LOST-TIME REPORT
Crews reporting: A0 A2 A4 A5 A9

Lost-time code and reason	MH this week	MH last week	MH last four weeks
11 Rework, plan change	41.0	14.0	98.0
12 Rework, damage	52.5	56.0	231.0
13 Rework, design error	163.0	151.0	630.0
14 Rework, other reason	39.0	24.0	84.0
20 Late start/Early quit	0.0	0.0	0.0
30 Travel/Transportation	28.5	6.0	42.5
41 Wait for surveyors	11.0	7.0	39.0
42 Wait for other trade	24.0	30.5	115.5
43 Wait for directions	10.0	0.0	22.0
44 Wait for equipment	32.0	42.0	127.5
45 Wait for materials	0.0	65.5	92.0
46 Wait, other reason	26.0	4.0	51.5
50 Interruption of work	5.5	0.0	15.0
60 Other reason	0.0	22.0	31.0
Total lost time (MH)	432.5	422.0	1579.0
(Total payroll hours for week)	2295.0	2320.0	9140.0
(Percent lost time)	19%	18%	17%

Lost Time by Crew

Crew code and foreman	MH this week	MH last week	MH last four weeks
A0 Knox, S. N.	52.0	58.0	377.0
A2 West, E. W.	96.5	62.5	305.0
A4 Williamson, T. J.	104.0	193.0	481.5
A5 Dupree, O. C.	122.0	66.5	227.5
A9 Gifford, D. L.	58.0	42.0	188.0
Total lost time (MH)	432.5	422.0	1579.0

Only project management can act to reduce lost-time manhours. Decide on appropriate actions and note here what you intend to do.

Figure 7.8   Superintendent's JOB-SIGHT® lost-time report.

Here, too, the superintendents look to achieve new exemplars and ever better unit rates. The 24.95 MH per unit for the first item represents a new best record for the average of the five crews working under the superintendent.

While the JOB-SIGHT® management system carefully avoids publicizing the unit rates from any of the reports, in practice many of the numbers become quickly known. Foremen, general foremen, and superintendents frequently express a great deal of curiosity concerning the averages and the exemplars. They want to see how well they are doing relative to the others. And they frequently feel competitive enough to want to be near the top. The informal competition that may develop among crews leads to finding better methods to install the work in less time. (Remember that craftsmen know better than any-

PERFORMANCE CONSTRUCTORS, INC.　　　WEEK ENDING 09/12/86
BIG RIVER POWER PLANT #2　　　SUPERINTENDENT WEEKLY REPORT
　　　NAME: *McLaughlin, R. M.*

UNIT-RATE REPORT　(Work hours divided by units placed)
Crews reporting:　A0 A2 A4 A5 A9

Code and work item	Unit	Work hours	Units placed	Unit rate for week	Four-week unit rate	Best 4-wk unit rate
71.4 Metal clad 480 KV	Each	181.0	8.5	21.29	24.95	**24.95**
72.3 Service 4.16–480 KV	Each	383.0	81.0	4.73	4.92	4.89
73.5 120/280V busway	Feet	237.0	1020.0	0.23	0.25	0.24
82.1 RMC 1" and less	Feet	371.5	1740.0	0.21	0.21	0.20
82.2 RMC 1-½" to 2"	Feet	233.0	850.0	0.27	0.28	0.27
86.1 Wire & conn als	Feet	457.0	920.0	0.50	0.53	0.50
Total work hours		1862.5				
Total payroll hours		2295.0				
Percent work hours		81%				

The best four-week unit-rate improvement for each crew (weighted for hours worked) was:

Crew code and foreman	Item code	Item name
A0 Knox, S. N.	73.5	120/280V busway
A2 West, E. W.	72.3	Service 4.16–480 KV
A4 Williamson, T. J.	71.4	Metal clad 480 KV
A5 Dupree, O. C.	86.1	Wire & conn als
A9 Gifford, D. L.	73.5	120/280V busway

Check off each foreman after you have told the crew how well they did. This week the crew with the greatest improvement in overall unit rates (weighted for hours worked) was: A9 Gifford, D. L.
Check here [ ] after you have told the crew how well they did.

Figure 7.9　Superintendent's JOB-SIGHT® unit-rate report.

one else how to improve their productivity. It's just that they usually have no incentive to do so.) The accurate and regular feedback provided by the weekly reports allows people to judge their own performance relative to standards set by their peers. Everyone likes to do well. Crews that work above the average take greater pride in their work and strive to maintain their superior position; crews below the average often respond to the challenge by trying to improve. And all without any management hassle.

To create the list at the bottom part of the report, the program computes, for each crew, the percentage of improvement in all its four-week unit rates. It then weights the results for the amount of time worked on the item. (A large improvement for only a few work hours would receive less weight than a smaller improvement made with many more work hours.) Regardless of how small the improvement, the program will find something positive about every crew's performance for the week. The report prints each foreman's name accompanied by the item which showed the most improvement.

The report asks the superintendent to talk to each foreman, praising the crew's progress. Recognition of exemplar performance offers positive reinforcement to continue to do well.

In addition, the program singles out the foreman whose crew made the greatest overall improvement for the week for special praise. In many instances, the greatest improvements come from the newest foremen (because they start from so far behind). Positive feedback from higher levels of project management encourages these new foremen to continue to improve. For a big job over many months, it's the *rate of improvement* in productivity that will ultimately determine a contractor's profitability. Setting continuous improvement as the expected standard, rather than some minimum productivity rate, will keep all crews reaching for new exemplars.

The Project's Weekly Report

Figure 7.10 shows the final report included here (the JOB-SIGHT™ management system actually includes other reports designed for specific uses on various jobs). The report calculates the percentage of work completed and projects the manhours based on alternative unit rates. The percent complete report at the top compares the percentage of work installed (the amount installed to date divided by the estimated amount) to the percentage of manhours expended (the manhours charged to date divided by the manhours in the estimate). Boldface type in either column shows which items are ahead (more installed) or behind (more manhours). Obviously, project management prefers to see all the boldface type in the "Percent complete" column.

Finding worth

The lower half of the report projects the manhours required to complete each item. The first column computes the performance ability ratios (PARs) by dividing the best unit rate into the four-week unit rate. The second column prints the amount remaining to install (by subtracting the amount installed to date from the amount in the estimate). The average four-week unit rate for each item appears in the third column. Multiplying the four-week unit rate by the amount left to install gives the manhours projected to complete each item. Multiplying the amount left to install by the best four-week rate in the fifth column gives, in the sixth column, the manhours required to complete each item if the remainder of the work could be accomplished at the exemplar unit rates. Subtracting the two manhour projections leaves the potential manhour savings in the last column—the number of hours that might be saved if the remainder of the project maintained

RCENT COMPLETE REPORT

de and work item	Unit	Estimated amount	Amount to date	Percent complete	Percent manhours	Manhours to date	Estimated manhours
.4 Metal clad 480 KV	Each	32.0	8.5	27%	28%	217.0	768
.3 Service 4.16–480 KV	Each	255.0	166.0	65%	71%	899.0	1275
.5 120/280V busway	Feet	2440.0	1550.0	64%	61%	449.5	732
.1 Fixtures & standards	Each	154.0	23.0	15%	19%	575.0	3080
.1 Cable tray	Feet	2045.0	855.0	42%	59%	752.0	1270
.1 RMC 1″ and less	Feet	4225.0	2050.0	49%	43%	540.0	1270
.2 RMC 1-½″ to 2″	Feet	2750.0	1020.0	37%	34%	336.5	1000
.1 Wire & conn als	Feet	2120.0	1080.0	51%	60%	759.0	1272
.5 Cable fireproofing	Feet	950.0	220.0	23%	21%	39.5	190
tals					42%	4567.5	10857

ANHOUR PROJECTION REPORT

de and work item	PAR	Amount to install	Four-week unit rate	Manhours to install	Best 4-wk unit rate	Manhours to install	Manhour savings
.4 Metal clad 480 KV	1.00	23.5	24.95	586	24.92	586	1
.3 Service 4.16–480 KV	1.01	89.0	4.92	438	4.89	435	3
.5 120/280V busway	1.08	890.0	0.26	231	0.24	214	18
.1 Fixtures & standards	1.02	131.0	22.30	2921	21.80	2856	66
.1 Cable tray	1.16	1190.0	0.88	1047	0.76	904	143
.1 RMC 1″ and less	1.05	2175.0	0.21	457	0.20	435	22
.2 RMC 1-½″ to 2″	1.08	1730.0	0.28	484	0.26	450	35
.1 Wire & conn als	1.08	1040.0	0.54	562	0.50	520	42
.5 Cable fireproofing	1.06	730.0	0.18	131	0.17	124	7
tal projected manhours				6858		6524	335
tal manhours to date				4568		4568	
tal projected manhours to completion				11426		11091	
stimated manhours to install				10857		10857	
anhours over (+) or under (−)				569		234	

re 7.10　Project's JOB-SIGHT™ weekly report.

exemplar productivity rates. The bold type shows cable tray as having the highest worth, 143 MH, the same item with the largest PAR.

In this example, all the current rates are quite close to the exemplars. The projected manhour savings are very small. When management works each week to locate and encourage exemplar performance and then to bring all crews up to the exemplar, the ratio between average and exemplar performance—the PAR—will be very close to 1. A small PAR indicates competent management. The fact that the job is currently projected to overrun the estimate by 569 MH may be due to a slow startup or to an inaccurate estimate; it is definitely not due to low productivity.

Note, however, that this report does not include a projection of lost time. Since none of the unit rates used in the projections includes lost time and since additional lost time will certainly occur before the job ends, a projection for lost time would seem to be necessary. A projection of lost time could be based on the current four-week average for lost time as a percentage of work time. If lost time averages 20 percent of payroll hours, then another 1715 lost-time manhours need to be added to the 6858-MH projection for a total of 8573 MH to complete the project (8573 × 20% = 1715).

For purposes of illustration, many work codes were omitted from the reports to simplify their presentation. On some jobs, the list of work-code items runs several pages. However, with the automatic analysis provided by the program, management can scan the reports to spot quickly the largest problems and the largest opportunities for performance engineering.

Report Graphics

Another important aspect of feedback reporting involves the use of graphics. Graphs can convey a great deal of information while remaining easy to read and understand. Figure 7.11 illustrates a JOB-SIGHT™ graph that tracks the performance of a single work item over a period of 16 weeks. The graph follows three weekly trends: the job average, the best crew each week, and the worst crew each week.

The three graph lines in Figure 7.11 show several important trends. First, the average unit rate for the job, after an initial rise in the first few weeks, shows a steady improvement thereafter. (A falling line means fewer manhours per installed unit, and therefore better productivity.) The worst-crew unit rates (not always the same crew each week) also show improvement, as do the rates for the best crew (again, not always the same crew). More importantly, the gap between best and average, the PAR, decreases—indicating that average performance is coming closer and closer to exemplar performance. The

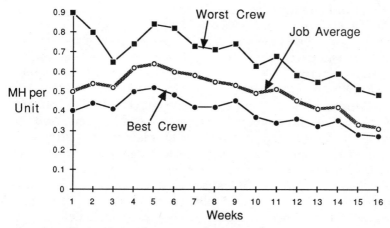

Figure 7.11   Best, worst, and average unit-rate trends.

spread between best and worst also narrows as all crews adopt similar work methods based on learning from the exemplars.

Graphs such as this can help management track performance over time and correlate changes in jobsite conditions with changes in performance. Such feedback allows management to discover how different jobsite factors, such as changes in equipment or crew assignments, affect performance.

Obstacles to Performance Feedback

The content and use of feedback reports has been explained. However, several questions concerning the troubleshooting process require further elaboration. One big question revolves around cheating. Many people will ask, "What good is it to develop and implement a costly performance reporting system since people will lie about their performance anyway?" A good question. It should be asked of every reporting system.

No incentives to cheat

A measurement system that fails to distinguish work time from lost time forces foremen to account for all their crew time as work time. Regardless of how long people stand around waiting for the truck to arrive to begin unloading the materials they need, the foreman must charge these hours to some work code. Now suppose she is working on only two items, one of which is well within the estimate and one of which is well over the estimate. Where will she charge her lost hours? To whatever item she is doing well on. To charge hours unnecessarily to items that are already showing poor productivity is foolish, for the even poorer rates will almost certainly bring her grief. It is human nature to bury the lost time where it is least likely to show—in the items that are going well. Studies have shown that 15 to 35 percent of a crew's time is normally lost (the time is discretionary as to which item it will be charged to). Therefore, foremen have tremendous leeway in making their actual unit rates come out close to the estimate. It's sort of a self-fulfilling prophecy, sometimes even a game. And the measured unit rates on the job will later be added to the estimator's file to be used again on another job. Thus the cycle repeats. No wonder so many field managers and their work forces distrust the estimate. Given the historical source of the information on which it's based, it is unlikely to be right for any specific item, but it may be right in total estimated manhours, since all the offsetting errors will hopefully cancel out.

Now, look at *a system that permits foremen to charge lost time to its real reason—lack of adequate management support.* In doing so, the manhours charged to work items fall, thereby improving the true unit rates. So what is to prevent foremen from deciding to make themselves and their crews look good by charging extra hours to lost time and fewer to work items? Feedback. If management takes the lost-time reports seriously and troubleshoots to solve foremen's problems, the crew that reports more lost time will have management problem-solving, trying to help. "You say you aren't getting support from the carpenters? Well, let's talk it over with their foreman and see if we can't work something out." Or "If waiting for equipment is slowing you up that much, we'll get another cherry picker on the job to work with your crew." After a few such "solutions" to nonexistent problems, either the foreman will stop trying to play games or management will have found him out.

On the other side, if management takes seriously the pursuit of exemplar performance, then the foreman who subtracts hours from work time to throw into lost time will soon find his crew singled out for careful scrutiny. Not because someone thinks the foreman is cheating, but because someone thinks the crew has a superior work method that might be worth passing on to others. It's more than a little embarrassing to be asked to demonstrate your competence at a task that you have lied about. In both cases, positive feedback in the form of supportive management will soon uncover the cheaters. No force or threats are necessary. And because foremen are among the smartest of individuals when it comes to figuring out how to get "the system" to work for them, they will quickly understand that they gain nothing by cheating the system and everything by cooperating with it. Under a well-engineered performance system, cheating is not only fruitless, it's foolish. All the incentives pull together to create a positive balance of consequences that make the system work.

Management leadership

Another question about troubleshooting revolves around effective leadership. Do good job managers need it, and can poor job managers even use it? Jobs are run by people with varying degrees of leadership skills. At one extreme, the "General Patton" type tells everyone exactly what to do and listens to no one. At the other extreme, Mr. Nice Guy promises everyone exactly what they demand but cannot possibly deliver most of it.

A performance reporting system, by explicitly providing everyone with the same kind of information aimed at the same problems and opportunities, forces cooperation and communication toward commonly accepted goals. On one large project, the business agent for the local union asked for, and got, weekly copies of the lost-time and unit-rate reports. He used the reports to push his foremen to better performance and to exhort them to report their lost time. He also used the reports to pump management for increased support for his crews to avoid the lost time, often coming up with creative suggestions himself. *With the right information, everyone knows what the problem is and can concentrate on the solution instead of trying to find someone else to blame.* By keeping after the problems, the business agent did as much to boost productivity on the job as did management. Both found themselves cooperating against a common foe—lost time—instead of fighting each other.

Performance reporting provides much-needed feedback. Strong managers can use it to gain support for their seemingly autocratic decisions. Weak managers need it to generate a consensus for cooperative decision making.

Secrecy

Yet another oft-questioned aspect of performance reporting lies in the area of the need for contractors to protect their estimates, both from their competitors and from their own labor force. Many contractors refuse to allow progress reports out of their office for fear that their competitors will somehow get them and learn the unit rates and prices used in the bid. This information will then be used to underbid them in the future. The second fear, that of giving reports to field labor, comes from the belief that if the labor force knows the estimate, they will never work harder to do better than the estimate. And should they somehow find themselves doing better than the estimate, they will slack off and coast. Both fears appear unreasonable. Even more unreasonable, however, is the response displayed by most contractors—to avoid performance feedback reporting altogether.

Any of the reports used as examples in this book could contain "secret" information. All of them could just as easily scramble the sensitive numbers in such a way as to make the reports meaningless to outsiders while remaining useful to the job. One contractor, for example, converts estimated manhours into "points"; subsequent recording of manhours charged to each task are also converted into points. Unit rates for her jobs are reported back to the field in the form of graphs, showing upward (or downward) lines representing "points per installed unit." As far as the people in the field are concerned, the more points they earn, the better the job. She uses a simple formula on her spreadsheet program to convert counts of manhours and amounts placed into points.

Separating lost time from work time and computing true unit rates for each crew reveals no vital estimating information. Neither does counting amounts installed according to site-specific criteria. For example, the use of a standard weighted unit of work may make sense in terms of counting the installation of many windows of different sizes but would have no meaning to someone working a different job.

Finally, just what would a competitor do with the information even if it was readily available? How much time would it take to figure out exactly what it meant? And how could a competitor be sure that the information was accurate? The fear of giving something away to the competition, when examined closely, turns out to offer little justification for concealing vital feedback information from field supervisors.

Similarly, hiding estimates from the field labor force yet failing to give them any targets at all can do more harm than good. In the example just above, the contractor's target on every job is to get more points each week than the week before. She effectively communicates this standard to her crews through her use of the feedback graphs. If the earned points for a particular task fall, everyone wants to know what went wrong and seeks to make corrections. Needless to say, most of her jobs make money.

And, without doubt, the vast majority of employees give their loyalty to the organization that hires them. They respond to the trust shown in them when given feedback information. Very few would abuse that trust.

Developing Feedback Skills

The methods engineering model underscored the importance of information in troubleshooting jobs and improving performance. Feedback forms a vital part of this information flow. Feedback tells people how well (or poorly) they are doing relative to the expected standards of performance (the exemplar). Without feedback, individuals may never know of their performance deficiencies and may therefore be unable to take appropriate steps to correct them. Management competence, in many respects, depends on the quality of feedback, both the feedback given to management and the feedback that management gives to the craftsmen in the field.

Improving the quality of feedback will certainly help improve performance. But just as importantly, people need the skills to use the feedback they get. It does little good to prepare reports for foremen if they do not understand how to interpret the information on the reports. So attention given to training field supervisors to read and act on feedback may be as critical as developing the feedback in the first place. Such training need not be fancy. Often a half-hour spent reviewing the report with a foreman and discussing what it means in terms of past and future decision making will be adequate. Frequent follow-up, to ensure that foremen and others are getting the most out of the reports, will also help keep the feedback as effective as possible.

Feedback can take many forms. Each contractor and each project may have different needs. But whatever form it takes and however it may vary from job to job, feedback performance reporting encourages the development of a competent labor force and a competent management team.

Chapter

8

Engineering
Field Performance

The previous discussions of productivity measurement and management have concentrated on explanations of theory and principles, using case-study examples to illustrate particular applications. They have emphasized that the purpose of measurement is to improve performance, and Chapter 7 examined one important management technique for performance improvement—feedback. Feedback provides management with exceptionally strong leverage with which to engineer improved performance in the field.

But, by itself, feedback is not enough. Three additional management techniques need to accompany feedback in order to obtain the maximum benefit from performance measurement. In addition to *feedback,* we need to concern ourselves with *standards, reinforcement,* and *job support.*

- Feedback
- Standards
- Reinforcement
- Job support

These four techniques are not new; they were first introduced in the methods engineering model in Chapter 4. But they deserve special emphasis because of their importance.

Setting Standards

Setting standards means letting people know exactly what is expected of them. Everyone works to meet some standard, even if it's only an internal standard set by the individual. Some individuals set their internal work standards quite low; they seek the minimum they can do and still keep their jobs. Others set very high standards for themselves. (Some set them so high that they spend their whole lives dissatisfied with their performance.) Most people, however, set reasonable work standards for themselves and tend to judge others by the same standards.

On a construction job where the work standards are unclear, craftsmen set work standards for themselves and their crews based largely on their past experience; some jobs may seem to require high standards, while other jobs may seem less demanding. Many contractors think that they set high work standards for their jobs, but in practice they fail to convey these standards to their work force. Others may set irrelevant standards that fail to bring out the best in their work force.

Standards and feedback

Unless people have a clear idea of what is expected of them, they have no standard by which to judge their performance. To be effective, feedback must compare present performance to the standard—the desired performance. Whenever present performance is below what is desired, people can alter their work methods (perhaps using the methods engineering model) to improve their performance. Most people want to know what is expected of them and will meet these expectations. Meeting work standards gives individuals a satisfying sense of accomplishment and a feeling of self-worth.

But we have seen that work standards should not be pegged to average performance. Only exemplar performance provides a worthy work standard. And most people, when they understand how the exemplar was achieved, readily accept it as a performance goal and strive to meet it. (After all, the exemplar represents the best historical record set either by themselves or by a similar crew doing similar work. The exemplar is set by them, not by someone in the office.) Since exceeding the exemplar automatically establishes a new exemplar and a new performance goal, the work standard continually improves, encouraging individuals and crews to do better.

One concrete contractor, engaged in a series of large concrete pours over several weeks, posted a billboard outside the site gate announcing to other subs and trades how many yards his crews had placed the day before. The billboard showed a graph with an upward-sloping line indicating that the crews were placing more and more concrete each day. Taking pride in their accomplishment, the crews always tried to beat their previous day's record. By the end of the month, the line had actually run off the scale at the top. The contractor set a simple standard—do better than the day before—and provided regular feedback as to how well the crews had worked to meet the standard. The result surprised everyone; the crews finished placing the concrete six days ahead of schedule.

Setting work standards and communicating them to field crews may require some thinking and planning. But it is always worth the relatively small amount of effort it takes. The alternative, letting crews set their own performance standards, may never lead to productivity gains.

Katz Kooling Kompany

Ever since the age of eight, Kevin K. (for Kimbrell) Katz has liked K's. As he likes to say, "It's a krazy business and you've got to be krazy to like it." Kevin's "kompany" does a little heating, ventilating, and air-conditioning (HVAC) work. But mostly Kevin fabricates sheet-metal work in his shop for other contractors. It used to be very profitable, doing the fabrication for others, but lately the shop has run into increasing competition. Labor turnover and nonexistent production controls have suddenly combined to cause large fluctuations in weekly output. Sometimes his shop gets weeks behind schedule, and even his regular customers have begun to complain about late deliveries. Kevin realizes that unless he can control output and improve productivity in his shop, he may soon be out of business.

Besides liking K's, Kevin also likes computers (or "komputers," as he calls them), and he has looked over many of the software programs that help contractors schedule work, do estimating, track progress, and handle accounting. Although Kevin has purchased and tried several of the programs, he prefers to write his own. He does most of his programing with an electronic-spreadsheet software package. Having just read an article on productivity measurement, Kevin has become intrigued with measuring the productivity of the sheet-metal fabrication shop. He likes the idea of weekly measurements but does not see the need for a complicated system of reporting. After all, he only has 12 people working on the shop floor. He realizes that if he could figure out a way to measure weekly productivity, he could set standards for shop production. And with measured standards, he could make better production forecasts and thus avoid promising delivery deadlines he could never meet. So Kevin sets out to develop a simple program to help measure productivity.

Counting by weighting

Kevin soon realizes that he has no effective way to count the work accomplished by the shop. Although his estimating handbook gives fairly detailed cost differences between various ductwork configurations, Kevin wants to separate the amount of time it takes to produce an item from the amount of money it costs. The shop produces such a wide variety of shapes and sizes that it seems impossible to count them all. So Kevin starts out looking for all the similarities he can find in the sheet-metal work rather than all the differences.

In talking with his shop foreman, Kevin learns that it takes just as much time to run folds 8 in wide as it does to run them 10 in wide through the machine. Eventually Kevin begins finding groups of similar sizes and shapes of ductwork that require nearly the same amount of time and effort to produce. He picks the simplest and most common duct size and shape (an 8-in by 10-in rectangular, uninsulated, low-velocity duct, 3 ft in length, with no grill or other cutouts) as his standard against which he weights the rest. He counts each subsequent size of rectangular duct in terms of how much more (or less) time-consuming it is to make relative to his standard duct.

Once he feels that he has established reasonable relationships among all the simple rectangular ducts, he then begins over again, this time adding a single grill to each. Then an air controller. Then other variations. Then insulation. He measures Y-ducts, curved ducts, transition pieces, and every other type he can find, judging each against his standard 8 × 10 duct.

Eventually he builds up a large spreadsheet matrix, which lists all the types of duct sizes and shapes down the left-hand side and which contains all the variations (such as grills, controls, and cutouts) across the top. Into each cell Kevin puts a decimal number that gives the assigned weight for that item. Table 8.1 illustrates a portion of Kevin's spreadsheet.

Productivity measurements

With his matrix, Kevin can look up the "degree-of-difficulty factor" for every size and variation of ductwork and get a pretty good idea of how

TABLE 8.1   A Matrix of Ductwork Measurements

	A	B	C	D	E	F	G
1	Rectangular ductwork						
2	Code	H″	W″	Simple	Grill	2 Grills	Controller
3							
4		6	8	1.20	1.50	1.85	2.00
5		6	10	1.10	1.45	1.75	1.95
6		6	12	1.15	1.45	1.75	1.95
7		8	8	1.00	1.35	1.60	1.75
8		8	10	1.00	1.35	1.60	1.75
9		8	12	1.05	1.40	1.65	1.80
10		8	14	1.15	1.50	1.75	2.00

long it will take to make the item, relative to making one of his standard 8 × 10 ducts. With the weighted measures of accomplishment, Kevin no longer has to worry about how to charge the manhours in the shop. (It would clearly have been counterproductive to have every person in the shop try to charge his or her time to every individual duct item, for most work is done continuously, with each person doing repetitive tasks, such as cutting or insulating.) Now, each week, Kevin counts the total number of each type of ductwork that has been fabricated. Entering the counts into the spreadsheet, he multiplies these counts by the appropriate weights from his matrix. Finally he adds all the weighted numbers together to get the total shop output for the week. By dividing this total count by the number of manhours worked for the week, Kevin obtains a single index measurement of shop productivity (given in units of standard ducts per manhour).

Searching through the past months' output, Kevin finds several instances of exemplar production for a single week. He chooses an average of his best three weeks as his standard for shop production. At a meeting with the shop employees, Kevin explains his new measurement system, why he thinks he needs it to stay in business, and how he will be able to use it, both to measure shop productivity and to schedule production orders. Each week thereafter, Kevin posts in the shop their productivity relative to their exemplar. Soon shop productivity rises and stabilizes around the exemplar.

Pleased with the results, Kevin toys with the idea of raising the standard but is afraid to do so. He fears that the shop workers will either rebel or demand a wage increase.

Without knowing its value, few contractors would have either the time or the patience to imitate Kevin Katz and develop such a detailed measurement system. Yet without numerical measurements, feedback often seems too subjective to the people in the field. And because it's subjective, it's suspect. People in the field will not readily accept management's evaluation of their productivity unless they can see the hard numbers themselves and understand how they were calculated.

In putting together a field measurement system, it must be kept simple so that the people doing the work can readily understand the measurements. Every contractor will have different requirements and different ways to measure, but however a measurement system is set up, it should be designed so that the measurements serve two important functions: *to establish exemplar work standards and to provide feedback regarding how closely current performance meets these standards.*

Giving Reinforcement

After a contractor has set standards and provided feedback, another critical step is necessary—giving the reinforcement necessary to encourage people to continue to meet the standards. In the example above, Kevin successfully set a higher standard for his shop but was unable to improve upon it once his work force met the standard. They were almost certainly capable of doing even better, but they lacked any incentive for doing so. This is the role of reinforcement—*to create an environment in which people want to improve.* They want to improve because they find reinforcements to superior performance.

Positive and negative reinforcements

Reinforcements may take many forms. Rewards, acknowledgment, prizes, bonuses, perks, praise, attention, tickets to the ball game, asking for advice, and pay raises all reinforce desired performance. Because these reinforcers act to encourage a desired performance, they are usually labeled "positive reinforcement." Negative reinforcement most often takes the form of punishment for undesirable performance. Children may be spanked to discourage unwanted behavior. Employees may be threatened with the loss of their jobs for failing to perform well.

Construction management often relies on negative reinforcers to push workers and crews toward desired performance standards. Threats of getting fired certainly stimulate individuals to meet minimum performance standards. But such negative reinforcers are generally incapable of stimulating individuals to exemplar performance. Only positive reinforcers can regularly bring out the best in people.

It is a curious fact, but research has shown that the most effective positive reinforcers are the unexpected or irregular rewards. (Weekly paychecks have little positive reinforcement value. The fear of losing the job and the paycheck, however, is a strong negative reinforcer that stimulates individuals to meet minimum performance standards, usually just showing up for work.) In the example of the concrete contractor given at the beginning of this chapter, unexpected positive reinforcement maintained the upward productivity trend. After the first week of setting higher productivity records, the contractor met his work force at the gate at the end of the day with his pickup loaded with cases of beer. Every crew member got a full case to take home—an unexpected yet totally appropriate reward for a job well done. Needless to say, the next week new records were set nearly every day even though no one promised any reward for the effort.

A balance of consequences

No matter how carefully a contractor attempts to structure positive reinforcements for superior performance, there will always be offsetting negative consequences that act to undermine the effectiveness of the reinforcers. In spite of the beer, for example, the crews did have to hustle every day in the heat to get the concrete placed, and there is a limit to how much effort an individual will put out. Peer pressure, in the form of unspoken work standards, may also act to limit productivity on some jobs; individuals who exceed such informal work standards soon find themselves under pressure from other workers to slow down the pace. Every performance improvement effort carries both positive and negative consequences. Competent managers recognize this fact and attempt to find positive consequences to offset the negative ones. In the end, it is the *balance of consequences* that will determine the level of performance on a job.

Bringing together standards, feedback, and reinforcement creates a work environment in which people know what is expected of them, receive regular guidance as to how well they are doing relative to these expectations, and find that their efforts to meet the expectations are adequately rewarded. To see how these three elements can combine to produce startling results, let us turn to another fabrication shop for a slightly different approach to the problem of productivity management.

Field and Fabrication

Bob Gyeser, a senior vice president at J&J Mechanical, figured to save money on jobs by doing more piping work in the company's fabrication shop. J&J did a lot of plumbing and pipe-fitting work, but recently its pipe-fitting business seemed to be running into stiffer competition. Bob had missed several jobs by a very narrow amount on the bid. He convinced top management at J&J to expand the fabrication shop to cut, fit, and weld sections of pipe for delivery to jobsites for installation. The prefab work, because it could be done under controlled shop conditions, would cut field labor costs. Within three months, Bob was sure he had made the right decision; two more jobs came in and the shop suddenly found itself with four full-time fitters cranking out "spools," the prefabricated, welded steel-pipe sections, for a number of jobs around town.

In fact, the shop seemed to be doing so much more business that Bob considered purchasing several new pieces of automatic cutting and welding equipment. But the high cost of the new equipment raised objections. Traditionally, construction companies keep their overhead as low as possible in order to weather inevitable downturns in business.

Bob's new equipment, although it promised to boost fab-shop productivity, could not guarantee enough new business to pay for itself. To justify the investment in equipment, Bob needed numbers. He needed to know just how much money the fab shop was making and how much more it could make with new equipment.

Comparing shop and field

J&J already measured field productivity in the form of unit rates for pipe installation and other work. Bob felt certain that the fab shop was helping to improve the field unit rates, but he could not prove it. He needed to find a way to measure fab-shop productivity separately from the field. And he needed to do it in a way that would not involve an enormous change in the present reporting and accounting system.

Bob first reviewed J&J's current reporting system for measuring the field unit rates, a fairly sophisticated system put into place only the year before. Each day the field foremen turned in time cards for the people in their crews. The foremen charged the number of hours worked to a series of standard work codes. The work codes grouped pipe sizes into a dozen classifications and included codes for many other types of work as well. At the end of each week a project engineer walked each job and counted the amount of work-in-place, calculating the amount accomplished during the week. The office then matched the manhours to the work accomplished to compute the unit rates (manhours per unit of installed work) for each job for the week for every type of work done. But Bob was interested only in the pipe-size codes. Here he had the field productivity measurements. Now all he had to do was to track them to see if they improved or not.

But tracking the field measurements turned out to be harder than Bob thought it would be. For one thing, the foremen did not charge their hours the same on every job; the project managers tended to "influence" where the hours were charged in order to get the measurements to come out as close to the estimate as possible. (Since the time cards had no separate lost-time codes, the foremen charged lost time to the work codes according to their own discretion.) Then, too, the amount of off-site fabrication of spools varied from job to job. If work backed up at the fab shop, the foremen tended to do their own work in the field, even though it was less productive. The foremen hated to wait for shop spools because it forced them to plan ahead in laying out work for their crews. (J&J foremen were not noted for their planning—another issue for a later time.) If the weekly unit-rate measurements ran over the estimate, the project managers blamed the fab shop for poor support; if the measurements came in lower, the project managers attributed the success to their field crews and their management methods, not to shop support. Bob would not find supporters for his automatic welding equipment in the field.

Measuring shop productivity

Bob turned to John Carltin, the fab-shop foreman, for help. Could John help devise a way to measure the impact of his shop on field labor rates? Bob and John agreed that they could not measure productivity in the shop with the same units as the field measured it—manhours per foot of installed pipe—since the shop did not install the pipe. All the shop did was cut, fit, and weld spools. But each spool varied so much in size and configuration that a simple count of spools would be misleading. And just keeping track of manhours per job wouldn't work either; the larger pipe sizes required far more manhours to cut and weld than did the smaller sizes. Then, too, several jobs usually came though the fab shop at the same time, since it was more productive to set up and do all the same-size pipe at the same time. It was hard enough keeping track of the manhours charged to each different job; there was no way the manhour charges could be tracked by each pipe as well. As Bob and John talked it over, however, they realized that the real accomplishment of the fab shop was welds. Count the welds, weight them for their degree of difficulty, and you had a measure of the shop's output.

But how to weight the welds? That weekend Bob took home the welding estimating manual and his calculator. First he calculated how many inches of weld were required for each pipe diameter (including saddle and lateral welds). From the estimating manual Bob came up with a degree-of-difficulty factor for each type of weld and each type of pipe. This degree of difficulty took into account the differing amounts of time required to lay out different welds and to handle heavier pipe sizes. Multiplying the inches of weld by the degree-of-difficulty factor gave a weighted number of "weld-inches" for each weld by pipe size. Then Bob grouped the pipes' sizes into the same categories used in field reporting and came up with average weights for each category. Finally, he designed a form to track each pipe size and weld and to figure the manhours per 1000 in of weighted welds.

The spreadsheet

Pleased with his success in developing the measurement system, he showed his work to his teenage son, Mike. Mike wrinkled up his nose at his father's crude hand calculations. "You gonna spend every weekend doing those calculations?" Mike asked. Bob looked at the forms, suddenly realizing how much work would be involved in computing all the productivity rates; and an error or two would destroy the usefulness of the measurements. "Do you have a better idea?" asked Bob. For the next half hour Bob sat transfixed as he watched his son use an electronic spreadsheet on the family home computer to lay out a program to calculate all the measurements automatically. All you had to do was enter the numbers once a week and, bingo, out popped the measurements. Mike then spent a few more minutes coming to a profitable arrangement with his father to finish the program and run it for him each weekend.

Table 8.2 shows a portion of Mike's spreadsheet. Given the pipe diameter (column A), the program calculates the circumference (column B); given the weld type (column C), the program looks up the weighting factor (column D) and calculates the weld-inches (column E) by multiplying the circumference by the weighting factor. Now all Bob had to do was give Mike the weekly counts of each pipe size by type of weld. These counts would be entered into column F, and Mike's program would multiply the counts by the weld-inches in column E to get the total weld-inches for each pipe size and weld type (column G). For example, Table 8.2 shows that six 4-in butt welds were made during the week. Multiplying 6 by the 30.2 weld-inches per pipe gives 181 weld-inches. Adding together all the amounts in column G gives the total weld-inches for the week; dividing this total into the total manhours for the week (and multiplying by 1000) provides a measurement of the week's productivity in manhours (MH) per 1000 weld-inches.

For the next two months, Mike picked up a nice addition to his weekly allowance while Bob got the numbers he needed. With John's help, Bob refined his first estimates of his degree-of-difficulty weights. (Mike simply plugged the revised weights into column D in the spreadsheet and recalculated all the past reports in less time than it took the printer to spit them out.) Bob and John soon discovered that, on the average, it took the shop 23.5 MH to produce 1000 weld-inches.

TABLE 8.2 An Example of Calculations of Weighted Weld-Inches

	A	B	C	D	E	F	G
1	Pipe		Weld	Weighting	Weld-	Number of	Total weld-inches
2	diameter	Circumference	type	factor	inches	welds this week	this week
3							
4	2.5	7.85	Butt	1.2	9.4		
5	3.0	9.42	Butt	1.6	15.1		
6	4.0	12.57	Butt	2.4	30.2	6	181
7	5.0	15.71	Butt	3.1	48.7		

Accounting for shop and field

Convinced that he now had a good measurement of shop productivity, Bob took the next step, trying it out on a real job. First Bob had a draftsman go over the isometric drawings for an upcoming small job to pick out and list all the welds that would be done in the fab shop (at least all the welds that the estimators had assumed would be done in the shop when they put together the bid). Bob gave the list of welds to Mike, who ran it through his spreadsheet to calculate a total of 5240 weld-inches required for the job. At an average of 23.5 MH per 1000 weld-inches, it should take the shop 123 MH to complete the job. Bob then went to Dorthea ("Dee") Myers, the project manager assigned to the job, and explained to her the system for measuring and accounting for fab-shop productivity. As an experiment, Bob would subtract the 123 MH from the total manhours estimated for the job and transfer them to the shop. Essentially, Dee would "pay" for the shop's services with field manhours and the shop would "earn" these manhours by producing work for the field. Although skeptical, she agreed to try Bob's system. (For the experiment, Bob promised Dee he would keep track of his shadow accounting system on Mike's computer, since no one wanted to get the data processing people in the office upset.)

By "removing" manhours from the field estimate, Bob automatically lowered the estimated unit rates for field installation. Dee would need to do the same amount of work in fewer field manhours, since the extra manhours were now in the shop's account. Thus the separate accounting for field and shop manhours permitted Bob to compare actual performance in the field and in the shop with his estimates of their expected performance. If Dee could beat her estimated rates, she would have performed well (although Bob recognized that she could control, to some extent, how many manhours her foremen charged to the pipe installation). And if John could turn the job out of his shop in fewer than 123 MH, he would have earned a "profit," doing better than the estimate.

χTracking shop productivity

Although Bob's attempt to measure the productivity in the fabrication shop proved successful, his idea about charging shop manhours against the field projects didn't gain much support. Distracted by more pressing business, Bob turned over the whole process to John and Mike, who continued to measure shop productivity for the next six months. Each week Mike graphed the shop productivity; the result is shown in Figure 8.1. John's shop started out averaging 23.5 MH per 1000 weld-inches. The average, calculated over the past six months,

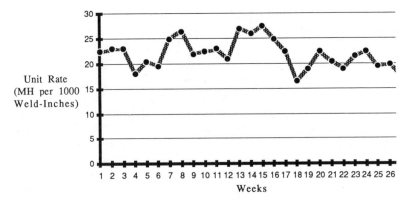

Figure 8.1   The fabrication shop's weekly productivity.

was down to 22 MH. Mike computed the trend for the improvement and showed that the current average rate (as projected from the past 27 weeks) was down to about 20.5 MH. The 3-MH gain, from 23.5 to 20.5 MH, represented a 13 percent increase in shop productivity. With these numbers, Bob figured the even greater improvements that would come if the new equipment was purchased. Unfortunately, business was off and J&J did not have either the money or the cash flow to justify the investment at that time.

No feedback

Bob hated to drop his measurements of fab-shop productivity, so he took them to John Carltin to ask him what he thought about the measurement system. Bob had not shared his numbers with the shop personnel before. Neither they nor John Carltin, their foreman, knew how well they were performing from week to week. Gathering the numbers had become just another paperwork exercise for John. Even Bob had lost some interest when he watched the large jumps in weekly averages graphed by Mike. To Bob, these jumps showed just how difficult it was to get good measurements of shop productivity. The especially large increases between weeks 13 and 16 in Figure 8.1 occurred over the December holiday period; when Bob commented to John that shop productivity was off, John had responded with large improvements in early January. But lack of regular feedback gave John little or no incentive to maintain the improved rate. As far as John knew, the 23.5 MH per 1000 weld-inches was the standard set for the shop; he had no reason to improve it.

When John and his shop people saw Mike's graph, they were

amazed. They had no idea that their productivity had been so irregular or that it had improved over the past six months. John immediately asked what happened in week 18, the week they set a record of 17 MH per 1000 weld-inches. No one could remember.

Regular feedback

Encouraged by the interest shown in the graph by the shop workers, Bob decided to keep up the measurements and send them to the shop each week. Mike added a "score" to the graph, each week dividing the current week's productivity by the exemplar from week 18. (Actually, without realizing it, Mike was computing a weekly PAR. The closer to 1.0 the score, the better the shop performance for the week.) The idea was to show the shop workers how far off they were from their best performance.

Within four weeks the shop hit a new exemplar of 16.5. And two weeks later it was down to 15! Apparently the feedback alone was enough to boost productivity. However, as Mike brought in the new graph for that week, John told him he knew it had been a good week but that he didn't think the boys in the shop would keep it up. After all, they weren't getting paid any more for the effort.

The need for reinforcement

That evening Mike told his father what John had said about not getting paid to do better. "Why can't you pay them for how much they do?" asked Mike, thinking he had come up with a bright idea.

"It's not that easy," said Bob. "They work under a contract and we can't change the wage scale."

"Well," commented Mike, "it sure doesn't seem right."

Bob thought so, too, and determined to see if there wasn't some way to encourage even better shop productivity and to sustain it. He felt the shop could be a real money-maker for the company if he could keep it running as well as it had the past six weeks. Feedback alone was not sufficient to reach the shop's real potential—incentives were also needed.

Suppose, Bob mused, that I'd been able to keep the manhour charge system going, pricing shop output according to the manhours required to do the work. Bob had originally intended to cut the shop's "price" for finished work in accordance with its latest productivity. He had started off "charging" 23.5 MH per 1000 weld-inches. In the following months the "charge" would have dropped to 22 and then 21 MH per unit. The improved shop productivity would certainly help J&J stay competitive. But what would have been in it for the shop personnel? If it meant working harder to meet a new standard each month, why would they have done it?

Bob recognized that the people who worked in the shop every day were smart enough to figure out all sorts of ways to increase production while cutting the number of manhours. In an operation such as a fabrication shop, many time-saving ideas come to mind every day. But unless there is a reason to try them out, most workers just keep their mouths shut, preferring not to rock the boat. After a while, they even stop thinking of ways to make the job easier, they just think about getting it done and going home. (During the initial period of productivity measurement, John had come up with a simple method of using different cans of spray paint to color-code pipe for various jobs. Another worker in the shop suggested a method to unload pipe onto the shop floor from the overhead crane so that it would be easier to sort and move to the cutting machines.) Bob's measurement system provided the feedback that the workers required in order to improve, but under J&J's labor contract Bob could see no easy way to offer incentives as well. The best incentives tie directly to the gains in productivity—the bigger the gain, the bigger the reward.

A "profit-sharing" proposal

Bob saw a possible answer. Suppose J&J tracked the "profitability" of the shop by keeping a record of the number of manhours the shop earned against the number that it actually spent to do a job. Using a 22- or 21-MH standard, the shop would continue to "charge" projects for work done, transferring manhours from the field to the shop account. Profitability would equal the excess number of manhours earned in any one month over the number of manhours actually worked. For example, if in one month the shop earned a "profit" of 40 MH, it would mean that the shop did 40 hours more work than management estimated it could do, a savings that would translate directly into real dollar profits for J&J.

That is, suppose the estimated unit rate for the shop was 21.5 MH per 1000 weld-inches and that the shop worked 840 MH during the month. At its estimated rate it should have produced 39,070 weld-inches. If its actual production was 40,930, it would have gained 1860 weld-inches, working at an average unit rate of 20.5 MH per 1000 weld-inches (840/40.93). Multiplying the extra 1860 weld-inches by the estimated rate of 21.5 MH per 1000 weld-inches (and dividing by 1000) gives 40 MH, the time saved that should have been required to produce the extra 1860 weld-inches had the shop not worked more productively.

Now, to encourage the shop to continue to turn a manhour profit each month, management should share the real profits with the workers. But how? Perhaps, Bob thought, they could split the 40-MH savings evenly, awarding 20 MH to the shop and 20 MH to management. Management would subtract its own 20 MH from the estimated manhours for shop work the next month and recompute a lower estimated unit rate for the shop. In the example here, the 20 MH would be subtracted from the 840 MH actually worked, giving 820 MH. Now dividing 820 by the 39,070 estimated weld-inches for the month would give a new unit rate of 21.0 MH per weld-inch, the new standard to use in figuring "profit and loss" for the following month. (Note that the shop actually worked the past month at a unit rate of 20.5 MH, so the new standard is reasonable relative to what the shop had accomplished in the past.) If the shop crew again worked 840 MH, they would need to produce 40,000 weld-inches to "break even" at the 21.0-MH unit rate. Any weld-inches above the 40,000 standard would again result in a "profit" to be shared between management and labor.

The work force (in this case four craftsmen and the foreman) might apportion their 20 MH evenly, each taking 4 MH. During the next month, they would be paid for these hours without actually having to work them. They might, for example, each take one-half day off or quit an hour earlier every Friday afternoon. During that month, the new unit rate standard of 21.0 MH per 1000 weld-inches would be used in the estimates to calculate shop production goals. (Assuming that the crew takes off the 20 MH and so works only 820 MH during the month, the production goal would be only 39,050 weld-inches, not the full 40,000.) If the crew beat the 39,050 standard, the gain would again be split; if they missed the goal, no one would profit, but neither would the shop crew lose anything. The same standard (21.0 MH per 1000 weld-inches) would then continue for the following months or until a new productivity record was set.

Under such a system, Bob thought, management would gain because it would be able to use lower and lower manhour estimates in figuring shop production, thus enabling it to bid lower and bring in more work and more profits. The work force would gain by earning paid time off every time they bettered their previous performance.

Bob felt that his incentive system would provide adequate reinforcement for continued productivity improvement in the shop. After all, the crew had already shown that they could get down as low as 15 MH per unit. Since the company could not pay additional wages for superior performance, extra time off might work. Maybe even throw in a company pickup truck for their personal use, Bob thought, when they reached some goal. Happy that he had a solution, Bob went off to try to sell his idea to his bosses. And what happened there is another long story.

Mutual reinforcement

Under such a system as Bob devised, both workers and management benefit. Workers get paid time off, and management gets a lower unit rate to use in estimating future work. Does such a system mean that labor must work harder? Probably not, since the minimum amount of time off would scarcely justify a frantic work pace, day after day. What it does mean is that labor will work smarter. They will start to look at the job they must do to see if they can find ways to do it quicker and more efficiently. They have a strong incentive to discover ways to speed up the shop output (a method for charging them for rejected welds will ensure quality) without increasing either the number of manhours or the effort involved.

As competition in the construction industry grows, innovative methods to tap the creative contributions of the labor force will become increasingly important. The continued evolution of the changing relationship between management and labor (both unionized and nonunion) reflects this need. *The intelligence of the work force represents perhaps the greatest underutilized resource in the construction industry*. To tap it, management needs to turn to creative methods that mutually benefit both sides.

Job Support

The fourth element of performance engineering—after standards, feedback, and reinforcement—is job support. Job support means removing all the obstacles to getting the job done. It means creating a work environment in which people find it easier to do the job (and to do it well) than not to do it. The methods engineering model in Chapter 4 stressed the importance of resources in obtaining superior performance. Job support means making sure that these resources are there when people need them. Individuals who know the standards, get the feedback, and accept the reinforcers still cannot do a good job if management fails to provide them with the support they need to do the work.

The George M. Lohman Construction Co.

High-rise commercial and residential work accounted for over 90 percent of the business of The George M. Lohman Construction Co. Over the years the company had established both a good reputation as a general contractor and the expertise to back it up. The company also practiced careful cost control methods; it kept overhead low and ran every job for a profit.

Dissatisfied with the excavation subcontractors in the region, the company had years ago established its own in-house excavation and foundation capability in the form of a small division. The excavation division, referred to internally as "the holely ones," bid each of Lohman's jobs as a subcontractor, often competing with other excavation subs. Over 80 percent of Lohman's excavation work was awarded to its own division, strictly on the basis of lower competitive bids. Barbara Sanger, an engineering graduate from Stanford, headed Lohman's excavation division.

Quantifying the problem

Although Barbara bid jobs separately, it was simply an accounting act. Her division did not function as a profit center. All the equipment they used was owned and maintained by Lohman in its large equipment yard near the river. And it was the poor quality of the equipment and its even shoddier maintenance that was lately causing Barbara to overrun her manhour estimates.

To help make a convincing case to her bosses to do something about the yard equipment, she asked her superintendent on one of the current jobs to keep track of the time his crews lost waiting while equipment was down for repairs. He was also to keep track of the overtime manhours he spent trying to catch up to the schedule when the equipment finally started working again. Table 8.3 shows the manhour charges collected by Barbara after seven weeks.

TABLE 8.3   Manhour Charges for Excavation Work

A	B	C	D	E	F	G	H	I
			Actual MH to date			Estimated	% MH	% Work
Cost code	Description	Regular MH	Lost MH	Overtime	Lost MH	MH	used	complete
2200	Overhead	154	0	0	154	400	39%	40%
2250	Preexcavate	139	0	0	139	140	99%	100%
2270	Soldier beams	684	33	7	724	770	94%	100%
2275	H-pile lagging	1658	34	21	1713	3800	45%	55%
2310	Cutoff soldiers	0	0	0	0	230	0%	0%
2315	Earth tiebacks	2486	654	1086	4226	5150	82%	45%
2322	Remove steel	0	0	0	0	165	0%	0%
2331	Support utils	164	0	2	166	460	36%	80%
2340	Dewatering	415	2	18	435	620	70%	80%
	Totals	5700	723	1134	7557	11735	64%	

In looking over the numbers in Table 8.3, Barbara sees she has the figures she needs to make her case. The manhours charged to earth tiebacks have already used up 82 percent of her estimated manhours, yet only 45 percent of the work has been done. A total of 654 MH have been lost because of breakdowns of the drilling rigs used to bore the holes for the tiebacks. Another 1086 overtime hours (actually 724 hours times the 1.5 overtime premium) have been charged to tiebacks as people stayed late throughout the weeks in an attempt to keep on schedule. Clearly management has not been providing the necessary job support.

Mismeasurements of performance

Confronted with Barbara's numbers, her boss agrees that the problem merits quick attention. Upon looking into it, he discovers that the equipment yard personnel have gotten excellent ratings according to Lohman's internal performance audit system! Puzzled, he looks up the criteria for the ratings. There he discovers that the yard is graded according to two criteria: getting the right equipment to the job when it is required and responding to on-site maintenance requests within an hour. Nothing in their performance standards requires that the equipment be in running condition at the site or that it stays in running condition after being repaired!

Measurements of job support

Often the number of lost hours on a project provides a good measurement of the adequacy of job support. And the lost-hour totals can help identify deficiencies in job support so that management can take appropriate actions to improve the support. All too often management neglects to measure the quality of the job support that it provides to the field. Management tends to forget that its primary role is to support the people in the field who work with the tools. Inadequate job support interferes with getting the job done. Unnecessary obstacles arise to block work accomplishment. After a while, people on the job come to accept weak support as normal working conditions, never questioning how much better they might do if the support improved. Measurements of job support and feedback to management are as important as measurements of field productivity and feedback are to crews in the pursuit of superior performance.

A Management Checklist

The simple checklist below suggests a means to evaluate the adequacy of standards, feedback, reinforcement, and job support on a construction project. After each statement, check the appropriate column indicating the amount of time the statement is true. By regularly asking such questions, management may spot possible shortcomings before they erupt to cause serious problems.

	25% or less	25% to 50%	75% or more
Setting Performance Standards			
1. All field supervisors (foremen, general foremen, and superintendents, for example) know their weekly targets for work to be completed.	[ ]	[ ]	[ ]
2. Management holds regular weekly meetings to set future targets and to plan for hitting these targets.	[ ]	[ ]	[ ]
3. Management sets written weekly targets for work to be completed and includes estimates of the manhours and equipment needed to get the work done.	[ ]	[ ]	[ ]
4. Throughout the job, management sets clear standards as to the quality and quantity of work expected of everyone.	[ ]	[ ]	[ ]
5. Each week, management evaluates the finished work and makes a point to spot those crews which have performed well at specific tasks.	[ ]	[ ]	[ ]
Providing Frequent Feedback			
6. Each week, the management team meets to compare actual performance against what was expected.	[ ]	[ ]	[ ]
7. Crews receive regular information on their performance.	[ ]	[ ]	[ ]
8. When field supervisors spot good performance, they quickly acknowledge it to the crew.	[ ]	[ ]	[ ]
9. End-of-week reports include information on work done versus targets and on hours used versus estimated.	[ ]	[ ]	[ ]
10. Every field supervisor knows each week how the job progressed and whether the targets were met.	[ ]	[ ]	[ ]
11. Weekly meetings probe the causes of failing to meet deadlines in order to find ways to avoid the same problems in the future.	[ ]	[ ]	[ ]
Giving Positive Reinforcement			
12. Management looks closely at crews that consistently perform well to find ideas that might be copied by other crews.	[ ]	[ ]	[ ]
13. Crew foremen are included in weekly schedule meetings.	[ ]	[ ]	[ ]

14. Top management rewards field supervisors for per-   [ ]   [ ]   [ ]
formance above expected standards.

15. Both before and during the job, project management   [ ]   [ ]   [ ]
includes representives from the work force in meet-
ings to plan and analyze work methods and procedures.

16. Management uses the work force effectively so that   [ ]   [ ]   [ ]
workers feel their time is valuable to the job.

Providing Job Support

17. Management carefully plans the work sequence so   [ ]   [ ]   [ ]
as to make the best use of equipment and
manpower.

18. Management and the work force run joint experi-   [ ]   [ ]   [ ]
ments to find the best method to install work.

19. Management sets and enforces clear safety rules   [ ]   [ ]   [ ]
and runs an accident-free job.

20. During the job, management closely follows tool and   [ ]   [ ]   [ ]
equipment needs to provide the best support possi-
ble for crews.

21. At weekly meetings, management tries to foresee   [ ]   [ ]   [ ]
possible problems and then takes actions to avoid
these problems.

22. Home-office management stays in close contact with   [ ]   [ ]   [ ]
the job and is thus able to make timely decisions
when needed.

23. Management closely watches materials orders and   [ ]   [ ]   [ ]
deliveries to make sure that either materials arrive
when needed or else work plans are changed before
late deliveries disrupt the schedules.

9

Implementing a Management System

The elements of a performance measurement and management system now having been described in some detail, a major question remains as to the procedures for implementing such a far-reaching change in management procedures. There is no single answer, only a few commonsense guidelines to help contractors avoid some of the obvious pitfalls. As an introduction to these guidelines, let us see what we can learn from the problems faced by one company that attempted to institute a performance reporting system.

Peerless Construction

The owners and employees of Peerless Construction Company take pride in what they have accomplished over the past decades. From a humble beginning, working out of the back of his pickup truck, Allen Foster Sr. built his company the way he built his buildings—solid and simple. When his son, Allen Jr., stepped into daddy's shoes, the company really began to prosper. Jobs came in from all over the state. Peerless outstripped its competition and began to go head to head with some of the biggest firms around. Soon it had a well-established share of the market. Its reputation and its low bids combined to push Peerless upward and outward. Everyone worked hard and everyone made money.

Stagnation?

But the times have not been so rosy recently. Jobs have not come through as expected. Old clients have drifted away, while rising costs and new price-conscious clients have cut Peerless's profit margins.

Peerless has watched newcomers take away jobs with low bids that left too much money on the table. "They'll lose their shirt on that job," Allen Jr. would say when he saw a bid well below his, but somehow those firms managed to stay in business and keep coming back for more. Allen Jr. felt uneasy but believed strongly that Peerless's reputation for quality workmanship and on-time delivery would eventually win back business once clients recognized that the lowest bid didn't always mean the lowest cost.

A couple of months ago Allen Jr. heard a speaker at a construction association national convention talk about productivity. "It isn't good enough," the speaker had said, "to do what you've always done. You have to get better. The competition is getting better. Either you invest in improving your productivity or you sink." The speaker's words jolted Allen Jr. What had been good enough for his dad had been good enough for him. But times had changed. The new watchword was "management systems."

Fear of change

Traditionally, Peerless's management took a hard-boiled view: the "get the job moving or we'll find someone who can" approach. Lately, however, the company hadn't been too successful with the get-tough tradition; several key superintendents had left, and one top project manager had jumped to a competitor. Many field people sensed a rising frustration in trying to get their jobs done. Others were beginning to coast, playing the game of covering their own tails at the expense of labor, suppliers, subs, and engineers.

Allen Jr. recognized a deeper management problem underlying these difficulties—field managers no longer exercised real control over their jobs. Control had diffused among vice presidents, accountants, labor representatives, lawyers, engineers, and purchasers. Yet field supervisors were still held accountable for getting the job done. Allen Jr., now hearing something new in the litany of complaints and problems that kept recurring at monthly senior-management meetings, proposed a series of management changes. New performance reports, productivity and cost measurements, motivational and training programs, and a revamped computer system would modernize Peerless's management structure.

After hearing about the proposed changes, Jim Blunt, Peerless's most forceful project manager, refused to admit that management might be the problem. "Hell," he shouted, echoing the feelings of many of the old-line project managers who feared a change in traditional management methods, "I know what to do. Just let me at those lazy jerks and I'll run them into the ground. We've got dead weight out in the field; too many paper pushers and not enough people push-ers. We don't need any newfangled 'systems'—we need old-fashioned 'fear of God.'"

Fear of sharing information

But Allen Jr. persisted in his conviction that Peerless needed to change. Over the course of a few months several ideas were re-searched and discussed by the office staff. The data processing depart-ment came up with better ways to collect project information in order to provide more current comparisons of actual costs to project esti-mates. The estimating department reorganized its procedures and de-veloped new bid forms that allowed estimators to run most of their work through the computer.

New reports were proposed and adopted. Yet when these reports came out, little in the way of new information appeared on their pages. Most reports were designed for senior management, not for field supervisors. No one wanted sensitive information on bids and es-timates to reach the field where it might fall into the hands of com-petitors or, worse yet, into the hands of the labor force, who might use the information to pace their own production rates. John Miller, Peerless's director of labor relations, adamantly insisted that he would be helpless in future contract negotiations if labor knew too much about the company's labor productivity. And, seeing a proposal for lost-time reporting, he shuddered to think of labor's reaction to Peerless's admission of responsibility for any job mismanagement.

Fear of field reaction

In the field, the reporting changes imposed increasing paperwork bur-dens without offering much in the way of solutions to problems. Field managers and foremen resisted the new reports because they saw in them the seeds of their own destruction. If they reported everything, they would eventually get hung for their mistakes. If they reported nothing, they would be held responsible anyway. Suggested revisions to the new reports were adopted, eliminating the requirements for some information and changing the reporting cycle from weekly to bi-weekly. These revisions undercut reporting accuracy and timeliness. The accounting, payroll, and data processing departments redoubled their efforts to overcome these shortcomings, putting increased pres-sure on field managers to report.

By the end of the year, Peerless had finally gotten a working report-ing system. The company had upgraded its computer hardware and was printing out detailed monthly cost reports on all aspects of every project. These reports were reviewed and discussed in depth at the monthly senior-management meetings. But senior managers shied away from getting field supervisors, particularly down to the foreman level, involved in the feedback process. Top management feared that foremen would only fight harder to resist reporting—and in doing so, management risked losing what little productivity gains it had managed to achieve.

The next step?

Still Allen Jr. was not satisfied. He and one or two of his top people went to productivity seminars, attended national meetings, and pursued the recommendations of the Business Roundtable's Cost-Effectiveness Study. They tried work sampling on one job, gave away belt buckles and caps on another, and set up a labor-management committee on a third. All with mixed success. Allen Jr.'s office shelves were piled high with literature from computer companies, consultants, seminars, book offers, and product manufacturers. Should they enroll their foremen in a local foreman training program or set up their own program or do nothing? Should they try collecting foreman delay reports? Would quality circles help? What else was new that they might try?

Having looked into the "productivity field," Allen Jr. found both too much and not enough. He found too much to keep up with and still run the company; he found not enough that really seemed just right for Peerless. Everything required too much time, too much money, too much risk, or too much effort. Productivity, it turned out, was easier said than done. Now, 16 months after starting, Allen Jr. is still looking, still interested, but unwilling to do any more than he has already. Business has picked up a little, so everyone is too busy to worry. If business improves enough, maybe they won't need any more productivity efforts. And if business turns down again, maybe they won't be able to afford it anyway.

As Allen Jr. reported at the last monthly meeting, "We still have room for improvement, but we've done a lot already. And we've got some things started that will help us in the future. But you know, we can't rush these things. Guys in the field have their own ways of getting the job done; our job is to make sure they do it, not to run it for them. We keep a tight rein on costs. We make them accountable for meeting the estimate. And we help them when they need it. After all, that's what productivity is all about, isn't it? The bottom line."

The short-term perspective

How familiar the Peerless story is. So many construction companies and contractors want to improve their performance but don't know how to go about it. They sense that attempts to change their current management methods promise long-term gains for the company but also promise to be very costly and very troublesome in the short term. And who needs more expense and more trouble?

Construction management has traditionally focused on the shorter-term aspects of the business, and for very good reasons. To start with, the construction industry is closely tied to the ups and downs of the national and regional economies. Small economic fluctuations in interest rates or consumer demand, for example, can produce wide swings in construction activity. Companies must be lean enough to get through the bad times and quick enough to take advantage of the good times. Then, too, construction companies are project-oriented, focusing their energies on completing projects they get. They cannot spend too much time worrying about projects that they may never get. Competition forces companies to give extraordinary attention to what is happening *now* in the construction market, not on what may happen a few years down the road. Finally, construction companies traditionally operate with very low fixed overhead. This not only keeps bid prices lower but also enables them to respond quickly to business changes. Layoffs are common. Only the largest companies can afford long-term commitments to overhead salaries not directly chargeable to specific projects. The overhead people who are on payrolls are usually overextended and project-oriented, with little or no time to think about longer-term issues. No one wants more headaches. Everyone already has enough to do coping with the daily pressures of project management, coordination, and support.

Because of this short-term perspective, many construction companies find it extremely difficult to invest time, money, and energy in researching, testing, and developing new management methods that, because business is so uncertain, may never be used. Yet it is exactly such a long-term viewpoint that is required for the development of successful innovations in management practices for long-term survival.

Implementing a Measurement System

Getting started on a system to measure field productivity requires dedication. It takes a serious commitment on the part of top management and a willingness to work to overcome the many obstacles and problems that will undoubtedly arise in the design and implementation of a measurement system. Yet measurements of field productivity promise to improve productivity vastly, provide superior job control, and generate invaluable information for estimating future jobs. As contractors recognize that the long-term benefits outweigh the shorter-term costs, they will want to start collecting field measurements. Before jumping into it, however, several issues in the planning and design of a measurement system suggest themselves as requiring special consideration.

Need for cooperative involvement

Many people in any organization possess the capacity to thwart changes, particularly changes that they see as threatening to their own position and well-being. Participation in planning and design remains one of the most effective means to ensure cooperation. By co-opting individuals into the planning and design process, they suddenly have a stake in making the program work. After all, it's now their system.

Individuals at all levels in a company need to feel some identification with a proposed change in order to overcome their natural resistance to any change. Such identification comes from participation and also from a shift in incentives. Proposed changes need to offer greater benefits in order to overcome the higher costs associated with change. When people recognize that they will get more out of a new reporting system than they must put into it, they are more willing to offer their cooperative involvement in making it work.

Parallel systems

While a new management reporting and control system may be needed, it does not mean that the present system need be junked right away. Most contractors have invested an enormous amount of time and money in their present reporting and accounting systems and cannot afford to throw them away. The best way to introduce a new system involves setting it up to run parallel to the existing system. This way it can be phased in slowly without upsetting the existing system, and it can be tested and refined without interfering with ongoing reporting needs.

Bob Gyeser's story with J&J Mechanical in Chapter 8 offers one example of a parallel system. Bob collected most of the numbers he needed from existing reports and then used his own personal computer to generate the new reports. In keeping his system separate, he avoided potential conflicts with the data processing department. Since the primary office computer is often used to run the weekly payroll, no performance reporting system, no matter how important to field management, will likely take priority over payroll. People want to get paid on time. The reports can wait.

Timing and pacing

Most contractors have come a long way without a performance reporting system and will certainly get by a little longer without one in spite of an impatience to start collecting field measurements. Timing and pacing are important for developing a successful system. It can't be rushed, but neither can it be left to coast on its own initiative. Implementation of a performance-based measurement and reporting system requires a balanced approach. Introduce elements of the system on appropriate jobs, testing pilot measurement and reporting methods before settling on a final design. Flexibility in the initial stages of design and implementation will encourage positive suggestions for improvements. Slowly evolving a successful system from one job to another also seems less threatening to project management than does an overnight revolution in companywide reporting procedures.

What to measure first

The magnitude of beginning a productivity measurement system may seem overwhelming at first. How can anyone count and track all the detailed work items on a job? The answer is simple—no one needs to. For most companies, counts of 10 to 15 aggregate work accomplishments should serve to profile job performance adequately. The story of Condo Constructors, Inc., in Chapter 6 illustrated a measurement system that counted only eight work items. Only if such an aggregate measurement displays a large performance ability ratio (PAR) and a large worth will it pay to develop more detailed measurements of the subaccomplishments that make up the task. By limiting the collection of detailed measurements to only those items which promise a large payback on efforts spent to improve them, a performance measurement system can be more easily established.

Performance measurements can be thought of in a hierarchical framework. The dozen or so very aggregate measurements at the top track overall performance. Those measurements with the highest PARs and greatest worth can then be disaggregated into smaller subaccomplishments to discover exactly where the problems and opportunities lie. It makes no sense to try to measure carefully every accomplishment at once since so much information may be generated that it overwhelms management's ability to act on it. Detailed measurements should start with the most critical items, those which have the greatest potential for improvement and payback. For example, contractors who use the critical path method (CPM) for planning and scheduling their jobs might start by measuring only those accomplishments which lie on the critical path. From a modest beginning, eventually a fully detailed system of on-site performance measurements will evolve.

Setting a baseline

A baseline defines an average of past performance. Knowing past performance gives contractors a reference point against which to measure future gains. For many contractors who have not used measurements before, the baseline will come from the first few months of reporting under a new measurement system. Initial measurement attempts, however, may contain some flaws that limit their credibility as reflections of true performance. But as confidence builds in the accuracy of performance measurements, the baseline will provide a means to assess performance gains. By figuring the difference between the baseline and future improvements, contractors can compute the value of their increased performance. And by keeping track of the costs associated with the development and implementation of a performance measurement and feedback system, they can also calculate the net benefit of improvement efforts over time. Not everyone will experience an immediate payback. The baseline gives a reference point for determining the longer-term return on investments in changes in management methods.

Counts of work accomplished

Perhaps one of the greatest obstacles to measurement lies in the inability of many contractors to develop an efficient method for counting the amount of work accomplished (and then charging manhours to the work items). Obtaining accurate and timely field counts takes time and experimentation. Rarely will units needed for field measurements correspond exactly to the units normally used in estimating. Estimators, for example, may bid rebar according to dollars per ton-in-place. Yet foremen, asked to count the quantity of rebar placed by their crews, can only point to the areas in which they have completed the work. They do not think in terms of tons.

To help convert field counts into useful measurements, one contractor asked her foremen to assign degree-of-difficulty factors to each of several categories of rebar placement, such as different types of floors, walls, and footings. Weekly counts of work accomplished showed as marked areas on the plans. Multiplying the volume of the areas completed (to match later concrete placement) by the difficulty factors (actually weightings similar to those used by Kevin Katz in Chapter 8) gave the contractor a reasonable aggregate measurement of the work accomplished.

Foremen represent a valuable source of common sense concerning the choice of measurements for field counts. *Whatever counts are used must make sense to the people in the field* (even at the risk of upsetting the accountants and estimators).

Reporting Measurements of Quality

In addition to the spreadsheet reports of productivity, management often needs feedback that reports on the accuracy (and sometimes the workmanship) of the installed work. Although accuracy may indeed affect productivity, such as affecting the amount of rework required or the additional time necessary to meet exacting standards, measurements of accuracy (and workmanship) primarily give management information about job *quality* rather than quantity. For example, one measurement of quality might be the fraction of the job completed *correctly* rather than the fraction of the job completed. (Hopefully, the two measurements coincide.)

Quality control

The measurements of accuracy developed in Chapter 2 included the number of manhours spent at rework and the amount and cost of materials wasted in rework. In addition to these, excessive rework can also cause schedule slippage, cut productivity, and undermine worker morale. Besides the rework required to fix it, inaccurate installation can hurt a contractor's reputation and may even lead to damaging lawsuits.

Contractor programs to control quality attempt to ensure high-quality work. However, continuous quality-assurance inspections can be costly. All too often, contractors try to save money by hiring quality inspectors who are less experienced (and less well paid) than the craftsmen whose work they inspect. In such instances, the on-site labor force may quickly lose respect for the quality-assurance program. Requiring approvals of their work by underqualified quality control (QC) inspectors can irritate craftsmen, causing them to attribute rejected work to the inexperience of the inspector rather than taking personal responsibility for the error. Once the work force relieves itself of responsibility for quality and places this responsibility on the QC inspectors, individual pride of craftsmanship is lost and overall quality plummets while rework soars. Such conditions have all too often prevailed on nuclear power-plant construction sites.

The problem is lack of feedback. Craftsmen who install work need feedback concerning its quality. If they are never told whether or not their work is acceptable, they cannot improve. In many instances, QC inspectors often break the direct link between the worker and measurements of work quality. As owner demand for increased quality leads to widespread contractor quality-assurance programs, construction quality could actually decline rather than rise unless the measurement system leaves the primary responsibility for quality on the only person who can achieve it—the individual craftsman.

Quality feedback

To be successful, quality reporting systems must provide feedback to the individual (or crew) who did the work. At the construction site of a large petrochemical plant, welding inspectors were required to certify every pipe weld. Each weld was tagged by the individual who did the work. During the week inspectors toured the site, checking on welds reported to the office as finished. Rejected welds were reported back to the office and later assigned to foremen for rework. Because of the difficulty of locating individual welders on the site and interrupting their ongoing work, no attempt was made to have welders redo their own rejects. The office did keep a record, however, of the number of welds made by each individual and the number of rejects. If any welders had 10 percent of their welds rejected in a week, they were warned; if it happened again, they lost their jobs as welders.

Such a system of hit-and-miss feedback caused the welders to attribute rejected welds to incompetent inspectors and a variety of superstitious behaviors. (One welder insisted that welds inspected on Mondays were rejected more frequently than welds inspected on Fridays—and he may have been right.) A welder who received a warning was *never informed which welds were rejected or why*. And welders who got no warning assumed that all their work was accepted. In fact, inspectors accepted only 92 percent of all welds. The 8 percent reject rate was quite expensive.

The methods engineering model tells us that if we want to improve performance, the first thing to check is the adequacy of the information given to the field. In this case the welders had not received good feedback on their performance. But soon afterward, in response to a suggestion, the office began giving welders copies of the inspectors' weekly reports on the welds they had made. Each week every welder got to see how many welds had been accepted and which ones had been rejected, along with the inspectors' reasons for the rejections. The top of each report showed the welder's percentage of *accepted* welds for the week. Within a few weeks welders were bragging to each other about "100 percent" weeks. The overall reject rate fell to 3 percent. A small change in the feedback system caused a drastic improvement in the quality of performance.

Productivity and quality

Such measurements of improvement in quality, however, must be compared to measurements of welding productivity. If the improvement comes because every welder now takes 3 times as long to complete a weld, performance may show a net loss. Somewhere between maximum productivity and maximum accuracy lies a cost trade-off. If high rates of production inevitably cause some errors, then accepting the need for some rework may be less costly than insisting on perfect accuracy at much lower rates of production. Such trade-offs face every contractor on every job. Intelligent decisions about how to make the trade-offs can come only from comparable measurements of jobsite performance.

Reporting Measurements of Resources

Another dimension of performance reporting (and trade-offs) lies in the management of the resources utilized by the construction process, which means that the costs of manpower, materials, and equipment must be measured. Manpower measurements include such labor costs as: hourly wage rates for various craft skills; differences between apprentice, journeyman, and foreman wages; overtime rates; and crew-size requirements. Management seeks to juggle the schedules, work assignments, and task times in order to minimize labor costs while meeting overall schedule and production goals. Measurements of labor costs in dollars (per day, to date, and/or projected) help determine how best to allocate manpower resources on the jobsite.

Similarly, materials and equipment costs, if affected by management decisions, need to be measured. If management needs to consider using alternative equipment in order to cut manpower requirements and increase productivity, measurements will help quantify the trade-off between the cost of the equipment and the expected manpower savings.

Feedback reports

Performance reporting requires a feedback system in order to provide each decision maker with the information that he or she needs to pick appropriate actions to improve jobsite performance. Such a feedback system should include weekly measurements of:

- Accuracy (and workmanship, if needed)
- Productivity

- Schedule
- Manpower
- Resources

The objective of performance reporting is that the information, once provided to the right people, will lead to improved decision making. Given timely, relevant, accurate, complete, and intelligible information (remember the TRACI attributes from Chapter 7), management cannot help but become more competent. Managers must recognize, however, that the reporting system will not necessarily include measurements of every goal and every condition at the jobsite.

Productivity and safety

Running a safe job is an overriding objective of competent management. Considerations of jobsite safety enter into every decision concerning trade-offs between alternative work methods. All too often, contractors pursue productivity at the cost of safety. Shortcuts on the job speed production while needlessly endangering the work force. On one site a contractor, eager to trim a few dollars off the contract cost, sent workers to hang drywall over open stairwells without first covering the openings. When one of the workers was killed falling through the hole to the concrete floor below, everyone finally learned the true cost of jobsite safety.

Every contractor ought to strive for high marks based on objective measurements of jobsite safety. Record all accidents and keep tabs on the effectiveness of on-site safety meetings. Be sure that all workers follow safety rules and appoint a safety manager at each jobsite. Pay specific attention to the OSHA handbook regarding fall-prevention regulations. (Falls account for most construction accidents.) Yet in spite of vigorous safety and accident-prevention programs, accidents may still occur. Competent managers should, through their preventive efforts, be able to minimize the seriousness of these accidents and to overcome their detrimental impact on the job.

↓ Troubleshooting Poor Reporting

Just as troubleshooting with the methods engineering model can locate deficiencies in work methods in order to help management devise strategies to improve, so, too, can troubleshooting locate deficiencies in the performance reporting system itself. Troubleshooting performance reporting includes the six steps in the performance audit. These six steps (described in Chapter 5) are:

1. Identify accomplishments.

2. Identify requirements.

3. Define exemplary performance.

4. Measure exemplary and average performance.

5. Compute the PARs and worth.

6. Apply the methods engineering model.

Problems in obtaining numbers from the field crop up in nearly all reporting systems. Often the source of the problems is the resistance of field personnel to paperwork burdens. They see little, if any, direct benefit in cooperating with the reporting system. Resistance to using new forms may be overcome by getting the people who must do the actual reporting to participate in the design of the forms they will use. Then, too, field personnel must fully understand how a feedback reporting system will benefit them by helping them to improve their own performance.

The application of the methods engineering model to troubleshooting the reporting system itself will help improve the system. Analyzing the information, resources, incentives, skills, capability, and motives of the people who must use the system frequently reveals that the causes of deficient reporting are a lack of *information* concerning how the system works and a lack of *incentives* to help make the system work well. Careful attention to system design at the beginning of a program can help avoid serious implementation problems later on.

Let us turn to a final story concerning how someone managed to put all the principles we have been discussing together and how this affected the owner, the contractor, the work force, and the project itself.

Peerless Construction (Continued)

In his continuing pursuit of performance improvement, Allen Jr. attended yet another presentation sponsored by his local contractor trade association chapter. After a brief business meeting, the chapter president introduced a man who represented Midwest Industries, the owner of a large project built recently in a nearby state. The talk and the slides showed how the contractor and owner had teamed up to develop a program to ensure high performance. Special training films were developed. Lectures introduced new hires to the job. Weekly foremen meetings discussed job progress, and awards dinners involved foremen in job-improvement efforts. Extra attention was paid to lunch areas, toilet facilities, and employee parking in order to demonstrate management's sincere interest in the welfare of the craftsmen. Surveys of work delays helped identify problems. Weekly subcontractor meetings sought solutions to problems and elicited suggestions for avoiding future problems.

In conclusion, the Midwest representative underscored the fact that the job was completed on time and within budget, that the work quality was high, and that only a few minor labor problems surfaced at the job. In fact, both Midwest and the contractor agreed that because the job went so well, because performance was so high, and because labor worked so productively, they should put together a presentation of the job in order to show other contractors and owners how to do it.

"Is this all they have?" thought Allen Jr., raising his hand to ask a question. "How much did your program cost and how much money did it save the project?" he asked as the speaker pointed to him.

"We don't have any hard numbers on that," the Midwest representative admitted, "but as you can see from the presentation, whatever we spent was well worth it."

Driving back to the office, Allen Jr. thought about what he had just heard and how it related to his own efforts to improve his company's performance. "Hell," he thought, "I could have done that same presentation on a couple of our projects. That's nothing new. I could even have done better." The fact that other companies were doing similar "job enhancement" programs didn't surprise Allen Jr. What did surprise him was that he felt so deeply dissatisfied with it all. All those fancy programs didn't add up to anything unless you could measure how much they cost and what they accomplished for it. Suddenly Allen Jr. became convinced that his own programs were worthless too. He needed measurements. And he was determined to get them.

A fresh start

Allen Jr. began by reviewing some of the "management systems" information he had accumulated over the past year or so. Some of it, he remembered, was quite good, but at the time he had been too busy to figure out exactly what to do with it. He found the series of articles he was looking for that explained how to set up jobsite measurements within a feedback reporting system and spent the next hour carefully reading it over again. It made a lot of sense. But the task of measuring performance and using the measurements to troubleshoot jobsite performance would require a lot of effort to set up. And some of the Peerless employees would undoubtedly oppose it. Allen Jr. thought specifically of Jim Blunt and John Miller, two of his old-line people. He would need to win them over if he was to make any changes at all.

The next day Allen Jr. met with Jim Blunt. Jim had a small project coming up that he would have to handle in addition to the big brewery job he was doing. The project was a small medical office building and the owner, a large developer in the area who regularly gave work to Peerless, had specifically asked for Blunt again. Blunt brought him luck, he insisted. Allen Jr. thought the office job offered an excellent opportunity to try out some of the measurement ideas he had. Jim, of course, thought otherwise. But after getting assurances that he could still run the project his way in spite of the measurements, Jim eventually gave in and agreed to help collect them. If they worked (which Jim doubted), they might even make it easier for him to run the two jobs at the same time.

Together, Allen Jr. and Jim laid out a simple report form that would require the foremen to charge all their crews' manhours to one of 13 work codes. Included in the 13 was a code for lost time. Because engineering manpower was short, they agreed that the foremen would also turn in counts of how much work they had accomplished each week. Jim would check up on them to see that they counted it correctly. After Jim left, Allen Jr. felt that he was finally making some headway. Although it was late, he was too keyed up to quit now, so he began to go over the office-building plans and the estimate to refigure the amounts of work and the estimated manhours for each of the 13 work codes. When he finished, he arbitrarily cut about 14 percent of the manhours (MH) from each of the work codes and put it into a "lost-time account," figuring that this would provide a reasonable starting point for measuring productivity and lost time on the job. Table 9.1 shows Allen Jr.'s preliminary spreadsheet.

TABLE 9.1   Work Items Taken from Estimate

	A	B	C	D	E	F
		Estimate for medical office building				Unit rate
1						
2	Code	Work item	Amount	Unit	Manhours	(MH/amt)
3						
4	110	Excavation	3200	CY	420	0.13
5	120	Foundations	1240	CY	1060	0.85
6	200	Steel	265	TN	510	1.92
7	320	Flooring	8200	SF	1680	0.20
8	340	Stairwells	12	#	600	50.00
9	400	Masonry	5150	SF	730	0.14
10	500	Windows	480	#	600	1.25
11	620	Interior walls	7660	LF	3900	0.51
12	670	Interior finish		NA	2100	
13	700	Roofing	2400	SF	260	0.11
14	800	Exterior finish		NA	500	
15	900	Other		NA	400	
16	999	Lost time		NA	2000	
17						
18		Total			14760	

Seeking cooperation

The next morning Allen Jr. met with John Miller, Peerless's director of labor relations. Allen Jr. carefully explained the benefits of an on-site measurement system and how it could induce greater cooperation (and higher productivity) from the work force. John didn't buy it. He felt that by letting the work force "get away with charging lost time" on their time sheets, management was extending an open invitation for labor to slack off on the job. "They will only work half a day and charge the rest to lost time," he fumed, "making us look bad and insisting that everything is our fault."

"Well," Allen Jr. replied, "maybe it is our fault. We'll never know until we ask."

Allen Jr. wanted John's willing cooperation to try the new reporting system, but he could see that by pushing, he was only making him dig in his heels further. Trying a different argument, Allen Jr. suggested that the two of them meet with a representative of the work force and see what happened. Late the next day Hank Lears, a carpenter representative, sat down with Allen Jr. and John to hear about the new reports. Rather than present Hank with the full reporting system, Allen Jr. began the meeting by asking Hank how management might provide better support for the workers at the job sites. Management needed to know what the problems were in order to do a better job, and only the people in the field could tell them what was wrong.

Hank shook his head. "Mr. Foster," he said, "my people got lots of problems out there, but we ain't gonna start complainin' to Mr. Blunt 'cause he's gonna tell us to either shut up or get out. We do what we're told and we don't worry about the screwups. Now, maybe I shouldn't say this, but I like workin' with you and John here; you always been fair to us and I know the work is fallin' off. So let me tell you this, I know you're losing money out there 'cause no one does nothin' 'less somebody tells 'em exactly what to do. You know what I mean?"

Hank's willingness to talk helped get John more interested in the idea of some kind of a cooperative effort. At least as an experiment. John also realized that the lost-time reports would work two ways: management would need to act on any reported causes of lost time, but the work force would be helping management find the lost time and solve the problems. It might be a way to begin to develop a more cooperative relationship between management and labor out in the field. ("Of course," he thought, "with Jim Blunt out there, cooperation is a laugh.")

Allen Jr. asked Hank how they ought to measure work accomplishment and lost time on the upcoming medical office job. Allen Jr. suggested that the foremen might use a daily time sheet to charge hours to work codes and to lost time, but he wanted Hank's thoughts on it. Hank agreed that the time sheets could be used, but he didn't want the foremen loaded down with a lot of paperwork. With Allen Jr.'s prodding, Hank and John laid out a time sheet remarkably similar to the one Allen Jr. and Jim had designed earlier (and not unlike Figure 3.3). But when Hank started putting down the work items to be measured, they differed radically from Allen Jr.'s spreadsheet (Table 9.1). Looking at Hank's 10 items in Table 9.2, Allen Jr. realized that Hank had listed items that foremen could count; Allen Jr.'s items in Table 9.1 represented estimating quantities rather than things foremen could see and charge manhours to. Allen Jr. decided not to show his list to Hank and to use Hank's list instead, even though it meant a lot of work to refigure new manhour estimates for each of the items.

The owner's point of view

The developer wanted a very short construction schedule in order to have the building ready for rental as soon as possible. Both Peerless and the developer agreed to work together closely to bring the building in early and below the estimate. To meet these goals, Peerless and the developer arranged to meet together every week to resolve any problems. The developer would review the weekly lost-time and productivity reports to help troubleshoot those problems which were within the owner's control. Peerless, on the other hand, would start the job immediately even though all the final architectural plans were still incomplete. From the developer's viewpoint, it looked as though the job was assured of success. The field reporting system proposed by Peerless was exactly what the developer wished all contractors would

TABLE 9.2 Work Items that Relate Directly to Accomplishments

	A	B
1	Work item	Unit of measure
2		
3	Formwork for footings	linear feet
4	Formwork for walls	linear feet
5	Formwork for floors	square feet
6	Place vertical rebar	linear feet of forms
7	Place horizontal rebar	square feet of forms
8	Place concrete	cubic yards
9	Set interior-wall studs	linear feet
10	Drywall	square feet
11	Install doors	count
12	Install trim	linear feet

do—provide hard numbers on job progress and demonstrate that the job was always under control.

Labor's point of view

Before starting the job, Allen Jr. had Jim Blunt bring his foremen into the office for a meeting to introduce the new time sheets and to explain the concept of reporting lost time. The foremen, always wary of anything that looked like more paperwork, were pleased that the reports were not too bad and that they allowed for a lost-time code. Although they weren't really sure of Peerless's motives in asking them to report it, they all felt it was a chance to get around Jim Blunt with some of the gripes they always had. After all, Allen Jr. himself had assured them in front of Hank Lears, John, and Jim Blunt that the reports would in no way be used to harass the foremen or their crews. The purpose of reporting lost time was to find out how and why it occurred and what to do to stop it from happening again. One of the younger and more aggressive foremen, Joanne Trainor, said she wished she'd had the forms on her last job—it had taken her a week just to cut an inch off both sides of every roof truss (after they were in place and she discovered that the exterior cladding wouldn't fit because the plans had a dimension error).

As the job got under way, the foremen and their crew members found that management was as good as its word. Hours reported as lost were immediately followed up on. Field personnel were frequently asked for their opinions as to why the time had been lost and what they thought ought to be done to avoid it in the future. As two-way communications between field and office increased, the number of unresolved problems decreased. One 30-year veteran exclaimed that it was the first time anyone had ever asked him to help solve a problem instead of blaming him for it. And management's tracking of the productivity unit rates for many of the work items showed a steady improvement. For the hours worked, the labor force performed well. Both Hank and John became believers in the new reporting system. And even Jim Blunt reluctantly admitted that it hadn't hurt the job.

An unexpected benefit: claims documents

However, in spite of Peerless's best efforts, the medical office building project turned out badly. First, unexpected excavation problems held up the job for several weeks, and when Allen Jr. asked for a contract extension for the delay, he was unable to get it. It seemed that some lease commitments had been made and that the occupancy date had already been moved forward several weeks in anticipation of an early completion. Second, eager to sign a big medical lab, the developer decided to make some changes to the plans to accommodate special laboratory equipment. The entire second floor's interior-wall plans were rearranged, the air-filtering and exhaust system redesigned, and extra reinforcing added. The stream of change orders from the architect and engineer threatened further delays, which Peerless had to meet through overstaffing and overtime. By the end of the project, Peerless was out over $150,000 in extra costs, most of them directly attributable to the compressed schedule and the changes. The big unanswered question was, who would pay?

The developer's attorney, unfamiliar with the project, at first insisted that each change order had been fairly priced and that no further money was owed. Peerless's attorney argued that the delays and changes were not the contractor's fault; the developer had been kept informed throughout the job of the manhour overruns and the reasons. When the attorneys sat down to review the contract documents, they were both shocked to find such a complete record of the job. The weekly performance reports clearly showed productivity losses whenever the job was overstaffed to stay on schedule. The lost-time reports showed that both Peerless and the developer had worked hard to eliminate the jobsite problems caused by the change orders. Some of the foremen's daily time sheets even included written comments on why time was lost on rework due to specific plan changes. One foreman, in her frustration, had written a page and a half explaining why it took 25 MH to add a few extra pieces of rebar; to accommodate the extra reinforcing at that point, the engineers had increased the depth of the floor slab 2 in, which meant that all the bracing and formwork already in place had to be removed and rebuilt.

Based on the document record, the developer's attorney reluctantly agreed that Peerless had presented a fair claim for overruns and that it would be silly to spend another $100,000 in legal fees to take it to court. Both sides reached an amicable settlement and agreed that if everyone kept such records, the lawyers might wind up out of business.

Costs and benefits

As the project was drawing to a close, Allen Jr. took the time to go over the costs and benefits of what he had accomplished with the changes in the reporting system. It hadn't been all roses.

First, the new forms, because they didn't report the work accomplished in the same format as the estimate, caused all sorts of difficulties with the data processing people who were trying to generate the regular cost-account reports. Second, follow-up on all the lost-time causes had nearly burned out one of the younger project engineers, who had wound up with the responsibility for making the system work. Not every lost-time incident was worth following up, but because Allen Jr. had insisted, other important matters were let go in order to prove to the foremen that lost-time reporting helped them get their work done. Third, the definition of the work codes originally sketched out by Hank Lears (Table 9.2) left much to be desired. While the people in the office wanted to add more items, the foremen wanted fewer. Allen Jr. realized too late that he should only have charged detailed hours to the critical items and to those which required many manhours. Much of the little stuff did not need a separate code and only irritated the foremen. And in spite of Allen Jr.'s determination, he still could not get a dollar figure on how much it all cost (or on what was gained).

On the plus side, Peerless had greatly improved its relationship with the work force, laying the groundwork for a more cooperative attitude on future jobs. In spite of the problems on the job, morale had been high. Many of the lost-time causes had been spotted early, before they got out of hand. Although the job had lost far more time than Allen Jr. had estimated it would, he sincerely felt that it would have lost at least twice as much time without all the effort to eliminate it. This alone saved as much as $25,000.

In addition, they had learned a lot. Allen Jr. realized that setting up a performance feedback system involved a lot more than just talk. It required a willingness to experiment, to listen to others, and to accept responsibility for problems, things that contractors rarely did easily. Allen Jr. felt convinced that he was on the right track and accepted the possibility that it might take years to evolve the right system for Peerless. But he was committed. And more importantly, he believed that, for the most part, Peerless's management was also committed. It was finally time to move the business out of the back of his daddy's pickup truck.

Management Commitment

Getting management to change the way it thinks and acts may be the single greatest barrier to improving construction productivity. As contractors often observe, "When work is slow, you can't afford to make changes, and when work is booming, you don't have to." Everyone recognizes that changes can lead to improved performance. But few are willing to act decisively to make changes.

Aside from the thousands of excuses for inaction, change seldom occurs unless management believes in and is committed to the change. Commitment requires that management understand two things:

- That the benefits outweigh the costs
- How to do it

Most people in construction management acknowledge the importance of performance improvement and can see that performance measurements, coupled with feedback, offer a means to achieve improved
performance. Yet they cannot readily figure the costs and benefits.
Nor do they see a way to implement the required programs easily. Because both the ends and the means to reach the ends remain unclear,
many in management find "performance improvement" only a catchy
phrase with little real meaning behind it. So current practices remain
unchanged.

Significant performance gains will not come about without a deep
commitment to change. And commitment demands a clear vision of
what needs to be done and why. This book has marked out one path-
way to improved performance through changes in management methods. It is up to each individual reader, however, to find his or her own
vision of what could be and then to create the commitment necessary
to bring this vision into reality.

Appendix

The Electronic Spreadsheet

Since measurement and reporting involve the collection, organization, and analysis of numbers, the use of computers can substantially improve our measurement capabilities. More and more contractors are coming to rely on computers to assist them. Computer programs now on the market (and many more to come) help with nearly every phase of construction—from planning and bidding to job management and cost accounting.

One multipurpose program, the electronic spreadsheet, offers an invaluable tool for productivity measurement and management. Most of the examples used throughout this book illustrate the use and power of the electronic spreadsheet, which is essentially a very large, empty ledger sheet. Table A.1 shows a portion of one.

Thousands of cells

Normally, spreadsheet columns are referenced by letters, and rows are referenced by numbers. The sheet in Table A.1 shows only 8 columns and 10 rows; it is, however, only the upper left-hand corner of a sheet that may exend more than 200 columns to the right and more than 1000 rows down. Some programs handle much larger sheets, containing over a million cells. (Each gridded box on the sheet is referred to as a "cell.") The user types words or numbers directly into the cells, much as one would fill out a ledger sheet.

TABLE A.1   The Electronic Spreadsheet (with no Data Yet Typed into Its Cells)

	A	B	C	D	E	F	G	H
1								
2								
3								
4								
5								
6								
7								
8								
9								
10								

However, instead of entering only words and numbers into the cells, we may also enter formulas that reference other cells on the spreadsheet. Thus, for example, instead of calculating the sum of a column of numbers, we can write a simple formula to add the column for us and display the answer at the bottom. Using formulas to calculate relationships between numbers on an electronic spreadsheet gives the spreadsheet its tremendous power. Once the formulas are in place, any changes we make to the original numbers cause the program to *recalculate all the numbers automatically*. This means that we can examine many "what if" possibilities, letting the power of the computer refigure all the numbers for us. Or, should we discover a mistake in the numbers we have entered, we need merely retype the correct number—and instantly the entire sheet is updated. The upper left-hand portion of a simple spreadsheet is shown in Table A.2.

After setting up the headings for Table A.2, the estimated amounts in column B and the estimated manhours in column F were entered. At the end of the week, when counts of work placed and manhours charged to the job are turned in, the numbers in columns C and G are updated. In columns D and E, formulas for the percent complete and percent manhours expended automatically figure the percentages for comparision. (For clarity, all the spreadsheets in this book include a row near the top showing the formulas used in the calculations, where appropriate.) In this simple example, we see that we can quickly compare the percentage of work done to date against the percentage of manhours expended for each work-code item to assess how well the job is going relative to the estimate.

TABLE A.2   Example of an Electronic Spreadsheet

	A	B	C	D	E	F	G
1	The R. T. James Construction Company, Inc.						
2	Project 88-23: The Main Street Firehouse						
3	Weekly Project Status Report for week ending:					11 Mar 88	
4							
5	Work	Amount	Amount	Percent	Percent	Manhour	Manhours
6	code	estimated	placed	complete	manhours	estimate	charged
7							
8	*Formula*			*(C/B)*	*(G/F)*		
9							
10	10220	1256	566	45%	45%	115	52
11	10230	223	223	100%	115%	54	62
12	10450	354	250	71%	66%	233	154
13	10480	3310	1544	47%	52%	510	266
14	11230	2000	500	25%	21%	400	82
15	11260	32	16	50%	22%	96	21
16	11270	780	360	46%	42%	288	120
17							
18	Total MH				45%	1696	757

Using formulas in cells

Table A.3 reprints an expanded portion of the same spreadsheet but shows the underlying formulas used to compute the percentages in columns D and E. Note how the formulas reference other cells to obtain the values needed to perform calculations. The formula in cell D10, for example, computes the percent complete for the first workcode item (10220 in cell A10 in Table A.2) by setting the value of the cell equal to the number given in cell C10 (the amount placed to date) divided by the number given in cell B10 (the total estimated amount). Using an electronic spreadsheet greatly simplifies the task of organizing jobsite numbers and calculating important relationships between the numbers.

TABLE A.3   The Underlying Spreadsheet Formulas in a Part of Table A.2

	C	D	E	F
5	Amount	Percent	Percent	Manhour
6	placed	complete	manhours	estimate
7				
8		*(C/B)*	*(G/F)*	
9				
10	566	= C10/B10	= G10/F10	115
11	223	= C11/B11	= G11/F11	54
12	250	= C12/B12	= G12/F12	233
13	1544	= C13/B13	= G13/F13	510
14	500	= C14/B14	= G14/F14	400
15	16	= C15/B15	= G15/F15	96
16	360	= C16/B16	= G16/F16	288
17				
18			= G18/F18	= SUM(F10:F16)

Work Sampling

Work sampling offers a method to gather information about the amount of nonproductive manhours worked on large construction projects. The method uses random sampling to determine the time that craftsmen spend at various activities throughout the day. Trained observers walk the jobsite at random times and places, classifying each worker according to the activity in which he or she is engaged at the moment of observation. Observers use a preset, limited number of activity classifications, generally divided into productive and nonproductive activities. For example, a worker carrying materials across the site might be observed as "working, moving materials," while a companion walking empty-handed beside him might be observed as "nonworking, traveling." The observations are generally made openly so that the workers and their representatives know that observers are conducting a sample study.

From the results of many such observations, a composite "snapshot" of the jobsite can be assembled and the percentage of workers engaged in each activity calculated. A cooperative review of the fraction of nonworking time and the reasons for it can lead to actions by both labor and management to improve productivity by reducing the time spent on nonworking activities. Work-sample studies carried out at power-plant construction sites generally reveal that an average craftsman spends 30 to 40 percent of his or her day engaged in nonproductive activities. Most such studies report an increase in the fraction of productive time as measured by subsequent work samples.

But what, really, does work sampling measure? It is not a measurement of productivity, for it counts only input (manhours at various activities) and not output (the amount of work-in-place). It measures behavior, not accomplishment. It cannot tell *why* a worker was waiting instead of working; it can only tell that a large fraction of people was observed waiting, not working. So the sample itself contains limited information concerning jobsite productivity; users must infer their own conclusions from observations of worker behavior. And what do users do with their inferences? In general they exhort the labor force to spend more time on productive work. At one nuclear power-plant site, the owner used a work-sample study to upbraid the subcontractors on the job to reduce their nonproductive time. Since the study's results came out two weeks after the sample was taken, no one knew what any workers were doing wrong at the time of the sample. So actions to correct the "problem" were limited to warning everyone to "stay busy." Sure enough, the sample taken the following month showed a dramatic rise in productive work time. The owner, the contractors and the labor force were pleased. But what really happened from one month to the next? Did productivity actually rise? No one knew.

But one electrician, bragging about how good his trade had come out in the study (up from last to second-best, the laborers always being first), pointed out that all electricians now carried around a 6-in piece of ½-inch conduit and a 12-in piece of wire in their back pockets. When the observers appeared on the site, every electrician that was not busy pulled out the conduit, stuck it up against the nearest wall, inserted the wire, and, holding on to it and pretending to pull, would shout, "I've got it at this end, go ahead and start feeding it through." It looked like work to the observers, that's for sure.

To avoid the problem of craftsmen altering their normal behavior during work sampling, the observations would need to be taken clandestinely. But spying on the work force is a sure way to create serious labor problems. Management wants the work force as allies, not adversaries. So to make work sampling a useful tool in pursuing jobsite productivity gains, it must be done on a cooperative basis with labor. The feedback that results from sampling must stress the positive aspects of the job and avoid building negative pressures, for the negative pressures are what lead the work force to invent whatever tricks they need to fool the observers the next time out.

Index

ABOUT THE AUTHOR

Louis Edward Alfeld, AIA, teaches in the construction management program of Washington University's School of Engineering. He is founder of Decision Dynamics, Inc., a leading consulting firm that specializes in applying human performance engineering to construction needs. A regular contributor to *Productivity and Management in Construction* and the author of many articles appearing in a wide range of construction trade journals, he has served as Director of Construction Industry Programs for the federal government's National Center for Productivity and Quality of Working Life and as a member of the National Research Council's Building Advisory Board committee on construction productivity. Mr. Alfeld is also a practicing attorney in Missouri, Illinois, and Massachusetts.

Engin.

TH438.A43 1988
  Alfeld, Louis Edward.
    Construction productivity.

                              15100900

7/28/89